# Conversations *with* Swami Muktananda

## THE EARLY YEARS

Swami Muktananda

# Conversations *with* Swami Muktananda

THE EARLY YEARS

Swami Muktananda

A SIDDHA YOGA MEDITATION PUBLICATION
PUBLISHED BY SYDA FOUNDATION

Published by SYDA Foundation
371 Brickman Rd., P.O. Box 600, South Fallsburg, NY 12779, USA

*Cover:* Looking east toward Gurudev Siddha Peeth, the mother ashram of Siddha Yoga meditation.

The photographs on pages 2, 14, 60, 168, and 282 are of Swami Muktananda.

**Acknowledgments**

Thanks and appreciation go to the editor of this second edition, Ed Levy; to the editorial assistant and indexer, Valerie Sensabaugh; to Professor William Mahony and Viju Kulkarni for their technical advice on the scriptures and *bhajans* in the Notes; to Hans Tuerstig for his Sanskrit expertise; to researchers Lissa Feldman and Diane Fast; to Laura Turley for the glossary; to Cheryl Crawford for design; to Suzanne Deck and Mara Sachs for typesetting; and to Osnat Shurer and Sushila Traverse for overseeing production.



Previously published as *Paramartha Katha Prasang: Spiritual Conversations with Swami Muktananda*



Second edition 1998

Printed in the United States of America

98 99 00 01 02 03 04 05 06    5 4 3 2 1

Library of Congress Cataloging-in-Publication Data
Muktananda, Swami, 1908–
[Paramārtha kathāprasaṅga. English]
Conversations with Swami Muktananda : the early years / Swami Muktananda
p. cm.
Previously published in English: Paramartha katha prasang. 1981.
Includes bibliographical references and index.
ISBN 0-911307-53-2 (pbk. : alk. paper)
1. Spiritual life—Hinduism.
BL1237.32.M84413 1998
294.5'44—dc21    97-52578
CIP

# Contents

# FOREWORD
## *to the Second Edition*

It was a great privilege and pleasure to be present at the question-and-answer sessions with Baba Muktananda recorded in this volume. They were a regular feast of wit, humor, and quick repartee—but above all, they were occasions on which one witnessed the sharing of Baba's profound understanding of the scriptures and of his equally profound state of inner perfection.

Most of these conversations took place between Baba and visitors to his ashram in Ganeshpuri, India. Often, these people would find Baba sitting on the porch outside his rooms, where his Samadhi Shrine now stands. I remember Baba wearing a *lungi* with a simple piece of cloth draped around his shoulders. Except for his piercing eyes and his strong, aquiline nose, Baba looked like a young boy. In those days, there were just a handful of ashramites, and people who visited on a weekday might easily be talking to Baba alone with only a notetaker present. On the weekends, twenty, perhaps thirty people would gather around Baba—devotees from Bombay and Baroda, from Pune and Pandharpur. Sometimes, those with questions would raise their hands and be called on by Baba.

There were many sorts of questioners and many sorts of questions. Some came with a burning desire to know the truth, and their questions would draw Baba's grace and wisdom the way a lightning rod draws lightning. Some wanted to test Baba's subtle understanding of Vedanta, or his status as a holy man and scholar. These interlocutors would come away astonished at the spiritual attainment that lay masked under Baba's simple exterior. Others came in order to add to their store of knowledge, carefully writing down everything he said. Baba would periodically remind them to be sure the knowledge they recorded so painstakingly did not just remain in their diaries but was implemented in their lives. Occasionally, there were those who came to see Baba perform miracles, as a kind of proof of his attainment. I remember, once, when the followers of a master who was famous for displaying his *siddhis*, his miraculous powers, asked Baba if he, too, believed in miracles. "The whole universe created by the Lord is itself a great miracle," Baba responded, "so what is the use of staging the feat of a smaller miracle within this great one?"

The greatest miracle, of course, was in the divine grace that flowed through even the simplest of his answers, and the way it flowed to everyone present. For although these responses may have been occasioned by a single visitor's question, they invariably touched everyone. Like the team of horses pulling Lord Krishna's chariot, all of whom took to heart the guidance given by Krishna's hand to any one of them, all those who were fortunate enough to attend these gatherings brought away from them whatever they needed to receive. It is a matter of great good fortune that after some time *Paramartha Katha Prasang* has found its way back into print as *Conversations with Swami Muktananda: The Early Years*, so that many others may join Baba in these timeless satsangs, hear the Master's teachings, and receive his grace.

*Pratap N. "Dada" Yande*
*Gurudev Siddha Peeth*
*Ganeshpuri, India*
*November* 4, 1997

***Pratap N. Yande*** *is lovingly known as Dada, "elder brother," the name that Swami Muktananda gave him shortly after their first meeting in 1961. Dada Yande, who was then working with the administration of the Maharashtrian state government, served Baba Muktananda in many capacities over the next two decades, from helping with the administration of his ashram to taking dictation for part of his autobiography,* Play of Consciousness. *Since Baba's mahāsamādhi in 1982, Dada Yande has continued his selfless service, and he now translates Baba's and Gurumayi Chidvilasananda's books into Marathi.*

# INTRODUCTION

Since the first time I had the darshan of Baba Muktananda, his divine words, which intoxicate one with the bliss of Brahman, the Absolute, touched my heart. The nectar-like drops from the ocean of his wisdom began to quench the thirst of my inner Self. The shower of his sublime teaching began to enliven my intellect by cleansing the mind.

I felt a keen desire to treasure his precious and soothing words, so that when I was not in his physical presence, I could remember him by reading what he had said. This would make me experience great joy and would strengthen the new understanding I had acquired through the inner awakening that had taken place in me by his grace.

In the beginning, I would collect Baba's words by remembering whatever wonderful things appealed to me in his informal talks. Therefore, the collection of his words of that time was small, and chosen according to my own personal interest and liking. Whenever I went for Baba's darshan, I would pick up whatever scattered gems of his words I could gather during the satsang.

From 1961, I had the privilege of being in Baba's presence all the time. The number of intellectual visitors who wished to understand the spiritual truths through words also increased. As a result, spiritual conversations began to take place in the form of questions and answers between Baba and the seekers. From these impromptu talks, I would remember and later record whatever I found interesting, inspiring, and enlightening. But when I saw that the treasure of his wisdom was limitless, I became more avid and began to sit with pen and paper to take notes. I would write down as much as I could catch from the conversation. There was no tape recorder at that time. Even though in the beginning these conversations were occasional, as time passed my notebooks started filling up. On weekends, the devotees would take them home to read and would experience great joy by drinking in Baba's nectar-like words. Seeing their delight, I would wish that such satsangs would occur more often so that they could be published in the form of a book. Baba knew my unexpressed desire and fulfilled it. As the satsangs became more frequent, he took the opportunity to talk at length. The drops of nectar became an ocean.

The monthly journal called *Sai Suman* began to publish them. Later the readers requested that these conversations be made available in the form of a book. As a result, the book *Paramartha Katha Prasang* in Gujarati, containing Baba's spiritual conversations of the years 1962 to 1966, was published in 1972. Later it was translated and published in Hindi. This book is its English translation.

The poet-saint Bhartrihari has said:

> Even though saints do not give direct teachings, one should attend upon them, because their casual talks become scriptures.[1]

This book of spiritual conversations is one such scripture, containing the spiritual truths revealed by Baba whenever the occasion presented itself. They are the words flowing out from a great saint's own experience. These words are Chit Shakti's self-inspired mantra. They present a true perception of reality and a guide on the path to liberation. For one who is open, this book is the revealer of spiritual mysteries; for one who is awake, it is a divine eye; and for one who is eager for Self-realization, it brings the contentment of fulfillment.

It is said, "There is no knowledge without the Guru." This is absolutely true. There is a great deal of teaching in the scriptures, but without a Guru, study of the scriptures bears hardly any fruit. It becomes dry and boring. Saint Nishchaladas has said:

> Without the Guru, the ocean of Vedas tastes like salt. But when the same water is showered through the cloud of the Guru's mouth, it becomes sweeter than nectar.[2]

The dry knowledge of the scriptures can at most inflate the ego, but it cannot impart the experience of inner satisfaction and peace. The state of the highest knowledge is so sublime and mysterious that it is difficult to reach it without the guidance of the Guru. It is said:

> Because Vedanta is manifold and doubts are many, and what is to be known is very subtle, without the Guru one cannot understand it.[3]

In the short span of human life, the quickest and the easiest means of attaining the spiritual goal is through the Guru. In order to acquire this knowledge from the Guru, the *Bhagavad Gītā* tells us:

> Learn That by humble reverence, by inquiry, and by service. The men of wisdom who have seen the truth will instruct you in knowledge.[4]

Baba Muktananda preaches the eternal spiritual truths expounded by the great saints and enshrined in the scriptures. Thus one finds in his talks many quotations from the writings of the saints and the scriptures. However, the spiritual conversations in this book reveal his experience of the Upanishadic knowledge, his grasp of the deep mysteries of yoga, his earnest interest in the philosophy of Kashmir Shaivism, and his immense reverence for great saints like Shri Jnaneshwar Maharaj, Saint Tukaram, Sundardasji, and others. Here there is no show of scholarship, but only the light of universal truth. Baba inspires everyone to realize the divine Consciousness that is within themselves. He teaches that one's true religion is the actual experience of the Self; that it is the religion of the Self. In this context, he has written about his own experiences in his spiritual autobiography, *Play of Consciousness.*

All kinds of people come to Baba. Some are seekers, while others simply come out of curiosity. Some are thirsty for knowledge, while others are in search of a true Guru. Some, being tormented by the sufferings of the world, are pining for mental peace, while others want to know how to solve the problems that arise in their spiritual disciplines. Some seek advice on worldly problems, while others want guidance in their personal life. Baba satisfies everyone with answers that are always clear and to the point.

Baba's answers to people's questions are always inspired. He always gives an apt answer, and in his answers, given in the most natural and informal style, one sees his frankness, his insight into the needs of the questioner, and his knack of making a person understand the point through direct or indirect suggestions appropriate for the occasion. Baba speaks often about the means to still the mind, about the harmony between the worldly and the spiritual, about idol worship, the significance of the "dos" and "don'ts" prescribed by the scriptures, about recognition of a true Guru, about the qualities necessary for receiving the Guru's grace, and so on. One will find many discussions on Baba's favorite topics—the waking, dream, deep-sleep, and *turīya* states of an individual; the unity of *jñāna, bhakti,* and yoga; the oneness of God with form and without form; the need for a Guru; true renunciation; the importance of chanting; the secret of a mantra; the technique of meditation; and so on. Each time he reiterates these subjects, his way of explaining the point is unique. Just as one strikes a pole with a hammer to dig it into the ground, Baba's repetition acts as hammer blows, which help truth penetrate into the reader's mind.

Sometimes one may find differences and contradictions in the answers given to similar questions asked by different persons at different times. But here one must keep in mind that these answers were given in a particular context and according to the need of the questioner at that time. For example, if a seeker was involved only in dry knowledge, Baba would impress upon him the greatness of the yoga of meditation. If someone was mad after *yoga siddhis*, Baba would explain to him the importance of knowledge. To someone too attached to worldly things, Baba would sing the praises of renunciation. To one whose renunciation was without discrimination, Baba would explain that one can attain God even while living in the world. If a person was entangled in the worship of God only with form, Baba would lead him toward the attributeless and the formless. If a person was opposed to God with form, Baba would tell him to see the Absolute even in an idol. If a person was self-willed, caught up in his own false ideas, Baba would advise him to accept the authority of the scriptures. If a person was enslaved by old traditions and completely stuck in religious texts, Baba would urge him to perceive the Truth that is beyond all religions. To an inert *jñānī*, Baba would explain the dynamism of Vedanta. To one caught too much in worldly affairs, Baba would teach withdrawal from activity.

Thus, Baba is more interested in the questioner than the question. He penetrates to the seeker's heart and mind. Each person is on a different level of understanding and in a different state of spiritual transformation. So Baba meets each seeker on his or her own ground and answers appropriately. If at that time it is necessary to give a long and loving explanation, he will do that; if a scolding is necessary, he will do that; and if it is necessary to strike with harsh words, he will do even that in order to drive his point deep into the heart. In order to make clear the context in which each of these conversations took place, a brief introduction of the questioner has been given before each dialogue.

Through these talks, a general reader will get to know the true meaning of many topics. He will come to understand the theory of reincarnation, miracles, the real meaning of *yogabhrashta*, the nature of *gurusevā*, the saints' and sages' way of behaving, their mission and their deeds, the process of shaktipat, and much more.

These spiritual conversations are the words of our Guru. It is not enough to say they are true and beautiful. One who wishes to turn toward God, who wants to attain something on the spiritual path, who truly desires supreme peace, should not only read this book but also contemplate it. He should absorb these teachings and act accordingly. Only then will this *guruvāṇī* (words of the Guru) take him across the ocean of worldly existence. In it is the Guru's divine message. Since Shri Guru is the embodiment of pure Consciousness, Shiva, his *vāṇī* (word) is the power of that Consciousness. Thus the *guruvāṇī* is priceless. It is said:

> There is no wealth on earth by which the disciple can repay his debt to the Guru for even one word of the knowledge received from him.[5]

With folded hands, we pray to our Gurudev to speak more because his nectar-like words are never enough; we thirst for more and more, like Arjuna, who requests Lord Krishna:

> Tell me more. I am never satiated with hearing Your nectar-like words.[6]

*Swami Prajnananda (Amma)*
*Gurudev Siddha Peeth*
*Ganeshpuri, India*
1981

---

***Swami Prajnananda,*** *known to thousands of Siddha Yoga meditation students as Amma, or "mother," moved into Shree Gurudev Ashram, as Gurudev Siddha Peeth was then named, in 1961. A former professor of Sanskrit at a college in Bombay, Amma was the first woman to live in one of Swami Muktananda's ashrams and was for years the only person to document his teachings and the experiences of his devotees. She was the editor of Shree Gurudev-Vani, an annual journal published by the ashram from 1964 to 1982; the author of the book, Swami Muktananda Paramahamsa: The Saint and His Mission; and an editor or advisor on all of the ashram's early publications. Swami Prajnananda, who died in 1993, was originally a disciple of Baba Muktananda's Guru, Bhagawan Nityananda.*

# Chapter One

## 1962

*For the past few evenings, Baba has been sitting on the platform around the bilva tree in the ashram garden surrounded by devotees who came for his darshan. A beautiful statue of Nataraj presented by a Parsi yogi, Mr. Boman Behramjee, adorns the platform. Currently satsangs take place at this spot, which is very enchanting in the evening. This evening a devotee asked the following question:*

## *The Scriptures Are the Form of God*

**Devotee:** *Is it proper to consider the scriptures authoritative?*

**Baba:** God and the scriptures are interwoven. To doubt the scriptures is to doubt God. To help you understand this, I will relate a true incident I once read.

In North India there lived a brahmin who was a great devotee of Lord Krishna. He had deep faith in the *Bhagavad Gītā*, which he studied and recited constantly. Since he had no time for any other occupation, his money dwindled to nothing. Money is like water in a pot. As you go on using it, less and less remains. Finally the poor man was reduced to such poverty that he and his family were forced to fast for three days, since he could not even receive alms from the town.

On the third day, when the brahmin was reading the *Gītā* as usual in a secluded place, he came across the following verse in the ninth chapter:

> I take up the burden of the well-being of My devotees
> who are always immersed in Me.[1]

At this point he stopped abruptly. He began to doubt the truth of these words, so he underlined them in red ink. He thought, "God promises He will take care of His devotees, but I have had no food for three days despite my long-lasting devotion. Why is this?"

While the brahmin was thinking in this manner, a handsome boy approached his wife with some food and told her to prepare a meal. His wife liked the boy so much that she invited him to stay and eat with them, and she asked him to call her husband from the secluded place where he was reading the *Gītā*. The boy went out and told the brahmin that his wife was calling him home for a meal.

The boy had a bleeding scratch on his arm. Pointing to it, the brahmin asked him, "What is this?" The boy replied, "It is the scratch from the line you made in the *Gītā*." Overcome with remorse, the brahmin fainted, and by the time he revived, the boy had vanished.

As this story strikingly illustrates, the *Gītā* is God's body. It is, in fact, God. For this reason, the holy books used for daily chanting are worshiped and adorned with sandalwood paste, *kumkum*, and flowers, along with incense and lights. Only when holy books are regarded with such reverence does the knowledge contained in them bear fruit.

## SUNDAY, NOVEMBER 25, 1962

*Since it was Sunday, many devotees were gathered at the ashram. Among them was Mr. J. L. Nain, a well-known barrister, the legal advisor to Shree Gurudev Ashram and a keen student of yoga. He asked Baba the following question:*

### *Live Mantra*

**Nain:** *Baba, when does a mantra become alive?*

**Baba:** A mantra is always alive, never dead, since it is the very form of God. "Mantra is My own form, O beautiful one," Lord Shiva said to Parvati. The name and the named are identical. The *rā* and *ma* are, in fact, Shri Rama. To say that the mantra has become alive is like saying that God has become alive. God was never dead. The real question is why mantras don't bear fruit even after they are repeated for a long time. The mantra that doesn't bear fruit can be called a "dead" mantra. A "live" mantra is one that has borne fruit for the one who gives it. To give a mantra to others when one has not benefited from it oneself is just an empty ritual. It benefits neither the one who gives it nor the one who receives it. How can one who has had no experience give any experience to others?

Those mantras by which the great sages and seers achieved tremendous power and attained Guruhood can be called live mantras, or Siddha mantras. That mantra which awakens the inner Consciousness, bestowing immediate results, is a live mantra.

## Thursday, November 29, 1962

*This afternoon Baba went to Kalyan to lay the foundation stone for the factory of Pepchemi Corporation Ltd. From there he went to Santa Cruz at 5:30 P.M., where many devotees were waiting for his darshan at the home of Mr. Yogendra Trivedi. Devotees continued to arrive throughout the evening. At 9:00 P.M. Mr. J. L. Nain, barrister, lovingly invited Baba to his house in Bandra. After being received there, Baba was asked several questions by Mr. Nain.*

### *Nāda-Bindu-Kalā*

**Nain:** *What is meant by nāda, bindu, and kalā?*

**Baba:** After receiving the grace bestowed by the Guru, the seeker hears the inner sound during his spiritual practice. This is *nāda.* In the beginning the sound is loud, but as the seeker concentrates on it, it gradually diminishes and finally subsides altogether. Afterward a Blue Pearl is seen, which is actually located inside the eye, even though it appears to be outside. This is *bindu.* As meditation progresses, this Blue Pearl bursts and the play of Consciousness becomes manifest. This is *kalā,* which grants the experience of realization.

## *The Life Span of a Yogi*

**Nain:** *Can a yogi prolong his life span?*

**Baba:** A Siddha yogi can prolong or shorten his life span, but for what purpose? What is the use of experiencing the impurities of the body, which is full of waste matter and disease? After realization of the ultimate knowledge, the yogi might wish to give up his body, but it is sustained by destiny and people derive benefit from it.

Swami Rama Tirtha has called the human body a "shit-producing factory." Composed of the five elements, it is by nature full of impurities. The Upanishads and Ayurveda describe the body in similar terms.

True happiness lies in becoming free from body-consciousness. Worldly life exists in the mind. Why would a person who has achieved the state of thought-free bliss choose to remain in the thought-enshrouded worldly state?

Siddha yogis continue living in the world only by the force of destiny. They have fully united their own will with God's universal will. The yogi who prolongs his life span beyond its destiny is indulging in "black marketeering."

*Baba stayed in Bombay for two days and many devotees came for satsang. At this time a noteworthy answer was given to a question asked by Prajna, a graduate in philosophy and the wife of Mr. Yogendrabhai's younger brother Niranjan.*

## Unity in Diversity

**Prajna:** *How does a realized being who experiences oneness everywhere manage to live in the world, which is full of diversity?*

**Baba:** In order to understand the realized being's experience of unity in diversity and diversity in unity, you should read Saint Jnaneshwar's commentary on the following verse from the fourth chapter of the *Gītā*:

> The *jñānī* is one who sees inaction in action and action in inaction.[2]

This subject is not easily comprehended, nor is it really a topic for discussion. It can only be understood through experience. For practical purposes, however, the analogy of the body and its parts would be appropriate for our understanding. A person experiences his body as one inseparable unit, but each part has a separate function. We don't eat with our feet or walk on our hands. We wear shoes on our feet and put a hat on our head. In the same way, the *jñānī* sees oneness everywhere, but treats things differently for the sake of practicality. Receiving a nice hat or a pair of shoes, he would put the hat on his head, not on his feet; the shoes would go on his feet, not on his head. The *Gītā* says that everything is the same in the eyes of the *jñānī*:

> The *jñānīs* look upon a learned brahmin, a cow, an elephant, a dog, or an untouchable with equal vision.[3]

In spite of this perception of oneness, however, a *jñānī* would not receive a dog with the same deference and respect shown to a brahmin. This is the *jñānī*'s practice of diversity in unity.

Let us take another example. The *jñānī* perceives the unity of the One in the apparent diversity of the world in the same way as a mother sees no difference between her sons and her grandsons, and considers them all her own. The *jñānī* perceives *chaitanya* (Consciousness) everywhere through his vision of the Self (*ātmadrishti*). Such *jñānīs* are not affected by individuality, just as the sun does not become wet when reflected in water. *Jñānīs* see the world, perform all actions, and have all sense experiences, but remain stable and unaffected within. Although the world is not different from God, He has created it of His own free will, with many forms. Shri Krishna says in the *Gītā*, "The world is created by My will."

The divine is one and indivisible, but diversities are created so that the world will function in a disciplined manner. The *jñānī* sees the world just as God has created it. He perceives its fundamental unity but acts in accordance with its diversity.

SATURDAY, DECEMBER 1, 1962

*This morning, returning to Ganeshpuri from Santa Cruz, Baba visited Dr. Dhirubhai Daftari, whom he once promised to visit on all return trips from Bombay. The doctor and his wife, Kanta, are deeply interested in spirituality. They are avid students of Vedanta and have great respect for sādhus and saints.*

## *Shaktipat Gives Rise to Knowledge*

**Dr. Daftari:** *I believe that shaktipat calms the wayward tendencies of the mind, but that it does not give rise to knowledge.*

**Baba:** That is not so. While the mental tendencies become calm through shaktipat, a thought-free state of mind is experienced from which knowledge—pure understanding—shines forth spontaneously. When darkness is destroyed, light automatically appears. One does not have to proclaim that the light will come; it is experienced. If the chimney of a lamp is covered with soot, the light inside is not clearly visible, but as one cleans the chimney, the light spreads by itself; nothing else needs to be done. It is the same with shaktipat.

*In the evening a group of devotees came for darshan. One of them asked Baba a question.*

## *Worthiness to Receive Guru's Grace*

**Devotee:** *How do we know whether we are worthy to receive the Guru's grace or not?*

**Baba:** Are you not part of God? If you are sure of this, then you are as pure as God. Everyone has the right to realize God. Surrender just once to the Guru and see what happens. Let him do what he considers appropriate. He will take care of everything. In fact, the receiving of grace is in your hands. In the *Gītā* it is said:

> I welcome people according to the feeling with which they surrender to Me.[4]

MONDAY, DECEMBER 3, 1962

*Divali Vrajlal Shah from Vile Parle has been staying at the ashram for the past three days with her family. She is a Jain and a keen seeker of dhyāna yoga. She often has discussions with Baba.*

## Good and Bad Deeds of Siddha Saints

**Divali:** *Do Siddha saints also have good and bad deeds?*

**Baba:** Those who are liberated, having become one with the supreme Reality, are not affected by good or bad deeds, which are like drops of water on a lotus leaf for them.

Virtues and sins are experienced in a particular state. Just as the summer heat is intensely felt in Ganeshpuri but hardly at all in the resort areas of Ootacamund or Simla because of their higher elevation, similarly, there is a state in which the effects of actions are experienced.

Existence of sin is like a drop of water before the ocean of greatness of a liberated being. Just as a drop of filthy water is transformed into pure holy water after falling into the rapidly flowing Ganges, in the same way, for saints established in the ultimate Reality, sins become virtues. If it were not so, how could a bandit become the great saint Valmiki by being with Narada? How could the robber Naroji become a good man after being with Chaitanya Mahaprabhu? And how could the murderer Angulimal become a monk under Buddha's influence? Isn't it change of sin to virtue?

Even if Siddhas appear to be bound by pleasure and pain resulting from good and bad deeds, such pleasure and pain do not really affect them. Their liberated state never changes. In summer they experience the coolness of Ootacamund. Even though they themselves are beyond both, they praise good actions and condemn bad ones.

## The Existence of Ghosts and Spirits

**Divali:** *Are there such things as ghosts and spirits?*

**Baba:** They don't have an independent existence like humans, animals, and birds. Those who have unfulfilled desires and meet untimely deaths become ghosts. Ghosts are not necessarily bad, and in any case there is no reason to fear them, since no one can ever harm a pure-hearted person.

The intermediate period between death and rebirth is long for some and short for others. Only a few fortunate ones are immediately reborn.

# Chapter Two

# 1963

*Lalbuva has lived in Ganeshpuri for the past few years and has recited the Bhagavad Gītā daily at the samādhi shrine of Bhagawan Nityananda. He is known as Lalbuva, meaning "the red sādhu," because of his red clothes. For the past twenty days he has read the Gītā daily at the ashram, sitting on the platform around the bilva tree. Today Baba also sat there.*

## Vision of Unity

**Lalbuva:** *I know the entire Gītā by heart. I once knew its meaning as well, but now I have completely forgotten it.*

**Baba:** How much more do you want to know? In the *Gītā*, the Lord says:

> I pervade the whole world with merely a fraction of My being.[1]

To know this much is enough. Whatever we see, sentient or insentient, is God's form. All our troubles arise because we see diversity in the world and are conscious of different names and forms.

A devotee had a gold statue of the deity Khandoba, sitting on a horse. Unfortunately, he became so poor that he was on the verge of starvation. Someone advised him to sell the statue of Khandoba, so he took it to a goldsmith who offered him three hundred rupees for the deity and seven hundred rupees for the horse. The devotee was enraged because the value of God was less than that of the horse. The goldsmith knew no difference between the deity and the horse. To him, both were only gold. For the devotee, the deity and the horse were different. So if you acquire the vision of the goldsmith, all your troubles will end.

*Today satsang was again held on the platform around the bilva tree.*

## There Is No Disparity in God's Creation

**Devotee:** *Why do we see so much disparity in God's creation?*

**Baba:** The way God is running the world is perfect. There is no mistake anywhere. I will give an example to explain this. One day a man was sitting under a berry tree smoking a pipe. Looking up at the tree, he thought, "Well, God does not seem to have much sense. Why has he given such a small fruit to this big tree and such a big fruit to that small, tender creeper bearing pumpkins? What disparity in God's creation!" After a little while, a berry fell on his head, and then he came to his senses. He exclaimed, "Oh God, no, it is not like that! You have made the world perfect! If You had given this tree a huge fruit, my head would have been crushed!"

WEDNESDAY, JANUARY 23, 1963

*Several devotees were assembled around the bilva tree platform this evening. One of the old residents of Ganeshpuri, Mr. Mardekar, and the panditji from Goregaon were among them.*

## The Law of Karma

**Mardekar:** *Tomorrow is my wife's operation. I am worried.*

**Baba:** Everyone has to go through the consequences of karma. Therefore, perform good actions and live through pleasure and pain resulting from past deeds. All days are not the same. Bad days will continue to follow good days and good days will follow bad ones. When an excess of sin is accumulated, we are born as animals or birds; whereas when good deeds predominate, we become gods. We are born as human beings when good and bad deeds are equal. Even gods have to take a human birth to undergo the results of their remaining karmas. The *Gītā* says:

> When their good deeds are exhausted, the gods return to the mortal world.[2]

One attains God-realization when all one's good and bad karmas are exhausted. I will tell you a story that illustrates this.

Once a great soul named Haridas, who was devoted to Lord Vitthal, lived in a certain city. This was to be his last birth. One day a devotee invited Haridas to his home for a few days. The devotee's wife became lustful toward the saint and urged him to sleep with her. Haridas replied that it was against the tenets of the scriptures to make love to a woman whose husband was alive. Hearing this, the wife went out and killed her husband. She returned to Haridas and said to him, "I no longer have a husband." The saint was flabbergasted and shouted, "What have you done? What do you think I am?" The woman became very angry. Wailing and lamenting loudly, she gathered a big crowd and accused Haridas of murdering her husband. The case reached the court and Haridas was found guilty. The judge did not have the heart to execute such a saintly person. Since the murder had been committed with his hands, the judge punished Haridas by having his arms cut off below the elbows and then released him.

The saint continued worshiping God, and eventually Lord Vitthal appeared before him and told him to ask for a boon. Haridas said, "After having seen You, what else could I possibly desire? However, I request You to clear one doubt for me. Why was I punished by having my arms cut off even though I had done nothing wrong in my life?" The Lord replied, "Your hands were cut off. That is why you have attained Me. One's destiny has to be lived out."

In order to satisfy him, the Lord showed Haridas his past life, in which he was an austere yogi. One morning while he was worshiping the sun, a cow passed by. Soon afterward a butcher ran up to him asking which way the cow had gone. "In that direction," he replied, pointing out the way with both his hands. The butcher found the cow and killed her. Then the Lord explained that in this life the cow had become the woman, the butcher had become her husband, and the yogi had become Haridas. The wife murdered the husband, and Haridas's forearms were cut off.

God-realization is only possible after fully going through the fruits of one's past karmas. It is said:

> The fruits of all the good and bad deeds performed in the past must be lived through, for the fruit of karma will never be destroyed in any other way, even after an eternity of time.[3]

## THURSDAY, JANUARY 24, 1963

*Jayantilal Kadakia and Lalit Sanghavi came from Secunderabad for Baba's darshan.*

### *The Importance of Patience in Sadhana*

**Lalit:** *An astrologer told me that after fifteen years I would reach a certain level of spiritual attainment, but wouldn't fifteen years of my life be wasted in this way?*

**Baba:** Whatever has to happen according to karma will happen. One does not become a father the moment he is born. He must grow up, get married, and then have children before he can be called a father. In the same way, one achieves results on the spiritual path at the right time. The aspirant should continue to practice with faith and patience.

Once upon a time, two yogis were doing sadhana under a neem tree. One day Narada happened to pass by, and they asked him what his destination was. Narada replied that he was going to Lord Vishnu. Both of them then requested Narada to ask the Lord how soon they would attain Self-realization. On his return journey, Narada gave each one a message from the Lord. One of the yogis was told that he would achieve his goal after twelve years. That is what the Lord had said. Hearing this, he immediately became disheartened, gave up his sadhana, and went away. As a result, his sadhana remained incomplete and he gained nothing from it. The other aspirant was told that the Lord had said that he would gain Self-realization after as many lifetimes as there were leaves on the neem tree. Upon hearing this, he began to dance joyfully, knowing that he would surely attain his goal no matter how many lives it would take. This aspirant continued his sadhana. As a result, he speedily went through the various types of short and long births and eventually realized the Self. Patience and contentment are essential on the spiritual path.

*Mr. Albert Rudolph from New York has come to Ganeshpuri for about a week on his yearly visit for Baba's darshan.*

## *Conserving the Shakti*

**Rudolph:** *I have been feeling a tremendous surge of energy since I visited you here last September. The shakti flows through both of my hands into the tips of my fingers and even seems to flow out through my fingertips. My right hand is automatically raised up in abhaya mudrā, and I feel as though shakti is flowing out of my palm. Is this all right?*

**Baba:** As far as possible, shakti should not be allowed to flow out of the body. When such sensations are felt in the hand, the first finger should be joined with the thumb in *jñāna mudrā*. Conserve your energy so that it may become more powerful and you can perform great tasks through it.

**Rudolph:** *In America many people come to me with all kinds of problems and questions. They claim to experience peace just by sitting near me. Sometimes my shakti flows into them, curing their diseases. Is it all right to allow the shakti to flow into others in this way? Afterward I frequently feel tired and my body aches. Sometimes this condition lasts throughout the entire day, but after a while I feel healthy and fresh again.*

**Baba:** There is nothing wrong with this. Service done selflessly without desire is not wasted. The shakti will be restored with meditation. However, if there is self-interest, it will be depleted.

## Seat of the Guru

**Rudolph:** *Sometimes I feel a sensation like a strong vibration between my eyebrows. I feel as though I have two eyes in my forehead from which something is coming out with a hissing sound. What could this be?*

**Baba:** Between the eyebrows there is a two-petaled lotus, the seat of the Guru. Progress beyond this point depends entirely on the grace of the Guru. The sensations you experience are caused by Kundalini Shakti, which is trying to move upward from this point. Through concentration on the region of the two-petaled lotus, we can know anything we desire in the world, but it should be kept a secret as far as possible. With increased meditation on this spot, one is inspired with noble thoughts. A thumb-sized light is situated here, above which is a thousand-petaled lotus of brilliant light where Shiva and Shakti become united.

**Rudolph:** *People who come to me have various kinds of experiences concerning me. Sometimes they see light, fire, and so forth in place of my physical form. One person claims that I talked to him at his home, but I know nothing about it. Sometimes when sitting in the company of others, I have strange experiences. The breath, or prāna, suddenly goes up into the head, resulting in deep meditation. At other times, even while sitting on the ground, I feel as though I am floating high in the air.*

**Baba:** Whatever is happening is good. Others have experiences concerning you because the shakti that has passed into them from you is working in them. You need not know about these experiences.

**Rudolph:** *Since I still have many impurities, I don't like people to hold me in high esteem.*

**Baba:** The Self is ever pure. Since it never becomes impure, you are pure.

**Rudolph:** *So you really believe that? Some of the people who come to me seem impure.*

**Baba:** The Self is supremely pure. What you are seeing are their old *samskāras* and mental attitudes.

*When taking leave, Rudolph again asked Baba some questions.*

**Rudolph:** *What kind of sadhana should I do from now on?*

**Baba:** Nothing particular. Just keep meditating.

**Rudolph:** *I don't sit for meditation regularly. When I suddenly feel an urge, I wish to sit down calmly.*

**Baba:** That is all right.

**Rudolph:** *When will I attain perfection?*

**Baba:** Let the shakti work in its own way. Everything will happen at the right time.

**Rudolph:** *I had a premonition when I was young that two of my students would become very great and world famous.*

**Baba:** You continue doing your duty and sadhana; leave the rest, the fruits, to God. Let everything happen according to His will. He will do whatever He wishes.

**Rudolph:** *I request your blessings for my mother and brother.*

**Baba:** Blessings are there, of course.

## Saturday, January 26, 1963

*Today the Managing Director of M/S. Mahindra and Mahindra Ltd., Mr. Harish Mahindra, came for Baba's darshan and satsang.*

# Recognition of One's True Self

**Harish:** *Will I be able to make progress on the spiritual path?*

**Baba:** Every human being is a part of God. How can he ever change? There is no difference between God and man. Just as mangoes alone grow on mango trees, similarly, only God is created from God. But because man, due to ignorance, has forgotten his real nature, he thinks that he is an individual being, imperfect and different from God.

In our scriptures we have a *pratyabhijñānyāya* (recognition), the essence of which I will explain by telling a story.

Once a king, accompanied by his young son, went hunting in a forest where he saw a beautiful deer. Leaving his son under a tree, he pursued the deer for quite a long distance. After a while, some tribesmen who were passing through the forest saw the young prince crying under the tree, and they took him home with them, assuming that he was lost. When the king returned from hunting, his son was nowhere to be found. He went home and sent search parties in all directions, but there was no sign of the child.

After several years, the king's prime minister was attending to court business and came upon the tribesmen's dwelling place. There he saw a young boy who appeared quite different from the other boys. Reminded of the lost prince, the prime minister asked him who he was. The boy replied that he was the son of a tribesman. The prime minister then asked the tribesmen about the boy, but they knew nothing except that they had found him several years ago under a tree in the forest and had brought him home. Hearing this, the prime minister was convinced that the boy was the lost prince, and he took him to the palace.

Even after the boy was told that he was a prince, he still considered himself a tribesman because of his deep mental impressions of having been with tribesmen for many years. The prime minister dressed him in beautiful, princely clothes and made him view himself in a large mirror, saying, "Look, this is what you really are." Seeing his real identity, the boy's illusion vanished, and he was convinced that he was really a prince. This understanding removed his former feelings of lowliness, and he began to behave like a real prince.

In the same way, if we become aware of our true Self, we will realize that we are really God and all sense of imperfection will be eliminated. Man has the right to attain his Godhood and, therefore, should not despair. Keep trying, have no doubts, and seek the company of saints. It is the duty of every saint to make you realize your real Self, just as the prime minister helped the prince to realize his true identity.

## SUNDAY, JANUARY 27, 1963

*Mr. Dwarka Khosla, a devotee, came today for Baba's darshan accompanied by an elderly seeker who has lived in the Aurobindo Ashram in Pondicherry for fourteen years.*

## *One Entity Pervades Everywhere*

**Seeker:** *Babaji, I see Aurobindo Ghosh in you.*

**Baba:** Your devotion to Aurobindo Ghosh has made this whole world appear like him to you. One sees as one really feels. Aurobindo is everywhere.

**Seeker:** *No, not in everything. I see Aurobindo only in you.*

**Baba:** God is everywhere. All the different forms in the world are made of God. Just as the same artist paints different pictures of a cow, a tiger, a man, and a monkey on the same canvas with the same colors and the same brush, so also this diverse and varied world is made of only one element. Only the forms are different; the substance is the same.

*Mr. Yogendra Trivedi, a trustee of Shree Gurudev Ashram, and his friend, Mr. K. K. Shah, the Secretary of the All India Congress Committee, came today for Baba's darshan. Mr. Shah, who is a good seeker, has great love for the Bhagavad Gītā.*

**K. K. Shah:** *We have begun experimenting with prānāyāma along with other treatments in our hospital near the Sabarkantha District in Gujarat. I believe the practice of prānāyāma could cure patients, since prāna is the most important aspect of the human body. Please give us three or four persons who will teach prānāyāma to the patients.*

**Baba:** All right.

## The Supreme Shakti Supports All

**K. K. Shah:** *When the child is in the mother's womb, it receives nourishment but does not discharge any waste matter. Breathing starts and the bowels move when the umbilical cord is cut after birth. Babaji, who protects the child when it is in the mother's womb?*

**Baba:** Only one shakti permeates the whole world, which exists only with its support. This shakti creates, sustains, and destroys the world. It also protects the child in the womb. This energy is also called *chitshakti* or *kundalinī shakti*, and is located at the base of the spine in the *mūlādhāra chakra* in all human beings. When it is awakened, one becomes aware of one's true self.

This entire universe is the manifestation of Brahman. Brahman pervades everywhere and is the sole element constituting all the apparently contradictory attributes visible to us. Fire is hot and water is cool, but the coolness and the heat consist of the same element, which is animate as well as inanimate. For example, the same potter makes many different pots out of the same clay on the same wheel. Likewise, this world, though having things with different names, appearances, and forms, has emerged from the same *chaitanya shakti*, an energy having the power to create the many out of the one and to reabsorb the many back into the one.

**K. K. Shah:** *People cannot comprehend this because they try to understand it with their limited intellect.*

**Baba:** Very true. A person makes himself something and believes himself to be that. He learns engineering and believes himself to be an engineer; he studies law and calls himself a lawyer. He forgets his original Self and believes he is someone whom he has created in his own mind.

## SUNDAY, FEBRUARY 3, 1963

*Some people from Aurangabad who had heard about Baba from the well-known Dr. A. N. Christian came for Baba's darshan. One of them, a doctor, began talking with Baba.*

### *The Power of Words*

**Doctor:** *This lady sitting here is not doing well. No medicine has had any effect on the pain in her legs.*

**Baba:** Remembrance of God's name combines all medicines. It is the medicine of medicines. The power of the Word is so great that the entire universe was created from it. The Word, or sound, exploded and became ether, the vibrations of which created air. Friction in the air created fire. The vapor of fire became water, and the sediment in water became the earth. To cure a disease is mere play for the mighty Word that has the power to create the world.

**Doctor:** *Is the power of God's name so great that it can relieve man of all diseases and worries?*

**Baba:** I will relate an incident that illustrates what power words have.

A man who had received his higher education abroad went to a saint to discuss with him how mantra repetition could be beneficial. The saint ignored him and refused to talk. The man lost patience and was about to speak, when the saint shouted, "Shut up, you ass!" Enraged, the man was on the verge of exploding, when the saint said, "Now can you see the power of words? If a bad word could cause such a violent reaction in you, then what effect, what transformation, would God's holy name produce?" Hearing this, the man fell at the saint's feet.

## Tuesday, February 26, 1963

*A journalist who is making an independent study of the various aspects of yoga has come today for Baba's darshan. He took sannyāsa on his own, calling it "samādhi sannyāsa," and assumed a new name. He recently came to Vajreshwari to practice yoga.*

## Three Kinds of Samādhi

**Journalist:** *No one has yet understood the supreme Truth.*

**Baba:** Everyone speaks according to his experience. Each person's words are the reflection of his own experience. I have heard that you took "*samādhi sannyāsa.*" What kind of *sannyāsa* or *samādhi* is that? According to the commonly understood meaning, I know only about three types of *samādhi*. One *samādhi* is that which is built over the burial site of a saint as a memorial. Another *samādhi* is the state of inertness in which yogis sit for hours. The third *samādhi* is the state of the Self in which one is not affected by any circumstances and remains in a state of equanimity. This is also called *sahaja samādhi.*

*The journalist did not answer Baba's question. Instead, he said:*

**Journalist:** *I had many doubts before I started on this path.*

**Baba:** According to Vedanta, doubt is merely a tendency of the mind. Doubts arise and subside, but the state of the Self always remains the same.

**Journalist:** *I want to reach that state which you have attained.*

**Baba:** There is no such thing as attainment or non-attainment. The one who seeks liberation is already liberated. The Self has no bondage or liberation. The divine shakti is infinite.

## Divine Energy Is Infinite

**Journalist:** *One's shakti is depleted by giving shakti to others and cannot be regained. Therefore we should not give away too much shakti, otherwise all of it will be irretrievably lost. Is this true?*

**Baba:** When the river merges into the ocean, it becomes the ocean, giving up its separate individuality. In the same way, how can a person's shakti be depleted when he becomes one with the absolute Reality, the infinite source of shakti? If a man who has earned a hundred rupees keeps spending one rupee here and one rupee there, his earnings will soon be used up, but the man with inexhaustible wealth need not worry. Divine wealth, divine shakti, can never be depleted.

### SATURDAY, MARCH 2, 1963

*Mr. V. S. Page, Chairman of the Maharashtra State Legislative Council, is a great scholar. He has made a deep study of the Tantras and Āgamas of Shaivism, and has assimilated Jñāneshvarī, understanding that they are both one. Even amidst worldly affairs, he lives like a true renunciant. He comes very often for satsang with Baba.*

**Page:** *When does one attain the ultimate stage on the spiritual path?*

**Baba:** That stage will surely come in its own time, just as when counting, one is followed by two, and two is followed by three, and so on until one hundred is reached.

## *True Bliss Is Not Relative*

**Page:** *Some years ago I had the experience of absolute bliss, but it has never returned, despite many years of sadhana. I have had many other experiences, but I always return to my ordinary state.*

**Baba:** Your present state in which you do not experience anything is higher than the experience you had. What you experienced before was mere happiness, not true bliss, because you are now unhappy in its absence. It means that that joy was relative. Happiness and pain are relative, but the experience of ultimate bliss, *sacchidānanda,* is non-relative and spontaneous. The thought-free state is the true attainment. Even after attaining that state, thoughts arise, but they do not affect the fundamental state attained. The completely still state and the state with vibrations come and go. They are also known as *nirāmaya* and *samaya* states. In fact, if the state of stillness remains undisturbed for too long, it could prove to be a problem, as in the case of Upasani Maharaj of Nasik. When his mind suddenly became still while eating, he would hold a morsel of food in his hand and remain in that state for two or three days at a time. If the state of stillness is attained even for a moment, it is sufficient. One need not remain in that state for hours.

## Thought-Free State Through Shaktipat

**Page:** *Where should one's attention be concentrated until the thought-free state is achieved?*

**Baba:** One should concentrate wherever the thoughts automatically settle down: at the top of the head (*sahasrāra*), heart (*hridaya*), or between the eyebrows (*ājñā chakra*). The effect of shaktipat is like an injection of medicine that spreads automatically throughout the body. The energy transmitted by the Guru works within the seeker without any effort on his part, enabling him to attain the thought-free state. One who tries to still his mind through knowledge has to practice for a long time with constant vigilance. This is not easy, but it becomes easy after shaktipat is received from the Guru.

**Page:** *Sometimes I feel that my breathing has stopped.*

**Baba:** It is going on within, in the *sushumnā.* Yogis end their lives in the *sushumnā.* The *prāna* of a yogi does not go out in the ordinary manner at the time of death, but merges inside in the *sushumnā.*

*Baba visited Manjusar, a town near Baroda, to attend a yajña called "Navakundi Vishnu Yajna" at the abode of a saint, Shri Girija-shankar Mugatramji. From there he went to Ahmadabad where he stayed at the home of Mr. Harsiddhashah, the grandson of the famous mill owner, Mr. Narsinhlal. Among the many devotees who came for darshan was Mrs. Shantagauri, the wife of the late collector, Mr. Chimanlal Kavi.*

## *Women's Right to Chant Gāyatrī Mantra*

**Shantagauri:** *Is it true that women do not have the right to chant either Om or the gāyatrī mantra?*

**Baba:** Who says so?

**Shantagauri:** *The head of our sannyāsa ashram.*

**Baba:** He speaks according to his interpretation of the scriptures. But I ask you on the basis of the Truth whether Gayatri itself is female or male? Gayatri is called *devī* (goddess). If women are not allowed to repeat *Om,* what about the repetition of *Om* that goes on constantly within, in rhythm with your breathing? Can anyone stop it?

## *Meditation*

**Shantagauri:** *How should one meditate?*

**Baba:** Many methods of meditation are described in the scriptures; however, the meditation that comes spontaneously through the Guru's grace is the best and easiest. When the *sadguru* bestows his grace on the disciple, he transmits his own shakti into him and awakens his inner *shakti, kundalinī.* With this, meditation comes spontaneously. This spiritual process of awakening the *kundalinī shakti* is called shaktipat. One who has this ability to give shaktipat is a Guru in the true sense.

## MONDAY, MARCH 25, 1963

*The following satsang took place when Baba stayed in Bombay for a few days.*

# *Discrimination Between Spirituality and Worldly Life*

**Devotee:** *I cannot maintain a proper balance between the spiritual path and worldly life. What should I do?*

**Baba:** If a person who earns just enough for his daily bread by breaking stones and sweating suddenly comes across a diamond, should he go on breaking stones? It is appropriate to give up the ordinary after gaining the extraordinary. But don't think that I am advising you to give up the world. Do both with discrimination. People nowadays want God on the one hand, and on the other they want their businesses to be successful, their children to study properly, their health to remain perfect, as well as their households and cars to run without any complications. A person should use discrimination if he wants to maintain a good balance between spiritual pursuit and worldly affairs.

## WEDNESDAY, MARCH 27, 1963

*Today in Juhu, Baba visited the home of a devotee, Shri Manilal Modi, proprietor of Gujarat Type Foundry. His son Ramendra asked Baba the following question:*

## Remembrance of God and Freedom from Debt

**Ramendra:** *We do not have peace of mind even though we do our actions truthfully. If we are harassed by others through no fault of our own, by what means can we keep the mind calm?*

**Baba:** This is known as undergoing the consequences of past actions and owing of debt. I like a person who repays the debt while remembering God. I call him a wise person.

**Another Devotee:** *But karma is inert.*

**Baba:** You speak merely from your reading of books. Do you know the truth? This whole world is made of one divine energy called *chitshakti,* which is conscious. The whole world is also conscious. How can anything in it be inert ?

### SUNDAY, MARCH 31, 1963

*Today Shri Dhamankar, a long-time active Congress Party worker, arrived unexpectedly. He had the following conversation with Baba:*

## The Detachment of an Avadhūta

**Dhamankar:** *I once asked Nityananda Baba what would happen to all the things associated with him after his death. It would be better if some arrangement for the future were made. Nityananda Baba simply replied, "All is dust."*

**Baba:** This is very true. He would always give the same answer. He was on the level of God. When the whole world belonged to him, then how could he have the feeling of "mine" for a small piece of land? Such great saints who are *avadhūtas* are completely detached from mundane affairs.

*The first meeting of the Managing Council of the Ashram Trust since its formation was held today. On this occasion Baba spoke the following words:*

**Baba:** Today the Ashram Trust completes one year of its existence. It is gratifying to note that everything is running in a well-organized manner. The Charity Commissioner, Mr. Godse, has said that from the point of view of discipline, our Ashram Trust is maintaining a very high standard, and he has expressed the hope that it will continue to do so in the future.

## *The Aim of the Ashram*

God's creation is also governed by certain laws. The sun and the moon rise and set at their appointed times. We have winter, summer, and the monsoon in accordance with the cycle of the seasons. If someone wishes to have another sun or summer during the winter season, it is just not possible.

This ashram is also a part of God. Just as nobody can meddle with the laws of God's creation, likewise, nobody can disrupt the discipline of the ashram. I request the workers here to keep in view the ideal of *paraspara devo bhāva*, "See God in each other," and consider one another as manifestations of God Himself. If a person is incapable of doing any work, let him do none, but he should not create obstacles for others.

The aim of this ashram is to impart spiritual knowledge to sincere seekers. One cannot be completely happy through the accumulation of external knowledge. At some point in life, one has to turn toward spiritual knowledge and take refuge at the feet of a Guru.

The tradition of saints has existed since time immemorial and will continue forever. This world has seen many changes and will witness many more, but the proclamation of the saints regarding Truth will survive as long as the sun and the moon remain in the heavens. Falsehood may undergo change, but Truth is eternal.

Nobody can destroy the tradition of the saints or their institutions, which are part of God. Since God is indestructible, they, too, can never be destroyed. Spiritual knowledge is the greatest of all knowledge. One gains this knowledge from a Self-realized *sadguru* through *gurubhakti* (devotion to the Guru), through Guru's grace. This knowledge is universal; it knows no bounds and is, therefore, indestructible.

TUESDAY, APRIL 2, 1963

*Three Sindhi women from Pune have come to stay in Ganeshpuri for a few days. This morning they had satsang with Baba.*

## *Worship God in Any Name and Form*

**Woman:** *In which form should I remember the supreme Lord? If the supreme Lord is One, then we should remember Him only in one form.*

**Baba:** The supreme Reality is One and yet manifests in various forms. You can remember the Lord in any form that you like.

**Woman:** *But the Bhagavad Gītā says that God manifests as light:*

> If the radiance of a thousand suns were to blaze out at once in the sky, even that would not be like the splendor of that Great Being.[4]

**Baba:** God is present everywhere. You may pray to Him in any form that appeals to you. If you were to consider this box as God and worship it, you would attain the same thing as by worshiping a stone idol of God. The main point is that you must remember God constantly.

**Woman:** *How can I know God?*

**Baba:** You will know Him only when He becomes pleased with you and reveals Himself to you.

**Woman:** *But when is He pleased?*

**Baba:** God is certainly pleased by your pure devotion. Remember Him constantly, chant His name all the time. You don't know about yourself, but He knows you. Leave it to Him and have faith in Him. We cannot bargain with God as we do in our worldly life. God may be pleased with one seeker who has chanted His name only seven times, while He may not be pleased with another even after he has done *japa* of God's name seven million times.

**Woman:** *Which name of God should I repeat and how?*

**Baba:** You can repeat that name of God that appeals to you the most, and you can chant it in any manner that is convenient for you. It is said that Valmiki was liberated even by repeating "Mara-Mara" (meaning killed-killed) instead of "Rama-Rama."

**Woman:** *Is it not contradictory to do japa and yet say, "You are my mother; you are my father?"*

**Baba:** Do you think that praying to God saying "You are my mother and father" is different from doing *japa* of His name or from constant remembrance of Him?

*A discussion followed in which references to the scriptures were made.*

**Baba:** You are discussing the scriptures through your mental cleverness and are thus trapped by your own cleverness. What is your ultimate goal? When you go to the market in Pune, you don't buy all the vegetables that are available, but just those that you want. All grains and vegetables contain nourishing substances. *Puri,* bread, *chapāti,* rice, pulses, grains—whatever you select will give you nourishment as well as satisfaction. Similarly, the scriptures are very numerous: Vedas, Upanishads, Puranas, Yoga Shastras, Sankhya philosophy, etc. Various methods of spiritual sadhana are described in these, but your life is short, so you choose the sadhana that appeals to you and start doing that. The end result of all the methods is one and the same.

## Friday, April 5, 1963

*Divaliben of Vile Parle came daily for satsang with Baba during his five-day stay in Santa Cruz.*

**Divaliben:** *At one time a Jain sādhu who lived in Abu was greatly respected. Wealthy people from distant places used to visit him. He had such powers that whatever he said would come true, but after a while he lost his power, and then the very same devotees who had previously revered him began to slight him. What could have caused the loss of his powers?*

**Baba:** During a certain period of one's sadhana one can know everything; whatever one wants to know will reveal itself. As one progresses, a stage is reached in which no thoughts or impulses arise. This stage is higher than attainment of powers; nothing can be known in this stage. The Jain *sādhu* at Abu used to show off to others whatever intuitions he had, and that is why he had all that trouble. The intuitions stopped, and therefore he also stopped talking about them. This does not mean he had regressed on his path.

**Divaliben:** *Why do the scriptures say that one should not eat tubers and that one should not eat at night?*

**Baba:** There is always some hidden meaning in what the scriptures say. Tubers contain a lot of sugar. At night at mealtime, insects are attracted by the light. But, in any case, how far can a seeker progress even after observing all these rules?

When I was staying at Kasara Ghat, five or six Jain women *sannyāsīs* came to stay on the ground floor of the house. The head of the group was afflicted by a ghost. If a person cannot cure himself of an affliction caused by a wicked person's black magic, what is the use of observing rules such as whether something should or should not be done and in what manner, or whether a certain food should or should not be eaten? What kind of *tapasyā* can it be that is incapable of expelling a ghost? And what sort of *tapasvinī* is one who can be possessed by a ghost?

## *Witness-Consciousness*

**Divaliben:** *Kindly help me that I may remain in meditation for a longer time, and that my mind may always remain calm.*

**Baba:** During meditation the mind may alternate between peacefulness and agitation. The Self witnesses both of these patterns of mind, but has nothing to do with either of them. The Self is not affected by anything, it is only a Witness. The Self always remains in the same state without undergoing any change, and that is your true nature. Remain steady in That.

**Divaliben:** *After attaining liberation, what is one's relationship with the body?*

**Baba:** After liberation, the body becomes an obstacle rather than a help. Because everything can be known without using the senses, the body becomes purposeless. When it is not necessary to hear through the ears, what is the use of the sense of hearing? When it is not necessary to see through the eyes, what is the use of the sense of seeing?

### MONDAY, MAY 20, 1963

*Shri Anandji of the Govindji Bharmal Company has come for a few days and is staying at the holiday camp. He came today for satsang with Baba.*

## Service to the Guru

**Anandjibhai:** *The Bhagavad Gītā states that we can attain knowledge by serving realized beings. What is the meaning of service here?*

**Baba:** It means that you should regard the lives of the saints and the great beings as an example and behave accordingly. Whatever work you can do for the Guru while staying with him is service to him. Through such service, a disciple's sins are washed away and he becomes worthy to receive the knowledge of Brahman. One must be worthy to gain the knowledge of Brahman, and this worthiness is acquired by service to the Guru. But in serving, one must also have an intense desire for liberation, without which even service to the Guru will not bear fruit. Many people did personal service to my Gurudev, Nityananda, for many years, but what they gained spiritually is best known only to themselves! A householder saint does not give the knowledge of Brahman even to his own son if he is not worthy of it. Shvetaketu had to go to another Guru even though his own father, Uddalaka, was a knower of Brahman. Liberation is not cheap. That knowledge which leads to the state of desirelessness, free from pain, in which only permanent bliss exists, is obtained by doing service to the Guru. In order to obtain it, you must be worthy of it.

Through service to the Guru, the disciple attracts the Guru's knowledge, and it flows into him automatically. The meaning of service is "I shall do Thy bidding." If your Gurudev tells you to go to Benares and you go to Mecca instead, this will bring your downfall. You will not gain knowledge by asking the Guru what he has studied or what he has achieved. You will gain it only by one-pointed service to him.

## The Time of Death Is Predetermined

**Anandjibhai:** *My doctors are advising me to undergo an operation, but I am afraid.*

**Baba:** Man does not die again and again, he dies only once. Death will come at its own fixed time, so you need not be afraid. If the time for a man's death has not come, he cannot die even if someone should try to kill him, but he will certainly die when his time comes.

In the same village from where you come there lived a man named Shiva Pengde, against whom there were forty lawsuits pending in the court. Even after a long, twelve-year search, the government officials could not catch him, and finally they gave up their efforts. Eventually, he even reformed himself. He gave large sums of money in charity and built many temples and ashrams. He changed so much that the government even awarded him a title.

Shiva Pengde's mother had been a widow from childhood, but during her widowhood she became pregnant. Owing to the birth of Shiva under such circumstances, his mother dug a pit in which she buried him alive. At that very time, the owner of the land happened to come there and heard a baby's cry inside the earth. He had it dug up and found the baby there. He then searched for and found the child's mother and told her to take care of it. The point of the story is that until a man's time of death has arrived, he cannot die. So do not be frightened. Go ahead with the operation.

## TUESDAY, MAY 21, 1963

*Today Satchidananda, a sannyāsī from Parle Sannyas Ashram, came to have satsang with Baba. Baba talked to him about shaktipat and about the futility of reading too many books.*

## Knowledge Is Gained from Within

**Swami Satchidananda** (presenting a book to Baba): *The author of this book is very learned and has written several books in Sanskrit.*

**Baba:** The books that saints and great beings wrote were inspired by their inner divine energy, for example, Jnaneshwar's commentary on the *Bhagavad Gītā*, known as *Jñāneshvarī*, and Tukaram's *abhangas*.

It is not my intention to criticize learning or the reading of books. What I want to convey is that when the same shakti that made them write is awakened within us, all that is written is understood without effort. If the knowledge that you seek in these books can be obtained from within your Self, then you won't have to look for it outside. That knowledge and that bliss are lying within us. We are a part of God; therefore, what is in God is in us too. It can be experienced only when the inner shakti is awakened, and the awakening of this shakti depends upon the grace of the *sadguru*.

THURSDAY, JUNE 6, 1963

*During Baba's seven-day stay in Santa Cruz, satsangs were held.*

## A Realized Being Is Beyond Virtue or Sin, Acceptance or Rejection

**Divaliben:** *Just as one has to reap the fruits of one's bad actions, one must also have to reap the fruits of one's good actions. In that case, isn't a realized being bound by his meritorious actions?*

**Baba:** Good actions with a motive are certainly binding. Good deeds done with a desire to gain merit are motivated. After God-realization, the results of a realized being's good actions are enjoyed by others. He may distribute sweets or clothes, he may perform *yajñas*, he may go on pilgrimages, or he may perform worship of God—the fruits of all these actions are enjoyed by others. Those who eat what he gives, those who develop faith in God through him, those who gain knowledge through him—they are the ones who enjoy the fruits of his good actions.

**Divaliben:** *Saints receive many offerings such as fruit, flowers, clothes, money, etc. What is the use of all these things to a realized being, since he has renounced everything?*

**Baba:** What you say is due to lack of personal experience. Nothing binds a *jñānī*. It is because the viewers are attached that they see duality between attachment and detachment. This is called misunderstanding the scriptures. Just as misunderstandings arise in mundane affairs, they also occur with regard to the scriptures. Seeing a snake in a rope is a practical illusion. Similarly, understanding just the opposite or not the real meaning of the scriptures is also an illusion.

The renunciation mentioned in the scriptures refers to a seeker's renunciation during the period of his sadhana. This is advised to save the seeker from obstacles and to develop detachment. For a Siddha, however, who has reached the ultimate goal of Self-realization, there is nothing to reject or accept. One who has to practice renunciation gives up his house, his possessions, his relatives, friends, everything. The reason is that he has to get rid of "I" and "mine," that is, ego. Even then, he still has to live in someone's house or under some roof, he has to retain some essential articles for daily use, and he maintains contact with some people, if not with his own relatives. He who desires liberation should destroy his ego through the attitude "all this is not mine."

In the eighteenth chapter of the *Bhagavad Gītā* it is said:

> What will he renounce who has completely annihilated
> his ego and attained true discrimination?[5]

Renunciation is possible only when the idea of "mine"-ness exists.

If a pot is filled with water, it can reflect the sun, moon, and stars, but if the water is removed, there can be no reflection. It is a peculiarity of the mind that external objects of the world continually create images in the mind; or, in other words, thoughts of worldly objects continuously arise in the mind. These give rise to likes and dislikes, which stimulate the senses. As a result, one experiences pain and pleasure. But if one's mind is completely dissolved, the outside objects cannot be reflected in it. Hence, for a realized being, there is neither acceptance nor rejection. His life proceeds according to his destiny. I advise you to give up such useless thoughts. If you go on thinking excessively, your mind will become dull and disturbed, and you will not be capable of grasping the Truth.

### TUESDAY, JULY 9, 1963

*Today a sannyāsī came to the ashram.*

## Know Vedanta from Your Own Experience

**Swami:** *At our ashram we are teaching Vedanta to the students.*

**Baba:** The Vedantic knowledge that is being taught in ashrams nowadays is like the academic knowledge of a college professor. Someone taught him something and he repeated it to others. Vedanta states that there are two things, the seer and the seen, and of these, the seer is real and the seen is unreal. Thus, from my point of view, I am the seer, you are the seen, so I am real and you are unreal. But from your point of view, you are the seer, I am the seen, so I who was previously real have now become unreal. Now, which of these viewpoints is correct? The kind of Vedanta that is being learned from books is like this, while in the Vedanta of one's experience, everything is Brahman. The seer himself appears as the seen.

**Devotee:** *What is the difference between a jñānī and a karma yogi?*

**Baba:** The *jñānī* acts considering the world as an illusion, while the karma yogi acts considering it real. From the spiritual point of view, both are the same.

## SUNDAY, AUGUST 11, 1963

*This morning several devotees gathered in the ashram hall for satsang. Among them were Mr. Nain, a barrister, and his wife, Rukmini.*

**Nain:** *Recently I have been reading Ashtāvakra Gītā, and while reading it, I am reminded of Nirvānashatakam of Shri Shankaracharya.*

**Baba:** The *Ashtāvakra Gītā* is even greater than *Nirvānashatakam.* In the scriptures, two methods of contemplation are described: *vyatireka* and *anvaya.* "I am not this, I am not that" is the *vyatireka* method, which is described in *Nirvānashatakam.* When this thought is firmly established, a stage arrives where nothing remains of which you can say "I am not this." On the contrary, you begin to experience that you are everything and everywhere, and you contemplate accordingly. This is the *anvaya* which is described in *Ashtāvakra Gītā. Sadāchāra* of Shri Shankaracharya and *Amritānubhava* of Jnaneshwar also describe this method of *jñāna* sadhana. Another saint sang:

> This entire world is filled
> By You and You alone.
> You are in You,
> You are in me.
> You are You,
> And I am also You.
>
> You are in the sky,
> You are in the water and in the earth,
> You are in the air
> And also beneath the earth.

In the thundering of the clouds
And in the lightning,
In the showers of rain
And in the *pralaya*—
What exists is only You.

In the infinite expanse of the sea
And in the flow of the river,
In the cooling moonlight
And in the sun's scorching heat—
What exists is only You.

In the virtues and in the sins,
In hell and in heaven,
In the beasts and in the birds,
In the gods and in the demons
And in all human beings—
What exists is only You.

In the earth and in iron,
In the stone and in gold,
In the four *āshramas*
And in the four *varnas*—
What exists is only You.

In the rich and in the poor,
In the wise and in the ignorant,
In the most humble
And in the proudest of all—
What exists is only You.

In the friend and in the foe,
Inside and outside of the house,
Above, below, and in the middle,
In the animate and in the inanimate—
What exists is only You.

You are in yes,
You are in no,
You are in You,
You are in me.
Everywhere it is only You, You, You, You,
You, You, and You.[6]

**Rukminiben:** *Baba, what is the meaning of the word yogabhrashta? The Bhagavad Gītā says, "A yogabhrashta takes birth in the family of wealthy and pious people." Is this true?*

**Baba:** The term *yogabhrashta* does not signify a man who has gone astray from his path of sadhana. If a seeker has reached the fourth or fifth stage of yoga while pursuing his sadhana, and if his destiny requires that he leave his body before reaching the final stage of yoga, then he will be reborn in a pious and rich family and will resume his yogic sadhana from the stage he had attained in his previous life. All knowledge comes to him from within spontaneously. He does not require a Guru because he receives guidance from within, from his own Self. This is what is meant by *yogabhrashta.* Whether such a *yogabhrashta* seeker completes his sadhana with or without a Guru, his final achievement, the state of perfection he attains, will be the same. One student may obtain a master's degree in one university and transfer to another university for his Ph.D. Another student may do his entire course of study up to Ph.D. at a single university. Both will obtain the same degrees.

**Nain:** *Should the mind remain blank during meditation or should one see light?*

**Baba:** A seeker must progress beyond the lights that he sees during meditation. The experience of the bliss of the Self that springs up from within during meditation is the true light. It is the divine bliss that is signified by the word "light" in the saying "The Self is full of light."

## TUESDAY, AUGUST 13, 1963

*Today Shri Pratap Yande, a devotee of Baba, brought some of his friends for Baba's darshan.*

# Sanyama Siddhi

**Pratapbhai:** *Two days ago I went to a friend's home. His Guru was there. He was able to materialize kumkum in a dish or a shower of flowers at will. I saw all of this with my own eyes.*

**Baba:** The *kumkum* was already there in the dish, but because your vision was obstructed, you were unable to see it earlier. Many such varieties of magic are practiced. In yoga there is a *siddhi* called *sanyama siddhi.* In order to obtain it, one must practice *trātaka* (concentration on an object). One can bring forth anything by *sankalpa,* that is, just by wishing for it with a concentrated mind. Anyone can develop this ability after practicing the technique for a certain period of time.

The *sanyama siddhi* is described in the *Vibhūtipāda* of Patanjali's *Yogadarshana,* in which it is said that by practicing *sanyama* on the moon, one may experience light; by doing *sanyama* on an elephant, one may acquire the elephant's strength; and by doing *sanyama* on the sun, one may obtain the sun's brightness. One may obtain the qualities of any object on which *sanyama* is practiced. One can even know another's thoughts by doing *sanyama* on his mind.

Once when Swami Vivekananda was in Hyderabad, he met a man who possessed the *siddhi* of materializing whatever was requested. Swamiji asked him to demonstrate his *siddhi.* It so happened that the man had been suffering from a fever for many days, and he asked Swamiji to place his hand on his head. As soon as Swamiji did so, the man's fever disappeared. Then, in order to demonstrate his *siddhi,* the man told Swamiji to ask for anything he wanted. Swamiji asked for certain dishes that he had eaten in foreign countries and that were prepared in those countries only. The man immediately produced them, and Swamiji even ate some of the items just to satisfy himself. Swamiji asked him about this performance, and the man replied, "What I have done is just fun; you have the real *siddhi.*"

It is possible to learn many such skills, but these petty attainments do not lead to self-improvement; they are simply a waste of shakti. In Kasara, a man used to materialize printed currency notes, but it was essential to use them immediately because the printing would disappear after eight hours. In Borivli as well, there was a man who could give thousands of rupees to anyone who asked, on the condition, however, that the money be returned to him within a fixed period of time, or else the magician would have to undergo great trouble. In Chalisgaon there is a man named Nariyal Baba who takes pieces of paper with written replies to your questions from the very same coconuts that you offer to him.

## WEDNESDAY, SEPTEMBER 11, 1963

*During Baba's four-day stay at Santa Cruz, Shri V. S. Page came for his darshan.*

**Page:** *How is it possible for a realized person to describe the state of perfection, since it is beyond the grasp of the intellect and, according to the scriptures, is attained only by transcending the intellect? With what intellect, then, can a realized being describe that state to us?*

**Baba:** If you were to descend into the depths of a well, you would perceive a totally different world there. As long as you were there, you could not describe it to the people outside the well because you would have no means of communication. At that time the senses would not be in use, and therefore no contact would be possible with the external world. After coming out of the well, you could certainly describe what you experienced there. The realized beings describe their experiences of that state of perfection in a similar manner.

**Page:** *The Tantra Shāstra describes shāktopāya, ānavopāya, shāmbhavopāya, and anupāya. What is meant by anupāya?*[7]

**Baba:** *Anupāya* is the shaktipat of Shiva.

*Today Anne Burian, a Canadian seeker, came to the ashram with Shri Sunil Damania, a devotee of Baba. After arriving in India, she changed her name to Savitri. For the past nine months she has been staying in the ashram of Swami Ramdas in Kanhangadh.*

## *The Importance of Having Only One Guru*

**Savitri:** *In America I had a Mexican Guru. Because of his grace, I had a very exalted experience in which I completely lost body-consciousness. I did sadhana while staying with him. For the past three years I have been in India, and I have been meeting many saints and sages. Today I have come here to obtain your grace.*

**Baba:** Why didn't you stay with the Mexican Guru?

**Savitri:** *He very much wished that I would, but I started feeling within that I should go to Tibet, and so I left for India.*

**Baba:** Instead of going to many saints, one after another, you should accept one great being as your Guru and practice your sadhana with him. This would be much better for you.

**Savitri:** *But this is not something within my control. God Himself takes me from one saint to another. My life is simply passing away in this manner. After taking me to a certain stage with one saint, God sends me to others in order to further my progress. I feel as though I have been born for a particular mission for which God is preparing me. For this reason, I have no control over anything that is happening. I act as God directs me. When I was in Almora I saw Shri Ramakrishna Paramahamsa in my meditation, and he told me, "Come home." So I left Almora and went to Calcutta.*

**Baba:** When we remain steadfastly with one Guru, his shakti works constantly within us and takes us to perfection in due course.

**Savitri:** *Perhaps it may happen so when the time comes; perhaps God will make me do so. Once while meditating in Canada, I saw myself in India in front of a banyan tree. That was my first encounter with India. Since arriving here, however, I have not seen that banyan tree anywhere.*

**Baba:** It is an auspicious sign to see a banyan tree in meditation. It indicates that you will find your Guru. It is not necessary for you to actually see that banyan tree.

**Savitri:** *What sadhana should I do now? Please bestow your grace on me.*

**Baba:** The grace is there already. Remain steady in the *sahasrāra,* remain intoxicated in bliss. Remember this ashram and come again whenever you can.

*Shri Pranjivan Thakkar, a longtime devotee, asked Baba before leaving the ashram about the difficulties he has been experiencing in his sadhana.*

## Agitation of the Mind Before It Becomes Still

**Thakkar:** *For the past month my mind has been restless. I feel as if I have gone mad, I am frightened, I have no desire to talk to anyone, nor am I interested in my work at the office. I cannot sleep at night. For no reason, all kinds of thoughts, good and bad, keep arising in my mind.*

**Baba:** This is a state of the mind. Just before the mind is about to become quiet, numerous thoughts arise. When a whirlpool is moving very fast, it appears to be motionless, but as its speed steadily decreases, it revolves around a larger radius and hence appears to be increasing in speed. After moving in this manner for some time, it suddenly comes to a halt. Similarly, when the mind is moving very fast, it appears quiet, but as its force starts decreasing, the mind appears to be more agitated. Ultimately, it reaches a state of true stillness. You need not be frightened. This stage will pass in due course.

**Thakkar:** *Please continue to bestow your grace on me.*

**Baba:** Grace is already present; it is with you, it has not gone anywhere. One more thing: you should try to reduce your weight. Give up eating salt for some time.

## Thursday, October 24, 1963

*Swami Rameshwarananda, who has been practicing hatha yoga for the past eight years, has come to stay in the ashram. He states that formerly he had several siddhis, such as the power to stop running trains, to materialize any object just by his mere wish, to know the news before it appeared in the newspapers, to know about events that were to take place in the future, and so forth. He also stayed for six months with Shri Vyasdevji (now known as Swami Yogeshwarananda) at Gangotri.*

### The True State of Liberation

**Swami Rameshwarananda:** *I have been practicing hatha yoga for the past eight or nine years, but for the last year or two I have been feeling disturbed. How can I describe to you the wonderful powers I had in the past? Now I have lost them all.*

**Baba:** It seems that you are a good yogi and that you have practiced hatha yoga quite thoroughly. Nothing has gone wrong, and you have not lost anything. Everything is with you. Real Siddhahood is attained when one feels that one has lost everything. This is a stage just prior to becoming a real Siddha.

Now you should give up hatha yoga and sit with a quiet

mind. The true supreme state is that in which nothing is being done and nothing is happening. Jnaneshwar Maharaj says:

> The real praise is to abide silently,
> The real worship is to sit quietly.
> The real *samādhi* is where nothing happens
> But remaining immersed in your own Self.[8]

Haribhakta, a *brahmachārī* from Katara, used to suffer from a headache. It could not be relieved even after the application of several remedies. Someone advised him to come here, and he came. He had attained a thought-free and immutable state. Still, he continued to do *japa* of the *gāyatrī mantra.* This caused vibrations to arise even in his thought-free state. The resultant vibration of the subtle *nādīs* in the *sahasrāra* was causing his headache. I told him to stop doing *japa,* and I kept him here for three days. His headache ceased immediately. Because I had given him such a simple remedy for his headache, he embraced me with overwhelming gratitude and joy.

**Rameshwarananda:** *I used to experience divine bliss during sadhana. I no longer have that experience.*

**Baba:** There is a state of supreme bliss even beyond the bliss of yoga. That for which you are meditating with effort, for which you are doing sadhana, is not in fact the supreme Self; but that which makes you meditate, that which makes you do sadhana, is the supreme Self. The *Viveka Chūdāmani* says:

> That on which the mind cannot meditate but which makes the mind meditate is verily Brahman. That which people worship is not Brahman.[9]

Try to understand the real meaning of this. You did a particular sadhana, and you think because of that you had an experience. It is not so. That from which you had the experience of bliss is the supreme Self. That supreme bliss is not dependent upon anything.

When a seeker passes from one stage to the next, he may feel as though he has lost all his gains from the former stage, but everything is still there. For example, if I move from one bungalow to another and I do not find there the objects that were present in the previous bungalow, it doesn't mean that those objects have been destroyed.

## SATURDAY, OCTOBER 26, 1963

**Rameshwarananda:** *Vyasdevji used to sit in one place for a long time with a steady gaze that was not disturbed even if anyone would come or go.*

**Baba:** This is the stage of a seeker, not of a Siddha or a perfect being. A Siddha is one who does not get dislodged from the Self even if his vision wanders about everywhere. One who remains established steadfastly in the Self even while seeing, hearing, and smelling is the real Siddha.

**Rameshwarananda:** *Are there different stages of kundalinī awakening, or shaktipat?*

**Baba:** No. There are three different degrees, not stages, of shaktipat, which are *ānavi* (mild), *mantrī* (medium), and *shāmbhavī* (intense).

**Rameshwarananda:** *Is shaktipat a theme of the Shaiva Tantra?*

**Baba:** This science is not limited to any one book. It has descended from the supreme Being through a lineage of Gurus. The primordial Guru is Lord Shiva. Jnaneshwar Maharaj has said that he received this knowledge from Adinath, Matsyendranath, Gorakhnath, and Nivrittinath, in other words, through the Nath lineage.

**Rameshwarananda:** *What are nāda, bindu, and kalā?*

**Baba:** When the *prāna* starts becoming steady, *nāda,* or sound, is revealed and is heard through the ears. In *Amritānubhava*, Jnaneshwar Maharaj says that the *turīya* state is beyond *nāda*. As one goes on meditating, one sees a blue spot. That is *bindu*. I can say without doubt that the great being who can describe this spot has realized God. The wise beings have described this spot in the most minute detail. The *kalā* of Chiti[10] shines in this very spot.

## THURSDAY, OCTOBER 31, 1963

*Today a Jewish gentleman named Samson, a retired railway officer, came to the ashram. He has been waiting a long time for the opportunity to speak with Baba.*

### True Realization

**Samson:** *I have been practicing meditation for several years but have never had any visions of God, nor have I attained samādhi.*

**Baba:** Meditation can be practiced through self-effort, but visions and *samādhi* are attained only through grace. Visions, however, will only satisfy the eyes. Arjuna and Lord Krishna were together for several years. Arjuna had a constant vision of Krishna right in front of his eyes, and yet he did not have inner satisfaction or peace of mind. This he had only when he heard the *Bhagavad Gītā* directly from Lord Krishna, that is, after he had received knowledge. Similarly, Namdev used to play and converse with Lord Vitthal, but he achieved internal peace only after gaining knowledge from his Guru, Vishoba Khechar.

Rama, Krishna, and other avatars are incarnations of God who come to this earth in human form in order to fulfill a particular purpose. Having a vision of them is not true realization. True realization is understanding their real nature. Having visions is not an attainment. The true vision is the experience of peace and bliss in your heart. Achievement of the state of supreme bliss and peace is the real God-realization. Just as the eyes enjoy form, the ears hear sound, and the nose perceives smell, similarly, the heart experiences bliss. To have visions, hear sounds, or enter *samādhi* during meditation is not the ultimate attainment. True attainment is to remain firmly established in the Self under all circumstances. Do you practice *japa*?

**Samson:** *Yes, I do japa of So'ham. How should I proceed further?*

**Baba:** How do you do *japa*? Do you utter the mantra with your tongue or does it occur in the throat?

**Samson:** *I repeat it with my tongue.*

**Baba:** As you go on practicing *japa* with the tongue, it will progress and start taking place in the throat. Then it is taking place in the subtle body. When it progresses to the heart, it is taking place in the causal body, and when it progresses to the navel, it is said to be taking place in the supracausal body. As you go on repeating *So'ham*, where your thoughts totally vanish, that is the abode of God. While doing *japa*, you should also experience its meaning. Keep in mind the idea "I am That." Whatever sadhana you have done so far will not go to waste. Just as one has to undergo the results of bad deeds, one must also enjoy the fruits of good actions. Meeting with saints and visiting their sacred places are the fruits of that. Nothing has been wasted, so you need not worry.

## Saturday, November 2, 1963

*This evening Shri Page and his family came to stay at the ashram for two days.*

## Pratīka Darshana

**Page:** *While meditating, I often see myself in front of me. Many times I have felt myself to be separate from the body. What is the meaning of this?*

**Baba:** To see oneself in front of oneself is called *pratīka darshana.* It is also called *drashtabhāva.* You have reached the stage of Witness-consciousness. After this, the attainment of God is not very far away.

### SATURDAY, DECEMBER 28, 1963

*Shri Pande, a college professor in Yeotmal and a representative of the Times of India newspaper, came to the ashram today and had a discussion with Baba.*

## Bhagawan Nityananda Was a Devotee of Truth

**Pande:** *To which sect did Bhagawan Nityananda belong? Which religious order did he follow?*

**Baba:** He did not belong to any particular religious sect or order. He was a pure Advaitin, that is, a believer in nondualism.

**Pande:** *Which type of nondualism did he believe in? Did he believe in the Vedanta of Shankaracharya or any other āchārya?*

**Baba:** Nondualism is only one. Bhagawan Nityananda was a pure Vedantin. He believed in the absolute Truth as propounded in the Upanishads. He did not believe in any one Vedantic or Advaita philosophy, nor did he put forth any different path or school of philosophy. He worshiped supreme Truth and had attained perfect oneness with That.

**Pande:** *The Bhagavad Gītā expounds four paths: bhakti, or devotion; jñāna, or knowledge; karma, or action; and yoga. Which of these did Bhagawan Nityananda believe in?*

**Baba:** He believed in the *Gītā*. He considered every word of it precious and invaluable. He did not believe in any one single path, but in all of them.

A devotee or seeker finds the path according to his own inclination and follows that path. None of these paths is wrong or imperfect, nor is one greater or less than the others. The *Gītā* contains instruction for followers of all the paths. It is folly to consider even a single word used in the *Gītā* to be wrong.

**Pande:** *Do you have any of Bhagawan Nityananda's sayings?*

**Baba:** He always remained immersed in his own Self, so when he did say something, who would be present and ready with a pencil and paper to take it down? Nevertheless, there is a book in the Kannada language called *Chidākāsha Gītā*. It is a compilation from memory of certain words and sentences that Nityananda Baba had spoken from time to time while staying in South India. This book cannot be considered his, nor did he wish to say anything new. A devotee once said to Nityananda Baba, "Give us some instruction." He replied, "What the poet-saints Narada, Mira, Kabir, Tulsidas, and others have said is just what I have said. It is not necessary for me to say any more."

Eknath Maharaj once had a desire to write a commentary on *Jñāneshvarī,* but after reading it, he realized that there was nothing more to be written about it. Ultimately, he wrote only the following verse:

> If, after Jnaneshwar, anyone tries
> to write more on the *Gītā*,
> It will be like dressing a dish full of nectar
> with pieces of coconut shell.[11]

Bhagawan Nityananda had no intention to establish a new sect. Just as in Sanskrit literature there is no poet greater than Kalidas, similarly, there is nothing greater than the knowledge of

Truth contained in the Upanishads. How beautifully Radhakrishnan has written about it in his book *Indian Philosophy*! Who can write better than this? What can be greater than that Truth?

**Pande:** *Yes. Radhakrishnan has not written anything of his own. There is nothing original in it. He has merely rewritten what is contained in the Upanishads.*

**Baba:** Anyone who has studied the scriptures thoroughly will not write anything new. Only a person with one-sided understanding starts a new sect. What is absolute Truth existed in the past, the same exists in the present, and the same will remain in the future. The absolute Truth never changes.

**Pande:** *Nowadays corruption, misconduct, etc., are prevalent all over the world. How can these be eliminated?*

**Baba:** Didn't much viciousness and injustice exist in this world in the past? The demons Ravana, Kamsa, Shakuni, Manthara, and Putana were here in earlier times. Even righteous kings had to fight wars, and respectable women were abducted. Duhshasana tried to strip Draupadi of her clothes in the royal court. Disharmony is the very nature of the world. It will continue. On the contrary, some people say that the present days are better than the olden times, and perhaps people are more humane now.

**Pande:** *How can the world develop?*

**Baba:** The world is already developed. To attempt to develop it is like developing what is already developed. How beautiful the old buildings are! In the past, earthen dams were made in such a way that the present-day concrete dams cannot match them. Wasn't that development? This world is described in the scriptures as the universal manifested form of God. Whatever is happening in this world today is merely a process of transformation, which appears to us as progress. Developing what is already developed is like trying to attain that which is already attained. The same elements keep manifesting in the world in different forms, and we view it as development.

**Pande:** *How can one attain God while living one's day-to-day life? Is it possible to enjoy material and spiritual gains at the same time?*

**Baba:** It is not necessary to give up this world in order to attain God-realization. One must attain it while living in this world. One must be kind and charitable. One must have a pure mind and act humanely toward others. One must not abandon Truth. Truth is dear to all, whether knowingly or unknowingly. For example, if a person is engaged in black marketeering, he would never proclaim it, but if he serves meals to brahmins in Benares, he would make it known to everyone. Therefore, acquire divine wealth.

# Chapter Three

# 1964

*Shri Sanjay Kumar, a columnist for a Delhi newspaper, came to the ashram today. He had a discussion with Baba and asked him some questions.*

## Religion and Politics

**Sanjay Kumar:** *Corruption is prevalent in our country. Our leaders give lots of speeches, but their words do not seem to have any effect. The public, however, is very much influenced by saints and sages. Can't they do something to remove corruption?*

**Baba:** In the Vedas it is said that only he who himself obeys can command others. Only he who has something himself can reform others. Only if one has character himself can he build the character of others. If one who is not detached himself tries to teach detachment to others, it will have no effect. It is the nature of this world to change. Rise and fall necessarily take place. If you perceive that society is now downfallen, progress and betterment are bound to follow. The *Bhagavad Gītā* says that whenever unrighteousness prevails in the world, God will incarnate to destroy it and reestablish righteousness.

## There Is a God

**Sanjay Kumar:** *The real saints and sannyāsīs leave society and go into isolation for meditation on the Self. The masses, therefore, do not benefit from them. Those who are sannyāsīs in name only and live among people appear to be lacking in character. Why is it so?*

**Baba:** Despite their leaving society, these saints keep working only for the world. Bhagawan Nityananda, for example, settled down in this jungle. He had given up everything. He had nothing except a loincloth. Most of the time he remained silent, uttering only two or three words after every five or six hours. In spite of this, thousands of people visited him and obtained peace and happiness, and experienced satisfaction and contentment in their lives. The happiness and bliss for which man endlessly strives, and for which he engages in innumerable activities, such as setting up factories, running about, and toiling the whole day could be had easily and naturally from Bhagawan Nityananda. Seeing him, one felt that there is God, and this made many people turn toward religion. Even rogues and scoundrels used to bow down before him. Thousands of his photographs have been sold. In homes and in shops people worship his image, offering flowers and incense, and pause for a while to pray and remember God. You must have seen photographs of Bhagawan in many shops and hotels. Isn't all this his work? Did people come to him in such large numbers for no reason? There are saints and *sannyāsīs* of all types. Some live in isolation, while some live among people. Not all saints living amid people are impostors.

**Sanjay Kumar:** *The basis of our culture is its religious tradition. In the past, all of life's activities were guided by religious principles, but today religion and politics are divorced. What is your opinion about this? Is it good for the country?*

**Baba:** Under the present political system, the seeming progress is merely an outward appearance. There is no basic achievement. In ancient times the sages conceived the system of government, while nowadays politicians do it. Formerly rulers were farsighted, while today only expediency prevails everywhere.

As the king, so the people. If a nation's leader does not believe in God, neither will the people. Why does all this happen? In the *Bhagavad Gītā*, Arjuna asked Lord Krishna the same question:

> O Varshneya! In spite of having no desire to perform bad actions, what is it that impels man to do so as if being forced?[1]

Lord Krishna answered:

Desires and anger arise out of *rajoguna,* which is never satisfied. This is the great sinner. Know this to be the greatest enemy in this world.[2]

## True Peace Comes from Turning Within

**Sanjay Kumar:** *Many seekers are practicing meditation in your ashram. How does this benefit society?*

**Baba:** Man's every action has as its aim the attainment of happiness, peace, and satisfaction. Happiness and peace can be obtained only by controlling the mind. When the mind that wanders amidst external objects turns inward, man experiences the happiness and bliss so dear to everyone. Having worked all day, the tired man yearns for a sound night's sleep. During sleep, the mind becomes quiet and is refreshed and rejuvenated. Thus it is proven that the mind wants rest.

Seekers living in the company of a saint who has really attained the inner bliss and peace of the Self spontaneously turn inward and experience that bliss as well. It is said that on entering the ashram of Lord Buddha, all one's thoughts would subside. Peace can be achieved only by abandoning all thoughts.

**Sanjay Kumar:** *Yes, but the entire society cannot come here.*

**Baba:** Whether the desire for inner bliss arises or not is an individual matter. One who has developed discrimination will certainly try to achieve that peace. It isn't possible for every individual of society to have such discrimination. This discrimination is the supreme means to achieve peace and bliss.

**Sanjay Kumar:** *Just as Bhagawan Nityananda gave you perfection and placed you here, have you prepared anyone to maintain the tradition?*

**Baba:** Someone will definitely get ready. Whoever is fortunate will attain it. Just as one player passes on his art, knowledge, and skill to another player, a potmaker to another potmaker, a doctor to another doctor, a teacher to his student, similarly, a yogi prepares another yogi.

## *Truth Is Beyond All Sects*

**Sanjay Kumar:** *There are photographs of saints of various sects in your ashram, and you have met some of them. When meeting these saints of different sects, did you encounter any feelings of hostility?*

**Baba:** As long as a man is bound by a particular sect, there is a possibility of feeling hostile toward other sects, but for one who has gone beyond all sects, such feelings do not arise in his mind. A sect is like a fence. When a plant is small, it requires a fence for its protection, but after it has become a full-grown tree, a fence is no longer necessary.

Mansur Mastana, a Muslim saint, wrote in one of his poems: "Give up the cloth for *namāz,* break the rosary, and throw the books in the river!" Sects are created by man, whereas the world is a creation of God. The world is full of diversity, but the basic principle remains the same. One who knows this secret does not feel hatred toward anyone. A Muslim will see Allah even in a temple of Rama, while a Hindu will see Krishna even in a church.

There is a Sanskrit verse that says:

> He whom the Shaivites worship as Shiva, the Vedantins call Brahman, the Buddhists call Buddha, the Nyayakas call the doer, the Jains call Arhat, and the Mimamsakas call karma, He is that Lord Hari who is the ruler of the three worlds. May He grant us the desired fruit.[3]

*Yesterday Shri Sunil Damania brought the famous Sufi saint Shri Gurdayal Mallik to the ashram. This morning Shri Mallikji, Shri Sunilbhai, and others had satsang with Baba in Turiya Mandir.*

## *The Individual Soul's Four Bodies*

**Sunil:** *Sharbaden is ill again. For the past year she has been suffering intensely.*

**Baba:** Everyone must undergo his destiny. It is inescapable. One's suffering can certainly be alleviated by surrendering to a *sadguru.* The individual soul has four bodies: gross, subtle, causal, and supracausal. Just as these four rooms are separate from each other, and as we walk from one into another we cease to exist in the previous room, similarly, these four bodies are quite independent of each other. When the individual soul leaves the gross body and enters the subtle body, the conditions of the former do not affect him at all. A similar situation occurs when a patient is given chloroform prior to an operation. As a result of the drug's effect, the mind becomes detached from the gross body and doesn't experience the pain suffered by it.

The *turīya* state is beyond all four bodies. In the dream state, the waking state disappears; in the state of deep sleep, both the waking and dream states disappear; but in the *turīya* state, the entire visible world disappears. In that state, the happiness and misery of this world do not have any effect on the mind. Attain that state by which the burden of destiny will become light.

*In the evening another satsang was held.*

## Worldly Affairs Must Not Be Neglected

**Devotee:** *Babaji, this man has become so engrossed in saints and sannyāsīs that he has forgotten his worldly affairs.*

**Baba** (*to Sunil*): While you are practicing spirituality, you must also do your worldly work with the same proficiency.

There was once a very wealthy and religious philanthropist named Nathkoti. The Mahadev idol was worshiped daily and bathed with cow's milk on his behalf. At one time when he wanted to build a new monastery, Shankaracharya went to see Nathkoti at his residence. He was told that Nathkoti had gone to his shop. Shankaracharya went there, but he didn't see him. He asked someone and was told, "See, there he is." Shankaracharya saw an ordinary, simple man picking up scattered grains of wheat from the floor. He questioned a few other people to confirm that the man was actually the owner. He wondered what that man would give him. Just then, the owner approached Shankaracharya and asked the purpose of his visit. After hearing about the plans for a new monastery, Nathkoti at once asked, "How much money do you want?" Shankaracharya replied that four lakh (400,000) rupees was needed. Without any hesitation, Nathkoti wrote a check for that amount. The moral of the story is that real wisdom lies in attending to worldly as well as spiritual work with equal efficiency.

# Sunday, January 26, 1964

*Mr. Albert Rudolph came today from New York to visit Baba as he does every year on his birthday. In the afternoon he came to Baba accompanied by Barrister Nain to act as an interpreter and began asking questions.*

## Let Events Take Their Own Course

**Rudolph:** *For the past four or five months, a lot has been happening in my head. Sometimes it feels as though it is going to explode. I had a similar experience last night.*

**Baba:** This is excellent progress. Shiva and Shakti unite with each other in the *sahasrāra* where you are experiencing this activity. As soon as this union takes place, you will realize God.

**Rudolph:** *When shall I attain that final state?*

**Baba:** Everything will happen in its own time. Have patience.

**Rudolph:** *I often receive indications of future events, and whatever I tell anyone comes true.*

**Baba:** Yes, when all the tendencies of the mind subside, you get such intuition from within.

**Rudolph:** *I have an opportunity to obtain* 104 *acres of forest-like land. May I purchase it in order to establish an ashram there?*

**Baba:** What is the price?

**Rudolph:** *It is about one and a half lakh* (150,000) *rupees, but I am not in a position to pay the entire amount in cash. I shall pay it in yearly installments.*

**Baba:** Do only what comes naturally. Don't be hasty. Whatever is going to happen will happen. Let events take their own natural course. Look what happened here. I never had even the slightest idea of building an ashram here, but such a beautiful ashram spontaneously came into being.

*Today Mr. Rudolph asked Baba about some of the experiences he is having.*

## Knowledge of Past Lives During Sadhana

**Rudolph:** *I poured water on my head this morning while taking a bath and immediately felt as though the top portion of my head had given way. I saw a lama entering into my head. Is the shakti of that lama working within me?*

**Baba:** During sadhana one keeps having this kind of new experience. Many dormant impressions from our innumerable past lives lie within us. These start manifesting during sadhana, resulting in numerous visions. Sometimes past lives are seen. What you saw today was probably a vision of some previous life. It does not mean that the shakti of any lama is working within you. During sadhana you will continue to have visions of worldly objects reflected in the Self. You will have many more experiences. I used to see myself riding a horse with battalions of soldiers in front of me and behind me during my sadhana. I concluded from this vision that I was a king during one of my previous lives. Similarly, whatever aspect of your sadhana that remained incomplete in your previous life as a lama is being completed now.

**Rudolph:** *I shall return to New York in a day or two. Will you give me some special instructions regarding my sadhana?*

**Baba:** No, you will receive indications from within as to what you should do. However, be regular in your meditation and continue to increase your love and devotion toward your Guru.

**Rudolph:** *Until now my life has been full of physical suffering, which began right at the time of my birth. As I was born, the nurse who was holding me dropped me from her hands, and I tumbled all the way down the staircase until I hit the last step. I was badly* *injured. During my childhood, I had to undergo fourteen operations, some on my chest and some on my head. Why did I have to experience all this? Was someone trying to take my shakti away, or was God preparing me to undergo suffering in the future?*

**Baba:** It was neither of these. It was a way of going through your destiny. Everyone must undergo his destiny.

**Rudolph:** *When will all my karmas be exhausted?*

**Baba:** Everything will happen at the appropriate time. With the practice of yoga, one's karmas continue to be destroyed. Keep up your sadhana with sincerity and enthusiasm.

## THURSDAY, FEBRUARY 6, 1964

*A Parsi seeker, Mr. Kanga, has been staying in the ashram for the past few days. He received initiation from Swami Shivananda, a disciple of Shri Ramakrishna Paramahamsa.*

### *Light Seen During Meditation Radiates from Brahman*

**Kanga:** *What is the nature of Brahman? I see light during meditation. What is it?*

**Baba:** The supreme Brahman is changeless and still. What you are seeing is a radiation from Brahman. The true nature of Brahman is absolutely changeless and ever steady.

*About seven or eight years ago an American woman, Hilda Charlton, used to come to see Nityananda Baba now and then, and during her visits she also used to see Baba. She has been in India for the past fourteen years and has met many saints. She learned the preliminaries of kriyā yoga from Yogananda Paramahamsa in California. Yesterday she came to the ashram to stay for a few days to get guidance from Baba in her sadhana.*

## Signs of the Awakened Kundalinī

**Hilda:** *My body becomes very hot when I sit for meditation. I feel intense heat within me. What should be done to cool the body down?*

**Baba:** Allow whatever is happening to happen. Do not try to obstruct it. It is not necessary to cool the body down. To experience heat within is a sign of the awakened *kundalinī.*

**Hilda:** *Formerly I observed fasts. Now when I sit for meditation with an empty stomach, I feel as if every cell in my body is dancing, and I have a desire to dance myself. What is this?*

**Baba:** This is the supreme bliss. The supreme Self pervades every cell of the body. A saint has said that Rama dwells in every particle of the body. When a seeker directs his love toward God, a feeling of happiness and bliss arises within, and he starts jumping and dancing. Just as this body is formed out of every particle of food eaten, this entire universe has come into existence because of God's presence in every particle of it.

**Hilda:** *During meditation and also afterward, I have numerous visions and I hear a variety of sounds. I have many more indescribable experiences, which disturb my daily life. I feel that everything is a nuisance. What should I do about it?*

**Baba:** In the spine there is a *nāḍī* called the *sushumnā* in which impressions of all one's previous lives lie dormant. While sitting for meditation or practicing any other kind of sadhana, these impressions begin to manifest. Therefore, during the purification of the *nāḍīs,* one has a variety of experiences. During my sadhana, many sounds would emerge from my throat, such as those of a camel or a tiger. The noise was so loud that the cows grazing in the fields around my hut would run away!

**Hilda:** *Sometimes I become so still and motionless that I start to wonder whether I have gone insane. I cannot understand what is happening to me, and I cannot concentrate on my routine work. At other times, so many thoughts crowd my mind that it is impossible to describe them.*

**Baba:** Yes, many seekers have such experiences. During my sadhana I also lost control of my mind, but after some time everything became all right. This is only a stage of the mind during sadhana. Just prior to becoming calm, innumerable thoughts arise in the mind. When all the thoughts and impressions have been expelled from the mind, it attains the *nirvikalpa* state. Before becoming still, it goes through considerable agitation. *Kundalinī shakti* is a live force; it is all-knowing. When we are engaged in worldly activities, it protects us and makes us do things correctly. Do you get the *khecharī mudrā*? Does your tongue get pulled in against your palate during sadhana?

**Hilda:** *Yes, it used to happen to me in the past, and it frightened me terribly. Seven years ago I came to see you, and you told me to remain calm. I believe that you know everything.*

**Baba:** Death comes at its preordained time so do not be afraid, have courage. Let things happen as they will. Let the shakti do its work, while you remain only as a witness. I told you the same before also.

# MONDAY, FEBRUARY 24, 1964

*On Friday Balwantrai Desai, a retired solicitor from Surat, came to stay at the ashram to see Baba and have satsang with him. He has studied Vedanta in depth and is interested in yoga. He has a keen desire to know about meditation and the awakening of the kundalinī. He has been to Pondicherry and Ramanashram, and several years ago he also met Swami Yogananda Paramahamsa. Today he had a discussion with Baba.*

**Balwantrai:** *There is a yogi named Kisan Maharaj who went into samādhi for eleven days. During this time, he did not eat, drink, or excrete anything.*

**Baba:** Yes, there are many such hatha yogis.

**Balwantrai:** *What is that state? Is that what is known as samādhi? Of what use is it?*

**Baba:** *Samādhi* is a state in which the intellect is balanced and the mind is still; it is what the *Bhagavad Gītā* describes as *sthitaprajña*. What can one gain by remaining in *samādhi* for eleven days? Only that people may be impressed and attracted to him.

**Balwantrai:** *How could he have lived without food and water?*

**Baba:** Have you read the *Yoga Sūtras* of Patanjali? Do you know about the *sanyama siddhi* described there? One *sūtra* says that by practicing control over the throat, one does not feel hunger and thirst. There are also some medicines that eliminate hunger and thirst. Another method is to eat a preparation of rice that is made by soaking the rice grains in milk and then drying them. This process is repeated several times over a prescribed number of days. Consuming this kind of rice also eradicates hunger and thirst.

**Balwantrai:** *It is said that the body of Swami Yogananda Paramahamsa did not start to decompose until several days after his death. How can this be explained?*

**Baba:** In the body there are ten kinds of *prānas,* or vital airs: *prāna, apāna, samāna, vyāna, udāna, nāga, kūrma, kukāra, devadatta,* and *dhanañjaya.* The first five are the main, or principal, *prānas,* and the next five are the subsidiary ones. Among these, the vital air called *dhanañjaya* remains in the body even after death. The *Yogachūdāmani Upanishad* says that *dhanañjaya* pervades the entire body and does not leave it even after death. The body of a yogi who has completely purified this *prāna* will not undergo any disintegration for many days after death.

## *The Ecstasy of Divine Love*

**Balwantrai:** *A woman named Indiradevi stays with Shri Dilip Kumar Roy in Pune. When she goes into samādhi, Mirabai talks to her, and she chants Mirabai's bhajans. Formerly, she stayed at the Aurobindo Ashram, but she left because of a difference of opinion with Mataji about this. What can we conclude about these experiences? Presently, Indiradevi's health has greatly deteriorated.*

**Baba:** This kind of experience is merely a state or emotion of the mind. The real ecstasy is that in which the seeker himself becomes the object of worship, and all the qualities of the worshiped object are manifested in him. Shri Ramakrishna Paramahamsa and Shri Chaitanya Mahaprabhu used to get into such exalted states of love.

When I was staying in Kasara Ghat, there was a woman who used to get into that kind of state. At these times, she answered correctly any questions she was asked. Many devotees of Nityananda Baba also experienced ecstatic states of love. These experiences, however, are merely manifestations of mental states. In the ecstasy of pure, divine love, the body is purified and all diseases vanish.

**Balwantrai:** *I have studied in great detail two or three cases of people who remember their previous lives, and I have concluded that some people actually do retain such memories. I have started believing in rebirth, but how can I learn about my past life?*

**Baba:** You will obtain knowledge of your past births before attaining final realization.

## *Alleged Incarnations of Sai Baba of Shirdi*

**Balwantrai:** *There is a sannyāsī who claims to be an incarnation of Sai Baba of Shirdi. Can this be true?*

**Baba:** Seven other people also claim to be incarnations of Sai Baba of Shirdi. Which one can be regarded as true? This is like the story of Laila and Majnu. Laila was a beautiful princess and Majnu was a poor man. He was madly in love with her and repeated "Laila, Laila" all the time. He lost all consciousness of himself.

The king took pity on Majnu and told the chief minister to provide him with food and clothes. Seeing this, numerous impostors claimed to be Majnu and were also provided with food and clothing. Once the king inquired about the expenses of Majnu and learned that the number of Majnus had increased. He conferred with the chief minister, who shrewdly devised a solution to the problem. He sent a town crier out with the following proclamation: "Majnu has gone insane because of his love for Laila, so he will be hanged tomorrow." Hearing this, all the Majnus except the real one disappeared.

I have also met two or three *sādhus* who claim to be incarnations of Sai Baba. One of them operated a factory with the money collected from his devotees and was later prosecuted by the government. I came across another incarnation of Sai Baba in Yeola. He used to put his hand on a person's eyes and give him a vision of Sai Baba. Later on, he married and led the life of a householder. A third man who claimed to be an incarnation of Sai Baba died in a car accident.

The truth is that Sai Baba of Shirdi was a completely realized being; he was a great Siddha. He became one with the supreme Brahman and merged into the totality. He can never be reborn. God alone incarnates, no one else.

**Balwantrai:** *A great saint was living in the home of a householder whose daughter-in-law committed suicide. Didn't the saint have the power to advise her and avert that calamity?*

**Baba:** Every creature's time of death is predetermined. Providence determines the time of birth as well as death. Even great saints and sages, let alone ordinary people, must die at their destined time. No one can prevent death; no one can avert the time of death.

**Balwantrai:** *I have seen many saints and I have visited Nareshwar, Ramanashram, Pondicherry, and other ashrams, but I never felt that any of the devotees or disciples had really achieved anything. I did not feel that anyone went there with a desire for God-realization.*

**Baba:** A man who has progressed in sadhana or who has attained something does not grow horns on his head by which you can identify his state of being. To know a *jñānī,* one must first attain that state oneself. One can know him by living with him for a long time. What can we understand about a person in only a day or two?

Besides, all kinds of people go to saints. Each person goes to obtain whatever he desires. A man with only two paise wants to buy a vegetable, and you start advising him to buy pearls instead. First of all, he does not want pearls nor does he have the means to purchase them. Is advising him to buy pearls wise or foolish? If a childless person goes to a saint to ask for a child and someone advises him to ask for *moksha,* of what use is it? Is that wisdom or foolishness?

## Friday, February 28, 1964

*Last Sunday Shri Sunil Damania and his friend Shri Sundarrao, a devotee of Swami Ramdas of the Anandashram, came from Khar, Bombay. They presented Baba with a copy of the first issue of The Mountain Path, published by the Ramanashram, in which the magazine's editor had written an article comparing three or four saints. The devotees here read the article, and today they discussed it with Baba. Many devotees were present, since today is a holiday because of Holi.*

## *No Saint Is Superior or Inferior to Any Other*

**Baba:** It seems that this gentleman (the editor) is capable of writing on the subject of philosophy, but he certainly cannot be an authority on saints and sages. Tukaram Maharaj says:

> To understand
> how the fish sleep under water,
> you have to become a fish
> and live under water.[4]

It is childish to compare saints and sages without having been a saint and without having personally experienced their state. Doing so is neither a sign of wisdom nor good manners. How can one describe America's New York City while living in India and without ever having seen it? To try to assess the state of a saint or to compare him with others is sheer ignorance. The state of saints is not like B.A. or M.A. degrees. As a matter of fact, the final state and attainment of every saint is the same. You may call it by many names: *nirvichāra, samādhi, sthitaprajña, turīyātīta, ātmabhāva,* or *īshabhāva.*

All the paths and means for God-realization indicated by our saints—such as the paths of knowledge, devotion, and yoga—are true. All paths ultimately lead a seeker to the same goal. There are many roads leading to the same place and different means for getting there. For example, several routes lead to Delhi, but the best route for a traveler is the one from the place where he is. A man staying in Calcutta need not travel through Bombay to reach Delhi. He can reach Delhi more directly via Kanpur and Allahabad. From Calcutta he can travel by any means: train, car, or airplane. One should choose the route and means best suited for him. The path to God-realization best suited to a seeker's temperament is the ideal path for him. Whichever path he follows, his destination will be the same. A verse in the *Shiva Mahimnah Stotram* says:

> Just as all rivers ultimately merge into the sea, You are the final goal for all people following different paths, straight or crooked, according to their temperaments and depending on which they consider best.[5]

A wise man will not judge saints and sages by their paths of sadhana, or say that one saint is superior or inferior to another because he is *jñānī, bhakta,* or a yogi. This is wrong understanding. To think that you know something when you do not is an illusion of knowledge.

Every seeker follows the path of God-realization according to his own inclination. A *jñānī* has no interest in *prānāyāma,* a *bhakta* is not drawn to intellectual analysis, and a yogi does not enjoy chanting. This does not mean that the paths of remembering God's name, chanting, and worshiping God are inferior means of sadhana. Jnaneshwar Maharaj says:

> A man who constantly chants God's name does not have to undergo any expiation or atonement, for no trace of sin remains in him. The yogic disciplines of *yama* and *dama* become irrelevant for him. All sins are destroyed in holy places, but his greatness is such that he surpasses even the holy places. About such a man, *yama* says, "Whom can I discipline?" and *dama* says, "Whom can I control?" because by chanting God's name, his mind and senses have become one with the Self. By this means, sinners are cleansed of their sins and need not go to Yamaloka. Chanting the Lord's name removes the misery of the whole universe and fills it with the bliss of Brahman.[6]

Also, Tukaram Maharaj sang the following:

> By chanting God's name, the body becomes the embodiment of Brahman. Such a person becomes so fortunate that God Himself feels indebted to him. I shall make the pilgrims stop their roaming to holy places; I shall make them abandon their pilgrimages and sit in one place. I shall make the sense pleasures bitter. I shall make the *tapasvīs* lose their pride, and I shall make acts of ritual and charity appear small. I shall attain the highest state of *bhakti* through chanting with love. I shall become one with the Supreme.[7]

After Self-realization, the sadhana by which one has attained it becomes just an addiction for a great being. Tukaram used to chant "Vitthal, Vitthal" and Ramakrishna Paramahamsa used to repeat "Mother, Mother" even after attaining oneness with the Supreme. In one of his verses, Tukaram Maharaj says of these saints:

> They have no interest in society, wealth, father, or mother. Narayana becomes their only object.[8]

Shri Ramakrishna Paramahamsa was very wise and a great *jñānī*. See how in the book *Gospel of Shri Ramakrishna* he has explained in simple and beautiful language the most intricate mysteries of *jñāna*. He may appear to have been an ordinary, illiterate peasant to some, but everyone knows that highly educated and intelligent people became his disciples. Could that have been the case if he himself were not intelligent? If educated and highly intellectual people surrendered to him, then of what value was their learning?

Ramana Maharshi was also a great yogi. During his sadhana he experienced all the yogic *kriyās,* after which he had numerous visions in meditation. He often had such deep *samādhi* states that he would be unaware of rats biting his feet, and he had to be lifted up and brought out of his cellar. He was also a great *bhakta* and composed a song full of love and devotion for Lord Shiva of Arunachala.

Ramana Maharshi did not establish any new path because Truth is only one; it never undergoes any change or transformation. No one can change it. The inquiry into "Who am I?" is the path of contemplation of the Self, developing Witness-consciousness and dispassion. It would be a mistake to call it a new path, for our saints and sages expounded it thousands of years ago. One with knowledge of the ancient Hindu scriptures would not consider this path new, but to one who has not studied the scriptures, it appears new. To regard the path of Self-inquiry—"Who am I?"—as new would be like using an old Japanese technique to grow rice in America and then claiming that a new type of rice has been developed. The Japanese people would say that this rice has existed in their land from ancient times, and for them there is nothing new in it.

"India has had only one or two great saints or Gurus, and all the others are inferior." Such a belief shows ignorance of Indian spiritual philosophy. India is a land of saints and sages. There is no dearth of saints and Gurus. There were brilliant *jñānīs,* great *bhaktas,* and saints in India in the past, they are here today, and they will be here in the future as well.

The realized Gurus and saints, ancient and modern, always proclaim the same Truth whether they are yogis, *jñānīs, bhaktas,* or karma yogis. They all have the same knowledge, realization, shakti, love, and perfection. The question of one being greater than another does not arise. The greatness of some saints comes to light while the attainment of others remains unknown, but this is no basis for arguing that one is superior to another. The greatness of saints and Gurus cannot be evaluated by such criteria as fame, *siddhis,* number of disciples, size of their ashrams, or the number of books they have written or that have been written about them. Only those with poor understanding would attempt this type of evaluation.

The Guru principle is all-pervasive; it is not limited to any one individual. The duty of every spiritual seeker is to respect the Guru principle in whatever form it has appeared, in whichever person it has manifested. It is best to surrender to only one Guru, but to disrespect the others is a sin. To do so is like being disrespectful to the Guru principle, God, and your own Guru. To say, write, or proclaim that your Guru alone is great and the others in the world are false is a display of stupidity. Many disciples become so stuck in such an idea that even years after their Guru has taken *mahāsamādhi* they remain prisoners of this narrow understanding, and yet they consider themselves to be very wise.

There is a beautiful illustration of this in the *Rāmāyana.* When Rama was returning from Sri Lanka with Sita and Hanuman in the Pushpak plane after defeating Ravana, the thought came to Hanuman, "There is no one like my Rama." Rama read Hanuman's thought. Just at that moment, Sita was handing her ring to Rama and accidentally dropped it into the sea. Rama told Hanuman to retrieve it, so he dived into the deep sea. On reaching the bottom, Hanuman was surprised to find a huge collection of rings exactly like the one Sita had dropped, all inscribed with the name "Shri Rama," and he could not recognize which of the rings was Shri Rama's. A saint was sitting there in meditation, and Hanuman asked his advice about the ring. The saint replied, "Take any one of these rings. There have been many Ramas like your Rama. Each time one returns home after defeating Ravana, one ring is dropped here, making this large pile."

In short, the essence of this is that all saints and sages are manifestations of Truth. They do not say anything new. If the disciple does not understand this, then by writing about his Guru according to his own limited thinking, he actually lessens rather than enhances the glory of his Guru.

## Saturday, February 29, 1964

*Shri B. C. Dalal, Secretary in the Ministry of Law, Maharashtra State, has been coming for some time for Baba's darshan. He came today accompanied by Mrs. Bharucha.*

**Mrs. Bharucha:** *Which name of God should I use for japa?*

**Baba:** Actually the Lord has no name, but nevertheless He has been given so many names. Muhammad called Him Khuda and Christ called Him God; among Hindus some call Him Rama, some call Him Krishna, and some call Him Shiva. He is called by different names according to the devotees' feelings, but all these different names are of one and the same God. You may do *japa* with whichever name appeals to you.

## *So'ham Is the Original Mantra*

**Shri Dalal:** *May I use the So'ham mantra for japa?*

**Baba:** There are innumerable mantras. The shakti is the same in all. *So'ham* (I am That) is a great mantra. It is the *ajapa-japa* mantra. Whether or not you consciously do *japa* with this mantra, it is automatically taking place with each inhalation and exhalation. The individual soul is initiated into this mantra by God while still in the womb. During the seventh month in the womb, he receives knowledge of his past and future and repents his past karmas. He prays to God, and God gives him the *So'ham* mantra. At the time of birth, however, when the individual soul comes into this world, he forgets the awareness of *So'ham* and starts crying *"ko'ham"* (Who am I?) instead. *So'ham* is the original mantra. Do *japa* with it.

## MONDAY, MARCH 16, 1964

*Today Shri Yogendra Trivedi's mother, Shrimati Bhanuben, who is a keen student of Vedanta, asked Baba some questions.*

**Bhanuben:** *What is the relationship between jñāna and the living out of one's karmas?*

**Baba:** The individual soul has different types of experiences in different states. The experiences in the waking state are different from those in the dream state. The pain of a boil is felt during the waking state but not during sleep. If given chloroform, the individual soul does not feel any pain while undergoing an operation because the drug takes him into another state. The experience in a dream is different. If someone beats or abuses you in a dream, you feel sad; if someone praises you, you feel happy; but these emotions vanish the moment you enter the waking state. Beyond the waking and dream states is the *turīya* state in which the individual soul has no experiences.

With the knowledge of Brahman the body is burnt into ashes, but one still must undergo one's remaining destiny. In the *Mahābhārata* during the war at Kurukshetra, Ashvatthama attempted to destroy Arjuna's chariot with the *agni astra*, but it inflicted no damage at all because Lord Krishna was protecting Arjuna with his willpower. Ashvatthama complained to his Guru, "What sort of mantra did you teach me that does not bring forth any result?" The Guru replied, "What I taught you regarding the *astra* is absolutely true, and you will definitely obtain the result of it." After seven days the war ended, whereupon Krishna told Arjuna to jump immediately out of the chariot. As soon as he had leapt out, the chariot caught fire and was reduced to ashes. Similarly, your knowledge of Brahman will certainly bear fruit as soon as you have lived out your entire destiny.

**Bhanuben:** *I can remain detached during moments of happiness, but I cannot do so during painful times.*

**Baba:** In order to achieve detachment from both pain and pleasure, you must remain steadily established in the Self.

*A seeker, Shri Karve, came today from Dadar to seek Baba's clarification regarding some problems in his sadhana.*

**Karve:** *During meditation I have body tremors and I perspire. I also smell a pleasant fragrance. Is this fragrance related in any way to the tremors and sweating?*

**Baba:** The fragrance has no relation to the tremors or the sweating. It has its place near the two-petaled chakra between the eyebrows. When the *prāna* becomes steady in that chakra, a divine fragrance emanates from within.

**Karve:** *Why are there so many kinds of fragrance?*

**Baba:** Sometimes you will smell fragrances hitherto unknown to you. When the intensity of the fragrance increases, it comes out through the *prāna* and can also be experienced by other people around you.

**Karve:** *Some people see lights of different colors during meditation. What kind of sadhana enables one to see these lights?*

**Baba:** One should see whatever appears naturally. One should not make any effort to have visions nor desire them. Why should one try to see the same thing again and again? Meditate peacefully and you will see divine light.

**Karve:** *What is the significance of lights of different colors? Does the red light appear when one is angry?*

**Baba:** All these are the colors of the inner Self. Do not think that they appear as a result of the three *gunas: sattva, rajas,* and *tamas.*

The red light is not caused by anger. Tukaram Maharaj says:

> Because of the ointment of divinity in my eyes, I saw the different lights: red, white, black, and yellow.[9]

*Baba has been in Santa Cruz for the past four days and will remain here for another ten days. Satsang is held in the morning and evening. Shri Sunil Damania came this morning with a letter.*

**Sunil:** *Babaji, yesterday I received a letter from the editor of The Mountain Path, published by the Ramanashram, requesting an article about Bhagawan Nityananda.*

**Baba:** Very good. Write to him as follows:

Whenever anyone approached Nityananda Baba requesting, "O Bhagawan! Please show us a new and easy path to suit this modern era," my revered Gurudev would reply, "This universe, which is a creation of Brahma, was created only once, and since then nothing new has come into existence. The past era, which today we regard as ancient, was new then. Since each era undergoes changes according to the times, we perceive a particular age to be either ancient or new, but in fact everything is now as it was in the beginning of creation. In a kaleidoscope, loose pieces of colored glass are reflected by mirrors on all four sides. As the instrument is rotated, the glass pieces keep changing position, resulting in the appearance of new patterns, but each pattern contains the same pieces of glass. Nothing old has disappeared, nor has anything new been added.

"Again, the sun is only one, but in different countries it appears to move at different speeds. In some countries the sun rises early, while in others it rises late. In some places it stays longer than in others. But the sun does not have the characteristics of being late or early, of short duration or long. The sun always is as it is. The knowledge of God should be understood in the same way.

"It is always one, it always remains the same, and it does not become more or less."

There is no question of easy or difficult paths for the attainment of knowledge. People find it difficult or easy according to their own mental inclinations, just as some people find the English language easy to learn and Sanskrit difficult, while the reverse is the case for others.

One kind of sadhana may be suitable for one person and another kind for another person. None of these different types of sadhana is easy or difficult in itself. The yogi finds Vedanta difficult, while the *jñānī* finds yoga difficult, and for the *bhakta,* both are difficult. The truth is that whatever appeals to a person will be easy for him. Despite the differences in the various paths of sadhana according to the seekers' inclinations, the goal is the same. Jnaneshwar Maharaj says:

> That state which the *jñānīs* call Brahman, yogis call *samādhi,* and Vedantins call *nityānanda* (eternal bliss) is the *bhakta's paramabhakti,* the deepest ecstasy.[10]

One who considers these paths to be different from each other is not wise; he is as ignorant as a child. The *Bhagavad Gītā* says:

> The ignorant, not the wise, consider knowledge and yoga to be different. One who establishes himself in either of these reaps the fruit of both of them.[11]

There have been many saints in India. They all proclaimed the same Truth. Many years separate the times of Jnaneshwar and Vasuguptacharya, the author of the *Shiva Sūtras,* yet both of them expounded the same principles. Kabir sang and Nanak spoke about the same Truth.

## *There Can Be No Incomplete Realization*

Just as all scriptures impart knowledge of the same Truth, the realization of all saints is the same. Realization cannot be partial or of different types. There can be disparities in worldly gains; for example, one person may have a bigger house or more money than another person. Gains in the mundane world can be estimated in percentages, but it is not so with regard to

God-realization. You cannot say that someone has attained twenty-five or fifty percent realization. The attainment of God-realization is either complete or none at all. There is no such thing as partial realization.

According to the Vedantic teachings, true realization is that after attaining which, nothing else remains to be attained, after seeing which, nothing else remains to be seen. For one who has attained the supreme bliss, not even the smallest part of bliss remains to be attained. That person is known as a saint. There have been many such saints in this era, for example, Ramakrishna Paramahamsa, Sai Baba of Shirdi, Upasani Maharaj of Sakori, Mugatram Maharaj of Manjusar, Narasimhacharya of Baroda, Abbajan of Pune, Ramana Maharshi of Tiruvannamalai, Bhagawan Nityananda of Ganeshpuri, Siddharudha Swami of Hubli, and Swami Ramdas.

Even after attaining divinity, saints behave in their daily lives according to the time and place in which they live, even though they are bound by no rules. In Benares there lived a wealthy man who was very charitable. During the winter he would give blankets to the *sādhus,* and during the summer he would give them umbrellas and water bowls.

Some *sādhus* remarked, "What sort of a philanthropist is he? Sometimes he gives us umbrellas while at other times he gives us blankets!" But in reality, their benefactor was being practical; it was the *sādhus* who lacked intelligence. He provided for them according to their needs. Similarly, saints and Gurus deal with their disciples according to the time, place, and their worthiness. In Ayurvedic medicine there is an excellent remedy known as *hemagarbha,* but that does not mean that the *vaidyā* should prescribe it for every patient. He gives each patient only the medicine that is necessary for him. Because he doesn't give *hemagarbha* to everyone, one cannot say that the *vaidyā* is incompetent.

The goal, the state, and the attainment of all saints is the same. The bliss experienced in the thought-free state achieved through *jñāna,* the *nirvikalpa* equanimity attained through yoga, and the ecstasy of chanting the name of Rama are all the same.

In Maharashtra there was a great *bhakta,* Namdev, with whom God Himself used to laugh and talk. He proclaimed, "God's name is God Himself." Gurudev Ranade used to give the experience of peace and bliss by awakening the inner shakti of his disciples, while Swami Ramdas imparted the same experience through the use of a mantra.

Bhagawan Nityananda's life was filled through and through with the principles of Vedanta. His greatness was amazing. He had knowledge of all the world's problems and he had the remedy for each of them. If someone complained of a stomachache, he would advise the right treatment or administer some medicine himself. If someone asked for food, clothes, or housing, he would provide those as well. To a seeker he would advise *japa,* meditation, or *sevā* according to the individual's capability. He belonged neither to modern nor to ancient times. He always taught pure Vedanta.

When asked about any other saint, Nityananda Baba would reply, "He is my own Self." He saw no distinction among any saints.

A saint called Amritrai lived in the Aurangabad district of Maharashtra State. He had attained the supreme state and was Self-realized. One day people of different sects gathered around him and asked him for some teaching. Having realized that this universe is the form of the supreme Self, he was always immersed in the Self and remained silent. When the people insisted, he sang the following verse:

> What can I say about anything? When there is only one eternal, blissful Consciousness, where can I find duality? When I have seen and realized Brahman, how can I give any value to this world, which is only an illusion? When I am deep inside the ocean of divine nectar, why should I dig a well? What can I say about anything?[12]

There was no discrepancy between Bhagawan Nityananda's philosophy and his daily life. According to him, the perception of Brahman and the practice of worldly life were the same. His teaching was that worldly life is also a manifestation of Brahman. If someone sought spiritual knowledge, he would impart that, and he would also give suitable instructions to those who discussed worldly problems. He would advise some people to become doctors, engineers, or lawyers, and others to start a business or industry. He did not tell everyone to study yoga and live in an ashram. If, however, a person said that in spite of doing everything he had not found peace, then Bhagawan Nityananda would advise him to meditate and become thought-free by turning within.

## THURSDAY, MARCH 19, 1964

*Today Mr. Niraj, a famous Hindi poet and a professor at Aligarh University, came for Baba's darshan accompanied by some friends.*

### All Problems Are Solved After Realization

**Niraj:** *There are so many theories about the creation of this world that one cannot easily understand which of them is correct.*

**Baba:** You are right. There are many theories about the creation of the universe. Which of these is true and which are false? How can one say that a particular theory is false? Those who have told us about the creation of the world were not ordinary men. The *Bhagavad Gītā* says:

> The *rishis* have sung about this subject in many different meters and styles, and it has also been explained with examples and reasons in the *Brahma Sūtras.*[13]

In the *Yoga Vāsishtha*, Rama asks the sage Vasishtha a similar question. Rama says, "You are a great seer; you speak only Truth. My mind is confused because some say the world has emerged from an egg, some say it arose from water, some say it evolved from an atom, and some say it came into being out of the supreme Brahman."

The fact is that whatever is visible can be described, but how can that which is not visible be described? About the invisible, one can only imagine in various ways or make guesses. Therefore, one says something and another says something else. The real answer to this entire problem is revealed only with God's grace. So far as the ultimate Truth is concerned, all saints say the same thing. There can certainly be different theories about the creation of the universe, but they are unanimous about the final attainment.

**Niraj:** *Bhagawan Buddha says it is "the void."*

**Baba:** Everyone says what he experiences. If I were to experience that, I would also say the same. All paths of sadhana lead to the same goal. You may follow any one of them: *bhakti, prānāyāma, jñāna*, etc.

**Niraj:** *I certainly respect Meher Baba, but he makes people call him God and he makes predictions about the future. How can modern people who have cultivated logical thinking have faith in him?*

**Baba:** Too much learning confuses the mind. By too much reasoning, one loses faith in God. A poet sings as follows:

> O Bhagawan, take away my intellect, take away this power of reasoning, take away my knowledge and learning. Fill my heart with devotion and faith; give me love.[14]

Getting rid of old mental impressions is not easy. You must always strive to make your mind devoid of thoughts. You must give up dependence upon books.

**Niraj:** *But how can this be achieved?*

**Baba:** Make the mind steady. Have dispassion. Give up the sense of "I"-ness and "my"-ness. Understand that pain and pleasure are illusory. I will give you an example.

Once there were two neighboring families who were close friends. A girl from one of the families was engaged to a boy from the other family. They developed great love for each other to such an extent that if one of them had any trouble, the other one would also become miserable. If one fell sick, the other one would not eat owing to worry. After some time, it so happened that the friendship between the two families broke up and the engagement was canceled. Eventually the boy and the girl each married someone else. The boy died after a year but the girl did not feel any grief, whereas previously, when she had felt that he belonged to her, his every sorrow gave her pain. This is what is known as the sense of "I"-ness or "my"-ness. When this sense disappears, there is no pain.

This world has as much reality as the son of a barren woman bathing in mirage waters and wearing a garland of flowers from the sky. You should try to become one with God. He alone is real.

**Niraj:** *Which is the simplest and easiest way for me to do sadhana?*

**Baba:** Steady the mind. You can realize the Truth only by making your mind steady. Artists, scientists, and musicians all excel in their work through concentration of the mind. A concentrated mind becomes one with the work. Absorb your mind in love.

**Niraj:** *How can I love? Shall I love God with form?*

**Baba:** The *Yoga Sūtras* say:

> Take refuge in a man who has complete dispassion. Unite your mind with him.[15]

Seek refuge in a Self-realized saint. Have love for him. As this love grows, your inner shakti will awaken and the mind will lose its unsteadiness and become pure.

The mind is as restless as a monkey. Your mind is very restless and you are aware of it. This very recognition will help you to make it concentrated. The mind becomes steady as a result of knowledge of the Self. Understand that you neither gain nor lose anything whether your mind pursues sensual pleasures or gives them up. You do not suffer any loss when a horse that is standing near you runs away and then returns, because you have no concern with its coming or going; it is the same between you and your mind. Just watch the mind. Become the Witness of the mind. I also passed through a state similar to yours. I am advising you to follow the sadhana that benefited me.

Always contemplate the supreme Brahman. In this way, you yourself become Brahman. Sundardas says:

> The mind that always thinks of a woman becomes a woman; the mind that constantly gets angry takes on the form of anger; the mind that continually dwells in delusion drowns in the well of delusion. The mind that constantly contemplates Brahman becomes Brahman. This entire world is only an imagination of the mind.[16]

**Niraj:** *Are miracles real? Is it possible to perform miracles through the practice of yoga?*

**Baba:** This entire world is one great miracle of the mind. It is all a play of Chiti Shakti.

**Niraj:** *I have heard that some yogis can make a dead man return to life. Doesn't this violate the laws of God?*

**Baba:** It is all according to the laws of destiny. Yogis always work according to God's laws.

**Niraj:** *I have heard about a twenty-two-year-old boy who can predict future events. He correctly foretells the winning numbers of racehorses. Is this all the result of yogic shakti?*

**Baba:** Even if one obtains such powers, they vanish after a short time. A bird flying in the air or a fish living in water—aren't these miracles, or *siddhis*? There are many such miracles. Some people can acquire *siddhis* according to their desires, but they can perform them only to the extent that they have progressed. If you can believe in this kind of magic, it would be much better for you to believe in the saints and Siddhas, who can take you across this ocean of birth and death.

**Niraj:** *We are thinking of building an ashram for seekers in Hardwar.*

**Baba:** First practice steadying your mind. Afterward, you can do whatever work comes to you by God's will. Do what destiny makes you do. It is not necessary for you to leave this world. Realize the Truth, and your concept of the world will automatically leave you.

**Niraj:** *We ourselves may achieve the goal, but what about our duty toward society? Wouldn't it be selfish? So many people in the world are starving and miserable.*

**Baba:** First realize the Truth and then you will only work to remove the misery of others. You will be working for society alone.

## SATURDAY, MARCH 21, 1964

*Shrimati Kundanika Kapadia, a famous Gujarati writer, poet, and editor of the Gujarati edition of the magazine Navneet, came today for Baba's darshan.*

### *The Place of Penance in Sadhana*

**Kundanika:** *How much bodily hardship must one undergo during sadhana? In other words, what is the place of penance in sadhana?*

**Baba:** While following a sadhana of sattvic practices, the body need not be subjected to any hardship. The body must be kept in good condition. One should do sadhana according to the capacity and limitations of the body. Many people practice *japa* for several hours and others chant God's name for hours while standing in water, but it is not necessary to follow these people blindly. We must progress slowly and steadily in sadhana, regulating our eating habits, conduct, and other activities as an aid to such progress. The *Bhagavad Gītā* says:

> Yoga destroys all sorrow for the one who maintains balance
> in eating, waking and sleeping, and other activities.[17]

**Kundanika:** *What should be done in order to conquer the senses?*

**Baba:** There are many means to gain control over the senses, but among them discrimination is the best. The senses do not work on their own. They act only according to impulses received from the mind. The senses start functioning when the mind is agitated. When the mind becomes free from all thoughts and emotions, the senses can easily be controlled.

## *The Mind Becomes Peaceful Through Discrimination*

**Kundanika:** *But the mind does not remain quiet.*

**Baba:** That is the nature of the mind. You must constantly discriminate. The mind becomes engaged in the objects of its liking. It wants everything to be pleasant. Therefore, you should always keep discriminating between what is permanent, or eternal, as opposed to what is temporary, or ephemeral; what is beneficial to you and what is harmful. Self-mortification does not work on the mind; the mind can only be controlled by discrimination.

The mind is such that where nothing exists it makes you see the whole universe, as one sees a snake in a rope or water in a mirage. It makes you see forms in the formless. It causes relativity to manifest in the Absolute. The *Maitrī Upanishad* says:

> The mind is the cause of one's bondage as well as of one's liberation.[18]

The same mind makes a friend into a foe and a foe into a friend. It takes you from heaven to hell or from hell to heaven. To focus the mind outside is bondage and to focus it within is liberation. The pleasure and pain of the body do not affect the Self. The Self is free from what the body has to go through. The *Bhagavad Gītā* says:

> O Son of Kunti! Pleasure and pain, heat and cold arise when the senses unite themselves with the sense objects. They are temporary; they come and go. O Bharata! Bear them.[19]

The *antahkarana* (inner psychic instrument) has two states: *chaitya* and *achaitya,* that is, live and inert. In the *achaitya* state, the individual soul does not experience the pleasure and pain of the gross body. In the *chaitya* state, however, the individual soul does experience them. Just as the rays of the sun can burn an object when focused through a convex lens, similarly, the *chaitya* state of the *antahkarana* is caused by the reflection of *chaitanya* (the life-force) onto it; that is the individual soul. When the inner psychic instrument unites itself with the objects of the world, the individual soul experiences pleasure or pain and becomes disturbed. It is only in the *turīya* state that pain and pleasure are not experienced.

*In the evening Shri Deshpande, a devotee, came to the ashram. He asked Baba the following question:*

## *The Self Is to Be Experienced, Not Intellectualized*

**Deshpande:** *My mind does not remain steady, nor can I understand God. What shall I do?*

**Baba:** God can never be understood by the intellect. The *Kena Upanishad* says:

> One who says he knows God does not know Him, and one who says he does not know God, in reality, knows Him.[20]

The supreme Brahman has no attributes and, therefore, cannot be known by any of the senses, nor can it be attained by the mind. The mind can contemplate the Self but it cannot know the Self, because realization of the Self is a matter of experience, not of intellectual thought.

Why do you want to steady the mind? There is one who witnesses the mind whether it is quiet or agitated. Know Him. That Witness has no connection with the mind and is not dependent on the stillness of the mind. However, you must first know what the mind is. The mind is a concept that creates trouble for many people. It is good to restrain it. A mind full of desires and hopes makes a person miserable, while the same mind when free from these makes a person happy. The mind that roams outside is sorrowful; the mind that turns within is peaceful. By making the mind contemplate God, it quickly becomes quiet.

### WEDNESDAY, MARCH 25, 1964

*Today Shri Niraj had a discussion with Baba.*

## The Integration of Yoga into Daily Life

**Niraj:** *How can one integrate yoga into the practical life of the world?*

**Baba:** Yoga is already interwoven in daily life. Every creature practices yoga. Yoga is for everyone. People generally consider it to be separate from worldly life, because they do not know the true nature of yoga. They feel that it is only for *sādhus* and *sannyāsīs* living in jungles or caves, and that the practice of yoga requires one to observe certain difficult rules, to undergo intense austerities, and so forth. In fact, it is not so. Everyone unconsciously practices yoga to some extent in everyday life. For example, regulated diet and conduct is a part of yoga. Students, artists, technicians, and others all have to fix their minds on their work; that is, the mind must be concentrated. This is also yoga. On waking up, you do not immediately relate to the outer world. For a moment the mind is devoid of any thoughts, and that experience is nothing other than *samādhi.* You see yoga practiced in all its aspects in the activities of daily life.

The final aim of yoga is *samādhi.* Meditation is the discipline and *samādhi* is its fruit. In *samādhi,* one achieves a thought-free state of mind and becomes united with the supreme Self. What the *Yoga Shāstras* call *samādhi* is called the *turīya* state in Vedanta.

**Niraj:** *How can the kundalinī be awakened?*

**Baba:** The *kundalinī* is already awake throughout the usual activities of worldly life, but its direction changes through the practice of *prānāyāma,* meditation, or *japa.* Its outward focus decreases gradually, and it becomes increasingly more inner-directed. Thus the *kundalinī* is awake in two respects: in outer activities and in the inner life. The latter is also called the awakening of the inner shakti, which can easily be accomplished by the Guru's grace. This is known as the *siddhamārga,* or the path of the Siddhas. When the *kundalinī* is awakened by the Guru's grace, all the yogic practices such as *āsana,* concentration, and meditation take place spontaneously. As soon as the mind becomes steady, *prāṇāyāma* occurs automatically; the seeker does not have to make any special effort to do it. This is the path of *gurukripā* (Guru's grace). It is a great science.

**Niraj:** *I want to follow this yoga. Will I be able to do it?*

**Baba:** Why not? Everyone is a part of the supreme Self and can, therefore, practice this yoga. Why then wouldn't it be possible for you? Try to receive the Guru's grace and thus attain it.

**Niraj:** *What is nāda?*

**Baba:** Just as there is this external space, there is an inner space known as *chidākāsha* in which sound arises due to the *prāna*. It is called *anāhata nāda*. This music goes on inside ceaselessly. The divine *nāda* is the vibration of the supreme Self in the *chidākāsha*.

**Niraj:** *I want to hear the nāda.*

**Baba:** It is already within you. As soon as the mind becomes one-pointed, this *nāda* is heard. Become one-pointed and you will surely hear it.

## Thursday, April 2, 1964

*Today a swami from a South Indian math came to see Baba and talked to him about the financial difficulties of the college he heads. After the swami's departure, Baba spoke to the devotees present.*

**Baba:** It is not proper to approach people for the sake of money or to go around asking for funds. In the first place, the head of a *math*, an *āchārya*, or a *sannyāsī* should not undertake that kind of work. This is not the dharma, or duty, of a *sannyāsī*. The establishment and administration of institutions such as schools and colleges is the duty of the government. Despite this, if a person still wants to embark on such a project, he should first carefully assess his strength, power, and resources before starting.

Worldly activities cannot proceed merely on the basis of promises such as "I shall give you money." "I shall give" is in the future tense. To have faith in such a promise is a mistake. From this, one starts getting entangled in a trap. The very nature of worldly life is such that even those who regard themselves as clever get into trouble. All work should be started only after considering one's current strength. Do not depend on the future, or your position will be like that of the bee who was once sitting on a lotus flower. Intoxicated by its nectar and fragrance, the bee was unaware that evening was quickly approaching. At sunset, the petals of the lotus closed, trapping the bee inside. The bee thought, "Well, the night will surely pass away, dawn will come, the sun will rise, and as soon as its rays fall on this lotus, it will open again. Then I can escape!" But meantime, while the bee was thinking in this manner, an intoxicated elephant came by and uprooted the lotus with its trunk and put it into its mouth. The bee was crushed between the elephant's teeth along with the lotus.

If you make even the smallest error in any dealings in this world, know that you are trapped. Any activity is like a small stream in the beginning. It slowly expands and assumes the dimensions of a sea, and then we drown in it. This applies not only to people living worldly lives but also to *sannyāsīs,* who have taken a vow in the presence of fire that "I shall not keep anything in my hand; I renounce everything." Even they get trapped in worldly affairs. A rare one among them has received the full grace of the Guru and can escape unscathed. Only one who is free and steady-minded is not carried away by others. In worldly affairs, he never believes in promises.

Man becomes infatuated by words that give him hope. This is called *māyā.* The Lord says in the *Bhagavad Gītā,* "It is very difficult to cross My *māyā.*" The power of the Guru's grace alone enables one to escape from the snares of *māyā.* I never tell anyone to give up anything, because the temptations of worldly life can entangle even renunciants and *sannyāsīs*. The vast pageant of this world is very tempting, deceptive, and difficult to conquer. Hardly anyone can escape from the clutches of this *māyā*. My advice is to have faith in the Guru and to meditate awhile in the midst of your daily life and activities. By remembering the Guru and spending even half an hour daily singing God's name, their grace will take you across this ocean.

Even in modern times, there are many instances of seekers who have realized the Self in this very lifetime after doing sadhana for a few years. What does this indicate? Such examples demonstrate that it is not difficult to realize God. After a while, one is sure to attain Him. In contrast, people spend fifty or sixty years in mundane activities and in the end do not gain any happiness or satisfaction. After years of exhausting effort, they remain empty. If you ask "Have you obtained any peace? Have you achieved whatever you set out to achieve?" they reply, "I have yet to achieve this thing and that."

Effort to attain God never goes to waste. It is always beneficial to the individual; one is freed from the cycle of birth and death. On the other hand, after undergoing much hardship and expending tremendous effort in worldly pursuits, at the end people find themselves where they started, having achieved nothing.

Just as a manufacturer requests a shopkeeper to display his goods along with the other goods for sale in his shop in order to make them known to the public, similarly, I advise you to remember the Guru along with all your other daily concerns—your business, service, house, family, wealth, and other worldly possessions. Reserve some time to remember God. That heart which has no love for God and takes no delight in singing God's name is of no value. Without Guru's grace, you get entangled in worldly life. Remember the Guru regularly and receive his grace. In that alone is the fulfillment of your life and the achievement of the supreme goal.

*Today Shri Dilip Mehta, professor of physics at K. C. College, accompanied some friends to the ashram. He regularly attends the discourses of Swami Chinmayananda. He had the following discussion with Baba.*

## The Guru's Grace and Recognition of a Sadguru

**Dilip:** *If a seeker begins his sadhana by obtaining Guru's grace, wouldn't it obstruct the evolution of his own inner power? Wouldn't it be harmful for a person to receive the Guru's grace if he lacks the basic qualifications of a spiritual aspirant such as knowledge and dispassion, which are necessary in order to realize God?*

**Baba:** Of all means of sadhana, the path of the Guru's grace is the best. The Guru's grace does not obstruct the evolution of the seeker's inner shakti. On the contrary, it helps his shakti to expand. As soon as the inner shakti is awakened, knowledge and dispassion spontaneously arise from within. It is necessary, however, to have a Guru who is capable of bestowing divine grace.

**Dilip:** *How can one recognize such a Guru?*

**Baba:** This is a simple matter. How did you come here? Someone must have aroused your curiosity by telling you about Bhagawan Nityananda and Ganeshpuri. Thus you came here and had satsang. How do you decide which college to join? First you make inquiries, meet the students and professors, talk to them about the colleges, and then finally decide which college to join. In our language it is called satsang. You go to a saint, remain in his company, and have a personal experience. You can truly know a Guru in this way.

**Dilip:** *Many great beings change the future of their devotees by their grace or their power. Doesn't this violate the laws of nature?*

**Baba:** What is your occupation?

**Dilip:** *I am a professor. I teach in a college.*

**Baba:** When an ignorant student comes to you, you give him knowledge and make him learned. Isn't that so? When a student comes to you, which law tells you whether or not to teach him? There is no such law, is there? Similarly, saints and great beings use their divine power or their own merits to uplift their devotees. There is no violation of any law of nature in this.

**Dilip:** *Is it true that a person with unfulfilled desires becomes a ghost after death?*

**Baba:** A person will always have desires until the time of *jīvanmukti*. This does not mean that all people become ghosts. Only those who perform undesirable actions and behave contrary to the scriptures become ghosts.

## SUNDAY, APRIL 26, 1964

*The second annual meeting of the Ashram Council was held this morning. The ashram trustees, Shri B. C. Dalal, Secretary of the Law Ministry of Maharashtra State, and some other guests were also here. They all requested Baba to say a few words. Befitting the occasion, Baba addressed them as follows:*

# The Need for Religious Institutions

My dear ones, you have all gathered here with feelings of love and brotherhood, and I am very pleased to see how selflessly all of you are serving the ashram.

Before starting any work, a thorough study and understanding of it will lead to the benefit of all. The title *trustee* signifies one who is worthy of trust, in whose hands everything can be entrusted with full faith. This signifies love of the Self.

Whatever is given in charity to a religious institution belongs to God. According to the Shastras, even one and a quarter rupee donated for a religious purpose is given to God. People donate to religious institutions purely out of love for God.

Vedanta is an unparalleled Shastra; it is the basis for all other Shastras. It expounds the knowledge of that supreme Principle, knowing which man becomes God, the *jīva* becomes Shiva. After attaining that supreme Principle, nothing else remains to be gained. In that state, a person feels that he is Shiva. One who has realized the supreme Self will always speak the truth and nothing but the truth. Tukaram Maharaj says, "God belongs to me and I belong to God." This is the doctrine of Vedanta, and it is religion as well. Religious institutions exist for this purpose: to help man achieve this truth. Such institutions must be well managed. That is practice of religion—putting religion into practice.

Some people complain that our government is not acting according to religious principles and does not provide protection to religion, but this is not so. The government is looking after and managing many religious institutions, and in this way it is working in harmony with religion.

What is the meaning of religion? It is that by which one can know the supreme Truth, that by which one attains eternal happiness. That is religion. Everyone undertakes activities in this world, such as industry, business, politics, and so on, in order to obtain happiness. Vedanta says that one who has not achieved inner happiness cannot understand the true state. Religious institutions are meant for that. There man gets peace.

There is no real happiness in wearing fine clothes or eating good food, and so on. True happiness is achieved only through knowledge of the Self. About this knowledge, the *Bhagavad Gītā* says:

> It is the king of all knowledge, the greatest of all secrets, the purest and the highest, and it can be directly experienced. It is easy to practice and is imperishable.[21]

The purpose of religious institutions is to impart this knowledge and enable people to experience it. These institutions do not belong to any one individual, neither to me nor to you nor to any swami. These institutions are open for everyone who has love for knowledge of the Self.

A person may progress to any extent but cannot have real happiness without realizing the Truth. There is no other way except the experience of *Shivo'ham*—"I am Shiva." The main goal of human life is to realize the Self. Whatever else one gains in this world is incidental, whether it is wife or husband, children, property, or wealth. The main purpose of a mango tree is to produce mangoes. Along with that, it provides shade, its dried leaves and branches are used for fuel, and its trunk provides lumber. These other uses, however, are subsidiary or incidental.

Similarly, the main purpose of religious institutions such as ashrams and *maths* is to remind people of the great Vedantic proclamation "That thou art." The fulfillment of material desires and relief from worldly miseries are the secondary gains of going to a saint. A trustee is one who with selflessness and impartiality fosters the main purpose of the religious institution.

When someone is devoted to attaining God, many people think that he must renounce the world, but that isn't so. If God is all-pervading, what can be rejected and what can be accepted? The *Taittirīya Upanishad* says:

> The supreme Lord created this cosmos, and then He Himself entered into it.[22]

This entire universe is the play of God. We are an inseparable part of that supreme Self. The realization of this is liberation. The reason we greet one another in daily life by saying "*Rām, Rām,*" "*Namo Nārāyan,*" or "*Shalom Aleichem*" is that we wish to see our own Self everywhere in everyone. The phrase on our ashram emblem, *paraspara devo bhāva*, "See God in each other," also means the same.

Whatever work is going on in this world is, in reality, the work of God. If one understands this, one can perform any work as an offering. To cooperate selflessly in God's work is real *yajña* (sacrifice). The aim of religion is to obtain true knowledge. The *Manusmriti* advises: "Whoever protects dharma is protected by it. Otherwise he is destroyed."

The Lord says in the *Bhagavad Gītā*:

> It is the supreme Self from which the activity of all beings arises, by which everything is pervaded. One who worships that supreme Self by performing his own duty attains liberation.[23]

Work done with this understanding will be beneficial to you, to the devotees, and to the religious institution.

## WEDNESDAY, APRIL 29, 1964

*Giridhari Sharad, a devotee, has returned to India after pursuing studies in the physical sciences for three years in England. While there, he maintained contact with the ashram through correspondence and read the ashram publications with great interest. He came today for Baba's darshan and asked some questions.*

### The Nature of the Self

**Giridhari:** *When I was in England, I read your poem entitled "Knowledge of the Self Is Easy to Attain." What is the nature of that Self? What are its attributes?*

**Baba:** The Self is beyond thought, cannot be seen, cannot be touched or grasped, nor can it be described in words. These are its attributes. In other words, the Self has no form, taste, smell, sound, or texture. It can neither be comprehended by the mind nor perceived by the senses. The senses are the instruments by which we acquire knowledge of the objects and matters of the world, but they do not have the power to know the Self because they themselves are illumined by the Self. Those who have directly experienced the Self tell us that it is self-luminous; it cannot be the subject of questions and answers. It is to be realized or experienced through sadhana. The nature of the Self is not like that of any other object in the world. It cannot be described or explained through comparison with anything else. Just as there is only one sun, and, therefore, you cannot say that it is like any other object or any other sun, similarly, there is nothing with which to compare the Self. In order to understand the Self, you have to realize the Self, for there is nothing similar to it.

**Giridhari:** *The poem also said: "Your Self is perfect light; the entire world is illumined by this light of the Self." Then is the light of the Self any different from the light of the sun? How does the light of the Self interact with that of the sun?*

**Baba:** There is no other light like that of the Self. It is incomparable. It is the Self that illumines the sun. Before the light of the Self, the light of the sun, moon, stars, and fire is nothing. The sun and the moon shine by only an infinitesimal portion of the light of the Self. The *Katha Upanishad* says:

> There the sun does not shine nor the moon, the stars nor lightning, let alone fire. Where can fire shine? By the light of the Self, all these shine. By the light of the Self, the entire universe is illumined.[24]

**Giridhari:** *If the light of the Self and the light of the sun are different, there must be some evidence to prove it.*

**Baba:** The only evidence is the words of the Self-realized Siddhas who have themselves experienced it.

**Giridhari:** *How can this be explained to the modern-day scientists?*

**Baba:** This is not the subject of common science. In order to understand any subject, you have to follow the particular process suitable for it. For example, if someone wants to become a doctor, he has to enter a medical college, attend the lectures of experienced doctors, and systematically undergo clinical medical training. The knowledge of the Self cannot be taught to scientists by these academic methods. One can know the Self only after Self-realization, and only a Self-realized master can make others realize it.

**Giridhari:** *In your book entitled Ādesh, you stated: "That which enables you to know what happens during the waking, dream, and deep-sleep states is the Self." But darkness prevails in the dream and sleep states. Does this mean, therefore, that one can see objects in darkness because of the light of the Self?*

**Baba:** The Self illumines darkness as well as light. When the light of the Self shines, even the sun appears to be dark. Even in darkness, the Self is always shining. A man sleeping in a completely dark room sees the procession of a king in his dream. By what light does he see it? The source of that light is the Self.

Light is of two types. One is ordinary or potential light, and the other is special or manifest. Ordinary light is concealed inside something, as, for example, fire is concealed or potential within wood. The light of the Self is within every individual. Just as a piece of wood cannot start burning spontaneously—fire manifests only as a result of friction—similarly, only when the light of the Self emerges as a result of sadhana is it fully manifest. This light is the special kind of light.

**Giridhari:** *Is it advisable to take these teachings on faith, or is it better to evaluate them logically?*

**Baba:** To accept any statement without the verification of personal experience is like accepting the stories told by one's grandmother during childhood as true. When someone tells you that Dasharatha, the father of Rama, was the king of Ayodhya, or that there was once an emperor called Napoleon, or that there is a city called

Patna in Bihar, you believe it although you have not seen them. But how can there be any question of disbelieving or believing in the Truth, which is manifest? The Self is not a thing of the past. It is a reality that is manifest and can be directly experienced. You can see the sun with your own eyes. How can any question arise about believing in its existence, when it is a reality you see for yourself? The Self is the eternal Truth existing in the past, present, and future. Vivekananda asked Ramakrishna, "Have you seen God?" and Ramakrishna replied, "Yes. God appears to be very far away to you, but I see Him very close to me."

## SATURDAY, MAY 9, 1964

*Shrimati Taraben Parekh came today for Baba's darshan and satsang. She is the daughter of Brahmaleen Swami Madhavtirth, founder of the Vedanta Ashram of Valad, and was born when he was a householder.*

**Taraben:** *What is meant by the term sahajāvasthā?*

**Baba:** It is the state of Witness-consciousness. Just as one naturally enters the sleep or dream states, this state also comes naturally. In this state, there is no ego or I-consciousness. When we are traveling, we observe our surroundings without becoming attached to anything. This state is the same.

**Taraben:** *Can one meditate with eyes open?*

**Baba:** Certainly. You can meditate in the way that suits you best. If you try to follow a method that is not suitable for you, then difficulties will arise. In meditation with the eyes open, the eyes see the outer objects but the mind is focused within. *Kumbhaka* does not occur even after the *prāna* has become steady. Even though the eyes are open, one does not see anything; even though words enter the ears, one does not hear anything.

To become free of the awareness of knower, known, and knowledge is meditation. When the mind abandons its usual nature and merges into the Self, that is meditation. The *Yoga Sūtras* say the same thing about meditation:

> Remaining unaffected in every situation is meditation.[25]

Being one with the Self is meditation. There are many definitions of meditation.

SATURDAY, JUNE 20, 1964

*Today Shri Rameshbhai Sumatilal Shah, the owner of Pannalal Silk Mills, came to the ashram for Baba's darshan with his family and some friends. He asked Baba the following question:*

## *The Bliss of Jīvanmukti*

**Rameshbhai:** *Baba, what is the state in which there is neither mental nor physical suffering?*

**Baba:** Pleasure and pain are not experienced in the *turīya* state. In that state, everything is seen as Brahman. This is what is known as *jīvanmukti,* or liberation in this very life. Waking, dream, and deep sleep are the three states of the individual soul. The Self does not have any such states. The Self is the witness of these three states, and the experience of this is *turīya.* Besides elimination of the non-Self, there is no other activity in *turīya.* When the mind ceases to be the mind, that is the *turīya* state.

In the waking and dream states, one sees unreality instead of reality, while in deep sleep one sees neither. In deep sleep, the individual soul is not conscious of "I" or "you"; it is unconscious even of nonduality. In the *turīya* state, however, it sees everything as Brahman. There one sees reality, and there is an awareness of nonduality. One who has knowledge of the Self no longer sees the world as world. The various dualities such as right or wrong, the Guru and the disciple, and bondage and liberation all become one. Such a realized person does not consider the triad of doer, deed, and fruit of the deed as different from the Self. He sees everything as the Self. Such a person has no mandatory duties. Since he does not experience duality, he is always nonattached. This is the fifth state in Vedanta, called *asansakti*. This is *jīvanmukti*.

Until one constantly experiences the bliss of *jīvanmukti*, one must repeatedly contemplate the meaning of the Vedantic teachings. If the mind has accepted that everything is nothing but Vasudeva, or God, but that idea does not remain steady and the mind and body continue to crave the pleasures of worldly objects, then faith will not become firm. If faith is not firm, the mind will remain restless and will stop the search for the Self. As a result, there will be no experience of the bliss of *jīvanmukti*.

A hollow gourd normally floats in water but sinks if filled with iron; similarly, if the mind is full of desire, hatred, and so forth, it cannot remain in the continuous awareness of the Self. The company of saints and sages is an antidote to this poison of the mundane world, enabling one to again experience the bliss of the Self.

In order to experience one's true Self, one should remain in solitude for some time each day. If possible, one should go into complete seclusion for about seven days every two or three months. During these periods of solitude, one should abandon all thoughts and practice watching what is happening within. In this way, one gets into the state of Witness-consciousness.

Love for the Self arouses yearning for realization of the Self. If you want to concentrate the mind while meditating on the Self, you must not let it wander here and there. By such practice, the mind melts away and desires are eliminated.

When the inner shakti starts expanding as a result of contemplation of the Self, many seekers have various visions, hear divine music, and see different colored lights, flames, and spots of light. A seeker should not pay too much attention to these, or else they will create a hindrance to his love for the Self. In order to disengage the mind from these, the best way is to continuously repeat the Vedanta *sūtra: neti neti,* "not this, not this." The means to Self-realization is the Self itself. If you remain constantly in the awareness of the Self, the mind easily becomes still. If knowledge of the Self remains steady, bliss also remains constant. This is the ideal of *sthitaprajña* in the *Bhagavad Gītā.* In this state, one remains undisturbed even in sorrow and adversity.

## WEDNESDAY, JULY 1, 1964

*Miss Hilda Charlton comes to stay in the ashram now and then and has satsang with Baba. There was a question-and-answer session today.*

### *The Lights Seen During Meditation*

**Hilda:** *What are the different stages in meditation? What is the sequence of the different experiences? I used to see lights and hear sounds. I also used to have visions, but I no longer have any of these experiences. I went to Rishikesh to practice meditation, and there I would become one with the inner Consciousness while meditating. I would often lose awareness of the gross body. What will follow after these experiences? I ask this question because I plan to return to America and I feel I should know what to expect.*

**Baba:** Why? Just before leaving, won't you come to see me? Or when I go to America, won't you visit me there?

**Hilda:** *Yes, I shall certainly come here again, and if you come to America, what more could I wish for! Babaji, please do come to*

*America. But now, please tell me what stage will follow in my meditation.*

**Baba:** I will write on this subject and send you a copy of the English translation. After reading it, you will have complete understanding.

**Hilda:** *I can't wait for such a long time. I will lose patience. Please tell me something now.*

**Baba:** Then listen. In the beginning several lights are seen during meditation.

**Hilda:** *Yes. I used to see many lights. I even saw them with my eyes open.*

**Baba:** There are different kinds of lights, many of them unimportant. The main lights are red, white, black, and blue. The *jīvātman,* or individual soul, has four bodies: the gross, subtle, causal, and supracausal. The red light represents the gross body; white, the subtle body; black, the causal body; and blue light represents the supracausal body. The red light appears as a large, expansive area within which you see a thumb-sized, bright white light. Afterward, within the white light, you see the black light. Within the black light, you see a blue spot. This shining Blue Pearl is of the nature of Brahman. Its appearance indicates the *turīya* state.

**Hilda:** *I see this Blue Pearl not only with closed eyes, but frequently even with my eyes open.*

**Baba:** This indicates that you are progressing well in meditation.

**Hilda:** *What should I do now?*

**Baba:** Nothing special. Just increase your meditation. The rest will happen spontaneously. The time will also come when nothing will happen; everything will vanish. Neither the lights nor the Blue Pearl will appear.

I have wrapped this shawl around my body. It is different

from me and yet I am aware that it belongs to me. You will feel the same way about your body; that is, you will develop Witness-consciousness, which is also known as the *nirvikalpa* state or *sahajāvasthā,* the natural state.

**Hilda:** *I experience this state even now, but only occasionally; it isn't constant.*

**Baba:** As your bliss keeps increasing, this state will gradually become steady. Try to increase that bliss.

**Hilda:** *When I was in America before coming here, I used to feel during meditation that I could leave my body from the space between the eyebrows and go wherever I liked. Is this possible?*

**Baba:** These are all the play of *prāna.* But the Blue Pearl that you see is important. It is the supreme Self; it is the *ātman*; it is the abode of God. This Pearl appears to be outside, but actually it is within. It is located right in the center of the eyes, ears, the crown of the head, and the back of the head. It is the supracausal body. The entire shakti dwells within it. With this body, we can go wherever we want. The Blue Pearl moves at tremendous speed. Its speed is such that within a fraction of a second it can go to America and return here. This Pearl appears in meditation as a scintillating, shining spot and then disappears.

**Hilda:** *I also see a brown light in the shape of a rupee coin. What is that light?*

**Baba:** That is also one of the lights, but the Blue Pearl is more important. Continue to meditate. After some time, you will acquire so much shakti that you will be able to give others the experience of meditation. You will be able to transmit shakti to others.

**Hilda:** *Oh! How beautiful! Baba, when I return to America, this is what I shall do. Here I have been able to cure some people. Should I continue to do this after returning to America? Is it advisable to do this?*

**Baba:** There is nothing wrong with it; however, instead of curing diseases, it would be better to guide others onto the spiritual path.

**Hilda:** *Baba, you have given me such clear understanding. My mind is satisfied. I used to think that Self-realization would happen suddenly like a bomb exploding, but now I understand that it comes easily and naturally. One does not even feel it. How wonderful!*

FRIDAY, JULY 3, 1964

*Today Hilda Charlton again asked Baba several questions.*

## *Great Beings Are One with Supreme Consciousness*

**Hilda:** *Do saints like Bhagawan Nityananda and Ramana Maharshi continue to exist in a subtle form even after their mahāsamādhi? After mahāsamādhi, some people have had their darshan and have received guidance from them.*

**Baba:** Before trying to comprehend this subject, it is necessary to understand the true nature of such saints. From the spiritual viewpoint, there are two classes of people: limited beings and saints. You must understand how a limited being becomes a saint. According to the Upanishads, that person is called a saint who has completely merged his individuality into the attributeless, formless *chaitanya,* or supreme Consciousness, becoming one with it. One who falls short of completely merging with *chaitanya* by even an iota remains only a limited being. He may perform any number of miracles, yet he cannot be called a saint. He may be able to travel to Kashi or Mathura while sitting here, he may perform many miracles or whatever he says may come true, yet he still is imperfect. It is said:

> He can disappear and then reappear, he can travel instantaneously to Kashi or Mathura, he can walk on water, his words may come true, and yet he is imperfect. He is not the child of a Guru.[26]

Just as salt dissolves in water and pervades all of it, similarly, a saint is one whose consciousness pervades everywhere.

**Hilda:** *How is it possible for saints to maintain their individual identities after completely merging with Consciousness? How can we say "This is Bhagawan Nityananda" or "This is Ramana Maharshi"?*

**Baba:** Just as there are many mangoes on a mango tree, such saints have the same relationship with Consciousness; or just as the sea has innumerable drops of water, similarly, the saints are different forms of one Consciousness.

**Hilda:** *What is the special quality of the samādhi shrines of these great saints that enables many people to have their darshan even after they have left their physical bodies?*

**Baba:** Listen to the following story to understand this. Once, in an assembly of sages, the topic under discussion was "Which is greater, austerities (*tapasyā*) or knowledge of Brahman (*brahmajñāna*)?" Vishvamitra declared, "Austerities are greater," while Vasishtha proclaimed, "Knowledge of the Self is greater." As the discussion proceeded, the arguments became increasingly heated. They could not reach any conclusion. Finally, they all went to the netherworld to seek the counsel of Sheshanaga, the king of serpents. Vishvamitra asked him to enlighten them on the subject. Being omniscient, Sheshanaga knew everything that had happened prior to their arrival. Yet he told them, "I will certainly give you the answer, but it would be helpful if you could relieve me of this heavy burden on my head." Actually there was no burden on his head. He holds the entire earth on his head as naturally as we wear a cap.

Vishvamitra said, "For ten million years I have done *tapasyā*, and I have controlled my *prāna* for many years through the practice of *kumbhaka.* By the power of this *tapasyā,* I will make the earth stand on my *yogadanda* (yoga stick)." As soon as he had placed it on his *yogadanda,* the earth started to sway.

Observing this, Vasishtha said, "If I have experienced the all-pervading supreme Self, whose nature is pure Consciousness, for even a fraction of a second, this earth will rest on my *kamandalu* (water bowl)." And, lo and behold, the earth did stand steady on his *kamandalu.*

Vishvamitra then said to Sheshanaga, "Your burden has been relieved. Now give us the answer."

Sheshanaga replied, "Where is the need for an answer now? You should all be able to understand it for yourselves."

This story gives you an idea of the great power of the *tapasyā* of those great beings like Vasishtha who experienced the supreme Self for innumerable moments rather than for just a fraction of a second. The *tapasyā* of these great beings after realization of Brahman is not for their personal use, because they have nothing left to attain. It is for the benefit of others. This power remains in their *samādhi* shrines. Actually, this power is the same as the all-pervading pure Consciousness. The same Consciousness is within you, and it manifests in different forms according to your faith; thus, you have the darshan of saints and sages. Just as the different objects perceived in the world are forms of the same *chaitanya shakti,* similarly, darshan of these saints is also a form of that same *chaitanya.* When devotees visit a *samādhi* shrine offering prayers and worship, then, according to their faith, they are blessed with the darshan of that saint. It is a manifestation of their own inner faith.

**Hilda:** *I had the darshan of Nityananda Baba even before I had met him in person. At that time, I didn't even know him. Therefore, I feel that even prior to meeting him, he was guiding me. How could this have happened?*

**Baba:** It is not at all difficult for *chaitanya shakti* to assume any form; in fact, it is very easy. The darshan that you had was to foretell your eventual meeting with Baba.

## The Inequalities Seen in the World Are the Result of Past Actions

**Hilda:** *When I return to America and tell people that God is all-pervading and that He has created this world, they will ask me, "If that is so, then why is there so much misery and poverty in this world?"*

**Baba:** God has not created any inequalities in this world. Pleasure and pain are seen by the individual, not by God. Moreover, an individual's outlook is relative. If you ask a wealthy man, "What is the world like?" in accordance with his own experiences he would reply, "It is beautiful and full of pleasures." But if you ask a poor man the same question, he would say, "The world is full of misery." The experiences of worldly pleasure and pain are personal and short-lived. In the state of realization, pleasure and pain are no longer cognized. In this regard Swami Rama Tirtha used to tell a beautiful story.

There was a lords' club to which no one except lords was admitted. At the very outset, the question arose as to who would sweep, who would cook, and who would perform all the other menial duties, since they all had equal status. They had a meeting and decided that they would draw lots. The lord whose name was drawn for a particular task would do it for that day. In this way, they all took turns performing the various jobs required to run the club such as sweeper, errand boy, cook, secretary, and president. Now, the lord who happened to be sweeping would be considered as a sweeper by passersby, but the lord himself knew that he was a lord, not a sweeper. Thus the views of the lord and the passersby were different.

Just as the lords in the club performed different roles according to their lots, similarly, in this world everyone lives according to his past deeds, but in essence the same Consciousness exists everywhere and in everyone; everything and everyone are equal. Pleasure and pain, wealth and poverty are all alike, but to an ordinary man they appear to be different.

Three years ago a man who had mastered the *Bhrigu Samhitā*[27] visited me. He told me that four births earlier I was a king, but now I am a monk. Similarly, people have pleasure or pain according to their past deeds. The supreme Self, however, is always the same.

An artist paints different figures—cow, horse, man, house, river, mountain, tree, and so forth—on the same wall using the same brush. These figures have different shapes and names, but in reality they are from the same paint. Similarly, everything in this world has in fact arisen from the supreme Self. The experience of pleasure and pain is dependent upon the thinking of the individual. The same set of circumstances will elicit different responses according to the individual's attitude.

"This is that Devadatta" is a sentence that is often quoted in Vedanta to illustrate one of its basic teachings, "Thou art That." Devadatta was the king of Benares. He developed a strong feeling of dispassion. Entrusting his kingdom to his son, he took *sannyāsa.* In his wanderings, he came to a town where someone recognized him. The man told his friend, "This is that Devadatta," by which he meant, "This is the same Devadatta who was formerly the king of Benares." To others, he appeared to be a *sannyāsī* and not a king because of the change in his clothes, place, and status. In fact, the same person was Devadatta the *sannyāsī* as well as Devadatta the king. Recognizing the real Devadatta even in the clothes of a *sannyāsī* is an example of the principle of Self-recognition according to Vedanta.

When you are asleep, you are not aware of pleasure or pain. Even in the waking state, you forget them when you are concentrating on some activity. This shows that pleasure and pain are not real, but are concepts of the mind and, therefore, cannot be lasting. I shall relate another story.

A fisherman once became friendly with a wealthy man. He used to take a walk every day on the beach, and the fisherman gave him fish. One day the wealthy man invited the fisherman to his home. On the appointed day, the fisherman went to the man's house, taking some fish as a gift. Both of them were very happy. They had their meals together, and then the man asked the fisherman to stay overnight. He was given a beautiful bedroom filled with the fragrance of flowers and perfume.

At midnight the host heard some noises in the adjacent room, so he got up and looked in on the fisherman. The guest, appearing quite restless, was sitting up in bed. The host inquired, "Haven't you slept?" The fisherman replied, "There is a strange smell in this room, and therefore I cannot go to sleep." Being perceptive, the wealthy man asked him, "Where is the cloth in which the fish you brought were wrapped?" The fisherman replied that it was outside. The host advised him to cover his face with that cloth and then go to sleep. The fisherman did so, and he immediately fell asleep. Thus, what was pleasant for the wealthy man was experienced as unpleasant by the fisherman, and that which was pleasant to the fisherman was intolerable to the wealthy man. Similarly, pleasure and pain are experienced according to the outlook of the mind. Only To A Degree. There is unanimity.

SATURDAY, JULY 4, 1964

## A Seeker's Experiences

**Hilda:** *I see a spider-like insect when I meditate with my eyes open. As I keep looking at it, it climbs up onto the ceiling and disappears. Is something bad happening?*

**Baba:** What you see is not a creature but a kind of network of light, which is actually within you although appearing to be outside. If you concentrate your mind on it, you will see spots of light. This is not a bad experience. Just be a witness to whatever you see in meditation.

**Hilda:** *Sometimes when I sit for meditation, I feel very dull and listless. How can I overcome this feeling?*

**Baba:** There is no need to do anything about it. Just continue to sit for meditation. All these will gradually drop away. Through meditation, the mind will be purified. The feeling of disinterestedness or listlessness is a kind of state of mind. As you continue to meditate, this state will change spontaneously.

**Hilda:** *During meditation I sometimes have visions of divine beings. I even feel that they are giving me their blessings.*

**Baba:** That is good. During meditation one may see various other worlds such as Siddhaloka, Chandraloka, and Indraloka. One may have visions of saints and sages. Sometimes one may also receive guidance from them.

SUNDAY, JULY 5, 1964

## *The Development of Shakti Through Self-Effort and Faith*

**Barrister Nain:** *My friend Albert Rudolph has some very exalted spiritual experiences. Are they the result of his sadhana in a previous life?*

**Baba:** The human body is a center of divine energy. This energy is so powerful that by its strength, Prahlad was able to bring God forth bodily from a pillar, Vishvamitra was able to create another world, and the *gopīs* were able to make Balakrishna dance in their homes.[28] This great shakti exists in everyone. In some people, however, it appears to be more active and in others, less. The same *chaitanya shakti*, or life-force, exists in the body, mind, intellect, and *prāna* of every being, but the level of development of these instruments varies from one being to another. For example, some are more intellectually developed than others. Therefore, what we must consider is how the development of the shakti can be accomplished.

All grains of wheat are alike. After sowing, they grow with the support of the soil. But whether they grow more or less depends upon the skill of the farmer. Similarly, the development of the dormant shakti within us depends on every individual's effort. The gross bodies of man, animals, birds, and so forth are all composed of five great elements (ether, air, fire, water, and earth). The basic constituents of all bodies are the same. Sundardas says:

> If you observe the gross bodies from Brahma down to a small insect, they are all made up of the same five great elements. If you consider *prāna,* it is the same in all beings. Both hunger and thirst are similar for all creatures. If you consider the nature of the mind, it is universally the same; it is always entertaining doubts and vacillating between one thought and another, and thus it is steeped in ignorance. If you consider the Self, it is also the same everywhere and at all times. Sundardas says: Where can you find any difference? One is just like another.[29]

In spite of the body, *prānas,* and mind being similar in all beings, the development of your *chaitanya shakti* depends on the subtle impressions (*samskāras*) of your innumerable past lives and on your own self-effort in the present life. For this development, both the awakening of the *kundalinī* and a deep faith are essential. Faith has great power. Faith is a great divine shakti dwelling within you. Surdas says that by the power of their faith, the *gopīs* milked a bull to quench the Lord's thirst! Because of the strength of her faith, Mirabai swallowed poison with no ill effects.

Faith arises as a result of one's feelings and mental tendencies, and may be placed in a worthy or unworthy object. The fruits we receive are in accordance with the object of our faith. The *Bhagavad Gītā* says:

> O Bharata! The faith of each person is according to his nature. Everyone has faith in something or in someone. A person is transformed according to his faith.[30]

In my early days as a monk, I went to a jungle called Anandavan in Khuldabad near Daulatabad. It was there that Eknath Maharaj had a divine vision of Lord Datta, and it has since become a place of pilgrimage in Maharashtra. Janardan Swami did his *tapasyā* there. I went there for the darshan of Bhagawan Datta. I stayed for three days. At that time I had such faith that I would meet Bhagawan there, that every day I looked all around expecting Him to appear from this direction or that. Ten years later I returned to the same place but had no desire at all to stay, because by that time I had become a Vedantin. I had lost all interest in the manifestation of God in any form. Had I stayed in Anandavan for two or three years when I first went there, I surely would have had the darshan of Bhagawan Datta in a physical form. At that time I had such unshakable faith.

## SUNDAY, JULY 5, 1964

*Today another meeting of the Ashram Council was held. In addition to the council members, some other devotees were also present. After the business of the meeting was concluded, Baba spoke a few words in the form of a blessing.*

*Earlier in the meeting, Shri Pratap Yande had reported on his discussion with Shri Shankarrao Raut, a trustee of the Shri Bhimeshwar Sadguru Nityananda Trust, regarding the program for the approaching Guru Purnima. Baba returned to this subject.*

### The Necessity of Following the Scriptures in Religious Ceremonies

**Baba:** What program are you planning to have at Nityananda Baba's shrine on Guru Purnima?

**Pratap:** *The trustees there are considering performing a rudrābhishek (ritual bath given to an image of Lord Shiva).*

**Baba:** Those involved in administering religious institutions should have a thorough knowledge of scriptural precepts. Charity is that which is given in the name of religion or for a religious purpose, and religion signifies God and the scriptures. Thus, knowledge of the religious scriptures is essential in order to properly administer such institutions. *Rudrābhishek* can be done on Mahashivaratri; worship of the Guru's *pādukās* must be performed on Guru Purnima. On such occasions it is best to consult experts on religious rites and rituals and act according to their advice.

After the *mahāsamādhi* of Nityananda Baba, an argument arose as to which day should be considered the thirteenth day. Should the days be counted from the day he left the body or from the day he was laid in the *samādhi* shrine? Swami Kuttiram, Swami Digambar, and other devotees said that Baba had told them to count from the day he was put into the shrine. If I had told them the relevant scriptural rule, my plight would have been like that of the priest in the following story.

Once a group of nine fishermen went on a pilgrimage accompanied by their priest. They had a good pilgrimage, doing everything properly according to scriptural rites. Nonetheless, desire is such a peculiar thing that it is impossible to predict when and where it will lead a man. The *Bhagavad Gītā* says:

> The turbulent senses violently carry away the mind of even a wise man.[31]

As the group was returning home, they spotted a toddy shop. The fishermen entered the shop and drank to their hearts' content. The priest said, "Look, we have not yet completed our pilgrimage; we have not yet reached our town. What are you doing?" The fishermen became fearful that the priest would complain about them to everyone on reaching home, so immediately upon arriving in town, before the priest had a chance to say a word, the fishermen told the townsfolk that the priest had drunk toddy while returning from the pilgrimage. All the townspeople began to reproach him, saying "You are a priest. Don't you understand that you should not have behaved like that? What have you done?" In this manner, the priest got into trouble even though he had not touched a drop of toddy.

Not wanting to get into trouble like that priest, I advised them to seek the counsel of Pandit Vare Shastri of Nasik, who is a well-known and accepted authority on this subject. I told them that he had a thorough knowledge of the scriptures, and that they should abide by his decision. Everyone agreed, and Pandit Vare Shastri was called. He said that the thirteen days should be counted from the day Baba had left his body, and so it was done.

Religion is not a business for idle people. It is not a pursuit for those who have nothing else to do in life. King Janaka ruled his vast kingdom according to the traditions of statesmanship, and although he was not a *sannyāsī,* he was a great *tyāgī* (renunciant), a great *jñānī,* and a Siddha. One cannot live religion merely by shaving one's head or wearing saffron clothes. These are merely a matter of custom according to the discipline of the four stages of life. Just by becoming a *sannyāsī,* one does not acquire the authority to give judgments on religious observances. For this, one must have knowledge of the scriptures.

Religion means friendship with God. Religion means behavior that is pleasing to God. Ordinarily, even in daily life, all the actions of a person who is dear to us appear good and pleasing. For example, followers of Nehru started wearing a jacket like his, and it became the famous Jawahar jacket. *Tulsī* is dear to Lord Vishnu, so devotees of Vishnu wear *mālās* of *tulsī. Rudrāksha* is dear to Lord Shankara, so his devotees wear *mālās* of *rudrāksha* beads. In this manner, you should consider what qualities are dear to God. These are truth, nonviolence, compassion for all creatures, and a pure and peaceful way of life. Love for these qualities is religion. Religion is Truth, the pursuit of which bears fruit immediately.

One must follow the scriptural guidelines in the performance of any religious ritual, and consult one who knows the scriptures. When we fall sick, we go to a doctor, not a lawyer. Similarly, with regard to religious ceremonies, we must consult a person with the appropriate expertise. The scriptural rules are quite explicit. It is said, "Any action, however good it appears, should not be carried out if it is contrary to the scriptures." This has been proven sound by experience. Guru Purnima is the Guru's day. On that day you must sing the glories of the Guru. The Guru is an essential aspect of religion. His status is great indeed. But unless one is a true disciple, the greatness of the Guru cannot be understood. I for one am a follower of the Guru. The Guru has been considered even greater than God. Sundardas says:

> The individual souls created by Govinda are drowned in the ocean of birth and death. Sundar says, "The Guru saves them from pain and suffering. Whatever the Guru says comes true. The greatness of the Guru surpasses even that of Govinda."[32]

Even the Lord is pleased by the worship of the Guru. Therefore, you should welcome, honor, and worship the Guru. It is the Guru who makes you realize God. On Guru Purnima, therefore, you must perform the worship of the Guru's *pādukās,* and perform *rudrābhishek* on Mahashivaratri. The scriptures have outlined in detail the methods for performing these different religious ceremonies, and it is our duty to follow them strictly. Even God Himself never transgresses any laws.

In this connection, I remember a humorous story. King Akbar once asked Birbal, his minister, "Who is greater, God or I?" Birbal replied, "You are greater, Your Majesty, because you can rule as you like, you can transgress laws, and you can punish a person whether or not he is guilty of any offense. God cannot do this. He has to act according to established laws and processes. God does not function according to His every whim and fancy." God and religion never transgress discipline or limits.

*An American woman, Laresa Gahan, has been staying at the ashram for the past seven or eight months. She came after hearing about Baba from Albert Rudolph in New York. Today she asked Baba about some doubts that were troubling her.*

## Devotion to the Guru Is a Great Sadhana

**Laresa:** *Baba, two different views prevail among your devotees. One group says that merely living in your company is sufficient; no other sadhana need be practiced. They believe that all our sadhana is done by Baba. We do not have to make any effort. Love, devotion, and service to the Guru will take us to our goal. The second group says that we must put forth effort, without which everything else is useless. They believe that, although Baba may guide us and give us inspiration, we must walk the path ourselves. Which of these two viewpoints is correct?*

**Baba:** Everyone gives advice according to his own understanding.

**Laresa:** *What is your opinion?*

**Baba:** There was a great Siddha of Maharashtra, Eknath Maharaj. A *bhandāra,* or feast, was held every day at his place, and a special type of sweet bread, *puranpolī,* was served. In the same village there lived a poor woman and her son Gavaba, who had an insatiable desire for that particular kind of bread. Without it, he would not eat his meals and would create a commotion. His mother implored Eknath Maharaj to let her son stay with him, because that bread was served at his place every day. Eknath Maharaj agreed, and Gavaba went to stay with him. Everyone started calling the boy Puranpolia.

After a while people began asking him, "Do you just eat *puranpolīs,* or do you ever do anything else such as praying, chanting, meditating, *japa,* or *tapasyā*?" Puranpolia would reply,

"Yes, I pray and worship Eknath Maharaj. I meditate on Eknath Maharaj. I repeat the name of Eknath Maharaj for *japa.*" In this manner, the boy was fully immersed in Eknath Maharaj. This was his only sadhana.

At that time, Eknath Maharaj was writing a book entitled *Bhāvārtha Rāmāyana.* It was still incomplete when he declared to his devotees that he would soon be leaving his body. The worried devotees said to him, "Maharaj, *Bhāvārtha Rāmāyana* is still unfinished." Eknath Maharaj replied, "Discuss the matter with Hari Pandit. If he cannot complete it, then Puranpolia will." Hari Pandit was Eknath Maharaj's son. He was a learned scholar, having studied the Vedas and Vedanta in Benares. The devotees thought that Hari Pandit would be able to complete the book. What could the illiterate Puranpolia write? Soon after Eknath Maharaj passed away, Hari Pandit sat down to work on the book, but he was unable to write a single word. Then Puranpolia, constantly remembering his Guru, began writing and completed the book within a short time.

The *Mahābhārata* contains another such example of devotion to the Guru. Dronacharya used to teach archery to Arjuna. Eklavya, the son of a Bhilla tribesman, requested Dronacharya to teach him as well. In those days the caste system was very rigidly followed, and so Dronacharya refused to take this lad as his pupil. Eklavya returned home, prepared an earthen idol of Dronacharya, placed it under a tree near his house, and considering the idol as his Guru, started practicing archery on his own. Because of his unshakable faith and devotion to the Guru, he would feel himself to be Dronacharya, and in that state he mastered the complete skill of archery quickly and easily. He became such an expert that he surpassed Dronacharya's other pupils.

One day a dog was passing by Eklavya's house, barking very loudly. Eklavya shot an arrow in such a way that it lodged right between the dog's two front teeth. The dog ran away yelping and passed Dronacharya and Arjuna. Everyone began to wonder who had the skill to shoot an arrow like that. Arjuna was not even able to remove the arrow. After some investigation, they discovered that this miraculous feat was performed by Eklavya. This is called *gurubhakti,* devotion to the Guru. Such devotion can make a disciple even greater than his Guru. Therefore, this is the best path of God-realization.

TUESDAY, JULY 14, 1964

*In the morning the devotees were sitting in the hall around Baba. Tehmina Bharucha asked Baba some questions.*

## *Yantras and Tantras*

**Tehmina:** *Are yantras and tantras valid?*

**Baba:** Just as there are so many other mechanical devices, similarly, tantric *yantras* are also a kind of device. For example, the nose of a dog is equipped with an organ that enables it to track down the real criminal. Once, two servants of a Christian man were murdered here near Akloli. No one could trace the murderer. The man's son was a high official in Delhi, and he brought a police officer, Mr. Kamte, to the site of the crime. Mr. Kamte brought with him two dogs trained in England. The dogs sniffed around the site of the murder and soon afterward led the police to the two murderers. The dogs even searched for and retrieved their shoes, which had been hidden in the river.

Similarly, there is an instrument fitted in ships that warns of rocks concealed under the water and dangerous spots in the sea. Just like these instruments, tantric *yantras* are mere tools. They are valid, but there is nothing extraordinary about them.

**Tehmina:** *Is it true that with the help of certain mantras or by doing a particular type of sadhana, we can read other people's thoughts or acquire the power to do anything we desire?*

**Baba:** Patanjali's *Yoga Sūtras* gives a description of *sanyama siddhis.* It says that by practicing *sanyama,* or concentration on an object, the seeker acquires the power of that object. Some yogis are able to stop speeding trains. Do you know the secret behind this ability? By envisioning a mountain in the space between the eyebrows and doing *sanyama* on it, the weight of the mountain bears down on the train, forcing it to halt. Similarly, *sanyama* on an elephant enables you to acquire the strength of the elephant so that you cannot be lifted. But what is the use of learning such tricks? God is beyond all these. He can be attained only after renouncing them.

## MONDAY, JULY 27, 1964

*A sannyāsī, Atmaramananda, came to the ashram today. He presented Baba with a scholarly book written in Sanskrit by a mahāmandaleshvar. Praising the author's erudition, he insisted that Baba should read it. At this, Baba said the following:*

# *The Pride of Learning*

**Baba:** The *mahāmandaleshvar* is a highly learned scholar who commands great respect. It seems that he has set out to prove his supremacy in scholarship. Listen to the following story.

About three or four centuries ago, there lived a great scholar named Vaman Pandit. He had proven his supremacy seven times at the universal competition of scholars. He had mastered all the scriptures and had also written many books. Wherever he went, he would carry a stack of books on the back of a mule so that whenever anyone raised a doubt in a debate, he could quickly provide the proof from the books. Normally, any book, article, or discourse is considered valid only if it can be supported by the scriptures. Without scriptural authority such works are valueless.

One day the scholar set out carrying his usual load of books. On his way he encountered Swami Samartha Ramdas, who asked him, "Where are you going with that pile of books?" Vaman Pandit was very proud. He retorted, "What can you understand anyway?" Swami Ramdas explained to him, "Look, a person may write any number of books, but whatever is written without God's grace will never endure. After five hundred years, no one will even remember your books."

Soon afterward, Vaman Pandit again went to Benares to participate in the universal competition of scholars for the eighth time. One afternoon as he was passing beneath a tree, he overheard two voices quarreling above him. One fellow shouted, "You get away from here; vacate this place at once!" The other fellow asserted, "Why should I? I am greater than you. You have won the universal competition only five times, while I have won it six times." The first fellow said, "Well, anyway, a scholar who has won the competition seven times will soon be coming, and you will have to vacate the place." Panditji looked up but could not see anyone. However, he understood that the voices belonged to two brahmin ghosts.

He was filled with remorse. He lamented, "After acquiring so much knowledge, fame, and respect, is this the state I am going to achieve in the end?" He jumped into the Ganges to drown himself, but by the grace of God, he did not die. After repenting in this way, whatever he wrote with God's grace was most beautiful, and even today research is being carried out on his works.

## WEDNESDAY, JULY 29, 1964

*Some relatives of Shri A. Shankar, a devotee from Hyderabad, came today for Baba's darshan. Two or three of them were seekers and asked questions.*

**Seeker:** *Is it advisable to control the mind, or might such control have a harmful effect?*

**Baba:** Allowing the mind to run loose brings about misery; hence, it is better to control it and keep it in check. If you desire happiness, renounce pride in your actions and control the various waves arising in the mind. If you do not practice even one of these two, the mind will become confused, and you will have to undergo the ensuing bad consequences.

**Seeker:** *Are birth and death determined according to one's past deeds?*

**Baba:** Birth and death are determined according to one's desires.

## *Perform Only Good Deeds*

**Seeker:** *After death, does one obtain another human birth, or might one be born as an animal or a bird?*

**Baba:** A human birth is not available over and over again. An individual soul progresses or degenerates according to his actions. He keeps coming back into this world until he achieves liberation. He must reap the fruits of his actions. The fruit of good deeds is a better state, and the fruit of bad actions, or sins, is an inferior state. Like humans, it is also possible for animals to achieve a higher state through good actions.

**Seeker:** *How can animals perform good deeds?*

**Baba:** Animals such as dogs, cows, and donkeys eat whatever dry or stale pieces of food they are given; they eat leftover food and they lie anywhere, never complaining about their living conditions. Despite all this, they work for people and benefit them. This is their selfless service. Aren't these virtuous actions?

## *A Discussion on Food*

**Seeker:** *Is it true that a person becomes tamasic by consuming tamasic food?*

**Baba:** It is not by food alone that a person becomes tamasic or sattvic. In ancient times many saints ate tamasic food, and yet they were considered to be great *tapasvīs*. In spite of their non-vegetarian diets, their minds were pure and sattvic.

Nevertheless, it is advisable for a seeker to consume only sattvic and pure food. Vegetarian food is also good for health. Someone once asked Bernard Shaw why he did not eat meat, and he replied, "My stomach is not a burial ground for dead animals." Man should always remember that the purpose of eating is to maintain good health and thereby lead a happy life, not just to satisfy the sense of taste.

The food that we consume acts on our bodies in three ways. First, food nourishes our *prānas*; second, it forms the seven elements of the body; and third, the remaining portion is excreted as fecal matter. Meat is devoid of *prāna*; hence, it cannot nourish our *prānas*. Its consumption only increases the fat on our bodies. Such food should be avoided.

## *Idol Worship*

**Seeker:** *Babaji, what is your opinion of idol worship?*

**Baba:** I do not object to idol worship, nor do I insist on it. I love my Gurudev, Nityananda Baba, so I have placed a large photograph of him here, which we worship every morning and evening. Saints such as Tukaram, Namdev, Mirabai, and Eknath Maharaj were able to cross over this ocean of birth and death by performing idol worship. Even in yoga, idol worship is accepted as a means of concentrating the mind. For those people whose minds cannot remain free from thoughts or steady on the formless, idol worship is all right.

We *sannyāsīs* worship our own Self with the understanding "I am Brahman"; we do not worship any other idol. Tukaram Maharaj says:

> This body is a temple of God. It is pure within and without.[33]

Idol worship is one of the methods of religious worship; it is a path leading to the realm of liberation. Tukaram Maharaj writes from his own experience:

> While I was meditating on God with attributes, I reached the attributeless Absolute. I have myself become Narayana.[34]

According to Vedanta, everything is only Brahman. Thus, for one who has realized the Self, God is everywhere, inside as well as outside. That which assumes the gross body is only Consciousness; that is, only the Self takes on a physical form. Then why not worship that very Consciousness itself?

We worship Gurudev considering him to be Chinmaya, the manifestation of Chiti. He can also be seen in meditation. Those who did not see him in his body see him in meditation. Some have had a direct experience of him. Therefore, can we say that Gurudev is not here now? He was here then, and he is here even now. Just as your relatives and friends feel love for your body, why shouldn't devotees of Rama, Krishna, or Shiva love the idol of their deity?

Nonetheless, while performing idol worship, it is essential to consider the idol as being conscious or alive and not to look upon it as a mere piece of stone. Only then will the worship bear fruit. There was once a devotee who worshiped the idol of Shri Rama daily. Several years passed by, but Shri Rama did not become pleased with him. One day a Krishna devotee suggested that he switch to worshiping Krishna and gave him a statue of Krishna. The man put Rama's idol away in a nearby window and installed on his altar the new idol of Krishna, which he began to worship instead.

One day, while he was performing *āratī* to the Krishna idol, the scented smoke of the incense began wafting through the window, passing over the idol of Rama. Seeing this, the man became angry, thinking that Rama had no right to enjoy the fragrance of the incense since He had not been pleased by his many years of worship and prayer. The devotee immediately jumped up and started plugging the idol's nostrils with cotton wool. At that very moment, Rama became pleased and appeared before him. The devotee wondered why Rama could not be pleased during all those years of worship, and yet now, when he was furious with Him and even hating Him, He was manifesting before him. Lord Rama explained, "Previously you considered this idol of Me as mere stone, but just now, when you felt that it was alive, I manifested Myself to you."

In short, if you have faith, then God is present everywhere and in everything. Whether you consider Him to be with or without attributes, it is the same. Everything has been painted with the same paint. God has no form, and yet all bodies are His. God is always satisfied; idol worship is for the satisfaction of the devotee. It is the devotee who derives fulfillment from it.

## *Religious Resolutions*

**Seeker:** *What is a religious resolution? If someone makes such a resolution and cannot fulfill it, does he commit a sin?*

**Baba:** A resolution is the outcome of a state of the mind. Making good resolutions is a Vedic rite, a way of religious worship. If you resolve to feed brahmins, then you must feed them with love; or if you resolve to perform *Satyanārāyana Pūjā* or *Shatachandī Yajña,*[35] then you must perform these joyfully.

It is true that if someone forces you to make a resolution, it has no meaning; it is not a religious observance. If the local priests in a place of pilgrimage force you to make some resolution and give money in charity, it would have no meaning. You should tell such priests to credit your account for the amount; you should not pay them in cash.

A resolution made voluntarily such as "Henceforth I shall not take wine" or "I shall not tell lies" is commendable. There is a prayer in the Vedas: "Let the resolutions of my mind always be auspicious." So you must cultivate the habit of having good resolutions.

**Seeker:** *If a saint gives a blessing through his will, does it come true?*

**Baba:** If a saint blesses you and you achieve success in your work, it is a result of his *tapasyā* and your good fortune, but there cannot be any success without self-effort. You should continue to perform meritorious actions. Such actions will never go to waste. Some karmas bear fruit immediately, while others do so after a lapse of some time.

## Thursday, August 6, 1964

*Shri Sunilbhai Damania came for Baba's darshan accompanied by Shri Hargovinddas Jani and his wife. Shri Jani has been staying at Ramanashram in Tiruvannamalai for several years.*

### *Devotion, Knowledge, and Yoga Are One and the Same*

**Jani:** *We go every day to a friend's house in Matunga in Bombay to hear a discourse on the Vichāra Sāgara.*

**Baba:** Very good. Knowledge (*jñāna*), meditation (*dhyāna*), and devotion (*bhakti*) are different paths of sadhana, but they all bestow the same final result. The *Bhagavad Gītā* says:

> Only fools, not the wise, consider Sankhya and yoga to be different.[36]

For the followers of the path of devotion, the examples of the *gopīs* and Narada's *Bhakti Sūtras* are instructive. A poet says:

> Constantly repeating "Krishna, Krishna," Radha herself became Krishna. She asked her friends, "Where is Radha?" Radha became so completely absorbed in Krishna through the ecstasy of love and devotion that, believing herself to be Krishna, she asked her friends, "Where is Radha?"[37]

This is the final attainment of devotion. It is also the final achievement of the path of Self-inquiry, "Who am I?" Who is Krishna? In his commentary on the *Vishnu Sahasranāma*, Shankaracharya describes who Krishna is in the first verse. He says:

> I bow to that Shri Krishna who can be known with the help of Vedanta, who is the Witness of the intellect, who performs actions very effortlessly, and whose nature is *sat, chit,* and *ānanda* (existence, knowledge, and bliss).[38]

For the followers of the path of knowledge, the philosophy expounded in the Upanishads is instructive. Sundardas says:

> The *jñānī* considers everything he sees to be Brahman; whatever he hears is Brahman; he speaks only of Brahman. For him, the earth, water, fire, air, ether, and *prānas* are all Brahman. For him, the beginning, the middle, and the end of everything is Brahman. This is his firm conviction. The *jñānī* considers the known and knowledge all to be Brahman.[39]

The phrase "Radha became Shyam (Krishna)" also has the same meaning.

For the followers of yoga, Patanjali's *Yoga Sūtras* are authoritative. Achieving a thought-free state by controlling the mental vibrations is, in fact, *jñāna.* In this state, awareness of the universal "I" arises; that is, the individual "I" becomes the universal "I." The great *bhakta* Tukaram says, "When I understood the real nature of Vitthal, I began to feel that Vitthal was present in everyone, and my mind became absolutely steady." This is truly meditation, a state without thoughts. Vedanta also gives a similar description of the final state.

Even though the spiritual practices of a *bhakta,* a *jñānī,* and a yogi are different, the final achievement of each is the same. You may refer to that final state as Rama, Krishna, the supreme Brahman, or *nirvikalpa samādhi.* It is like calling the same person by different names.

**Jani:** *I am returning to Ramanashram in three months. I have now decided to remain there until the end of my life.*

**Baba:** Do not bind yourself with such resolutions or restrictions. You should understand that whatever is here is also elsewhere, and thus you should remain serene. Our destiny determines where we will stay; we must not insist on any particular set of circumstances. Saint Tulsidas says:

> For one in whose heart Rama dwells, all waters are the Ganges, all mountains are *shalagrama*, all jungles are *tulsī*.[40]

When the mind acquires such a state, Rama will manifest from within wherever you may be.

**Sunilbhai** (observing a woman in deep meditation): *Baba, where is her Self now?*

**Baba:** The Self does not go anywhere, nor does it come from anywhere. Where can the Self go? The Self is all-pervasive. It pervades the entire universe. Human beings are seen coming to or leaving the earth, but where does the earth go? Similarly, it is the individual soul who comes and goes; the Self neither goes anywhere, nor does it come from anywhere.

## Saturday, August 15, 1964

*Shri Ramanbhai and Shri Harshadbhai, friends of Shri Maganbhai Hingwala, an old devotee of Nityananda Baba, came today. They had the following discussion with Baba.*

## Means of Conquering Mental Modifications

**Ramanbhai:** *It is very difficult to conquer rajasic and tamasic* *vrittis (passionate or dull thoughts). What is the easiest way to control them?*

**Baba:** Attend satsang and practice what you learn there. In this way, the heart will become purified. Saints who have gained control over their own senses are able to bring the senses of others under control. Have satsang with such beings, and your heart will be transformed. Ordinary satsang improves the understanding, but does not transform. If attending satsang is not possible for you, then develop your discrimination and faculty of reasoning.

**Ramanbhai:** *Even after much reasoning, my mind cannot be controlled.*

**Baba:** Yes, this is a kind of internal battle in which some skirmishes are bound to be lost and some won. One's mental tendencies will sometimes be positive and sometimes negative.

**Ramanbhai:** *But this undermines one's self-confidence.*

**Baba:** It is not easy to conquer rajasic or tamasic *vrittis.* Even a great devotee like Arjuna had to face this problem. He says:

> O Krishna, the mind is restless and vulnerable to disturbances. It is very powerful and very obstinate. The mind is as difficult to control as the wind.[41]

Arjuna once went to a Siddha mountain called Indraneel where he practiced intense *tapasyā* in order to please Lord Shiva and thus obtain the *pāshupat astra* from him. He controlled his *prānas* and achieved *sanyama siddhis.* The intensity of his *tapasyā* was so great that a fire broke out on the mountain. This enraged the beings in Siddhaloka, who all went to complain to Shiva. To appease them, Lord Shiva took the form of a tribal hill-dweller and fought with Arjuna.

If a powerful person like Arjuna could not conquer the mind, you can imagine how powerful the mind must be. It is possible to control the wind, but to control the mind is very difficult indeed.

*Buddhi yoga,* the yoga of discrimination, is an excellent means of achieving control over the mind. Lord Krishna also tells Arjuna, "Seek refuge in the intellect. Take the support of *buddhi yoga.*" So with the help of balanced thinking, try to control the mind.

**Ramanbhai:** *Too much thinking leads to doubts and fears.*

**Baba:** Doubts are bound to come up. Doubt is the very basis of this world. A yogi is one who has gone beyond doubt. Fear is a kind of addiction. Only one who conquers fear becomes happy. Until one attains Self-realization, fear will persist. But after Self-realization, where can there be fear? Where can there be sorrow?

Proceed steadfastly on your path. A state will ultimately arrive in which fear will drop away. Read *Yogadarshana,* attend satsang, and also develop your discrimination. Sundardas says:

> Discriminate when you see,
> Discriminate when you hear,
> Discriminate when you speak,
> Discriminate when you act.
> Discriminate when you eat,
> Discriminate when you drink,
> Discriminate when you sleep,
> Discriminate while you are awake.
> Discriminate always; that's the surest support.[42]

In this world, everything is full of fear. In the *Vairāgya Shataka,* the fifth-century philosopher Bhartrihari writes:

> Sensual enjoyment creates fears of disease, a high family fears its downfall, wealth fears taxation from the king, silence fears being misunderstood as weakness, military force fears the enemy, beauty fears old age, a virtuous person fears the wicked, scriptural knowledge fears debate, and the body fears death. Thus everything in this world is full of fear. It is only *vairāgya,* or dispassion, that makes you fearless.[43]

Everything in this world has a fear of something. As we

progress materially, fear increases proportionately. For example, the discovery of the atom bomb automatically increased fear. It is the normal way of the world. Therefore, if you really want to be free of fear and attain that which is eternal, give up the idea of "I"-ness. A poet has said, "You cannot obtain God until you give up the idea of "I"-ness."

Once a man was sitting at a place where he could hear echoes. When he said something, the same words were repeated opposite him. Thinking that someone was mimicking him, he started abusing the other person. He heard the same abuse addressed to himself. He was enraged and went and complained to his Guru. The Guru understood what had happened. He said, "You become silent. Don't say anything. Then the other one will also stop abusing." That is what eventually happened. It means that, similarly, if you also forsake your individuality, then all fears and doubts will end.

Saint Janabai, who was a servant and a devotee of Saint Namdev, says:

> I can reveal in just one sentence the key to obtaining the knowledge of Brahman. Give up your ego, and then you yourself will become Brahman.[44]

**Ramanbhai:** *But in attempting to do this some obstruction always crops up.*

**Baba:** It is like fighting with an enemy force surrounding you. If you want to avoid such fighting, have faith in the Self. Become worthy of God's grace and seek refuge in a *sadguru.*

## Monday, August 24, 1964

*Today Savitri Chadda came for Baba's darshan and posed some concerns.*

## *Paint Your Heart with the Color of God*

**Savitri:** *Swamiji, I know and accept that the world is not real; everything in this world is perishable. Nonetheless, since I live in this world, I have various worries. I have to look after my husband and children, so I think about them constantly. What should I do about this?*

**Baba:** Your heart will become saturated with whatever color you keep painting it. Desire, anger, greed, attachment, and egoism are the various colors for the heart. The individual soul experiences these. Water does not have any color of its own, but assumes whatever color you add to it, and if this colored water falls on a cloth, then the cloth also acquires the same color. Similarly, paint your heart with the color of Hari, then you will see the world full of Hari. All your worries will end and you will find happiness and peace.

**Savitri:** *What must I do to paint my heart with the color of Hari?*

**Baba:** Have satsang, practical satsang. If you go to a saint for two hours in two years, that cannot be called satsang, because for all the remaining time you are being painted with the color of the world. To acquire an unfading color, you must have the company of saints again and again.

**Savitri:** *The worries of worldly life constantly harass the mind. Just before leaving the house for satsang, some obstacle always arises. "Let me finish this work first and then I'll go. Let me finish that work also." This is what happens every time.*

**Baba:** Worry for the good of others is good. Worry for the welfare of your husband and children is all right. Even Gurus, who have achieved liberation, desire their disciples' liberation and think about it.

The fact is that everyone has his own destiny. Look at me. I left my home at the age of fifteen. My mother must have worried about me a lot, but I had to follow my destiny. Her worries were useless. You cannot add to or subtract from someone's destiny by worrying about him. So do your worldly work with a sense of duty, and at the same time remember that everyone must live out his own destiny. Perform your duties, but paint your heart with the color of the Lord. God alone is worthy of constant, wholehearted worship. This world is not in contradiction to God. Live in your home, look after your family, but also reserve some time for God.

## Sunday, August 30, 1964

*This morning Barrister Nain was present for satsang.*

**Nain:** *What is meant by uparati?*

**Baba:** *Uparati* is the mature state of Vedantic contemplation. It is a stage. The practical aspect of dispassion is *uparati.* In this state, meditation occurs only on the Self, nothing else. Shankaracharya has explained this in his book *Aparokshānubhūti*:

> To turn away from worldly objects and thoughts is called *uparati.*[45]

*Uparati* is one of the six assets of a seeker.

**Nain:** *Many yogis do not perform any action; they simply remain in one place. What is their state?*

**Baba:** Such lack of activity often indicates disinterestedness. True *uparati* is a state of neutrality based on the understanding that the world has no reality.

# A Seeker's Spiritual Maturity Determines His Sadhana

**Nain:** *Some people say that spirituality must be practiced in a particular manner such as worship, chanting, meditation, mantra japa, etc., while there are others who do not even believe in visiting temples, making pilgrimages, or worshiping idols.*

**Baba:** Advice should always be given according to the spiritual maturity of a particular seeker. Guidance is always based on the disciple's worth and ability. To advise the same type of spiritual discipline for everyone is mere obstinacy.

As soon as one listens to and understands Vedanta, one loses the desire for pilgrimages and idol worship. Immediately upon attaining knowledge of the Self, idol worship and such things automatically drop away. Idol worship is a matter of mental inclination, a kind of mental understanding. On attaining full knowledge, all doubts about these matters automatically disappear.

I believe in the incarnations of God, but I do not say that the incarnations alone should be adored and worshiped. I would say, "Worship Him from whom the incarnations came." An incarnation is an effect that has some cause behind it. Catch hold of that cause. Everyone has his own path. Everyone has an equal right to aspire for God. Arjuna was a warrior; hence, his path was karma yoga. Hanuman had a preference for serving God. Although Ramakrishna Paramahamsa was constantly established in the *nirvikalpa* state, he supported the worship of God as manifested in an idol. God is everywhere. Why can't He be present in an idol? Actually, a devotee sees his own Self in the idol. It is a miracle of faith that one can attain God even through an idol.

# Monday, August 31, 1964

*Today some followers of the Jain religion came for Baba's darshan. Among them was a seeker named Jayantilal.*

**Jayantilal:** *Does a human being have another human birth after his death? If so, after how long?*

**Baba:** It depends upon the karma and desires of the person. If one has performed good actions, one has to enjoy their fruits for years in a heavenly body; if one has performed bad actions, one will be born into a lower species. A fortunate one immediately receives another human birth. If a person is doing sadhana and dies before completing it, he or she is immediately reborn as a human being.

**Jayantilal:** *Can one acquire the power of knowing the future in this life?*

**Baba:** This is not a great accomplishment. Many have acquired this ability either through yoga, palmistry, or astrology. This power can also be acquired through spiritual practice. In general, such powers reside in everyone. It occasionally happens that something we say subsequently comes true. This power can be developed further through sadhana. These powers relate to the *savikāra* state (state with form).

The *nirvikāra* state, or the state of void, is beyond these attainments. If you want to know the future, you have to disturb that *nirvikāra* state. You are sitting so peacefully now, but if you wish to say or do something, you have to disturb this state.

*Today Gyan Chand, a friend of Hira Nayan of the Lahera Printing Press, came for satsang with Baba. He has a special interest in Vedanta, which he sometimes expounds to others.*

## *Knowledge Does Not Bear Fruit Without the Guru's Grace*

**Gyan Chand:** *Swamiji, I have read the Upanishads and various books on Vedanta such as the Ashtāvakra Gītā. I have also studied the Yoga Vāsishtha and Rāmāyana with special attention and given discourses on them. Since retiring from my job as a municipal inspector, I have been spending my time in satsang. From the worldly point of view I am happy in all respects. I have been keenly interested in reading spiritual books for the past thirty years, but now I feel that despite all my reading, attending satsangs, and giving discourses I have achieved nothing from the point of view of spirituality. What could be the cause for this? Does my destiny come in the way?*

**Baba:** Destiny is always a factor. In addition, your practice may not have been thorough enough. A seeker should be perfect in practice. Knowledge bears fruit immediately for a person who has detachment, discrimination, control over the senses, self-restraint, and sincere longing for Self-realization. Otherwise, his knowledge is like a parrot's repetition of words.

**Gyan Chand:** *How can practice become perfect?*

**Baba:** Understand and contemplate whatever you study. Practice meditation. Practice making your mind *nirvikalpa,* thought-free. Just as effort is required to achieve success in any worldly field, similarly, you have to do *tapasyā* to go beyond jivahood and become Shiva. In this the Guru's grace is a very important factor; therefore, obtain that. To obtain the *sadguru's* grace, you must consider him to be none other than God Himself.

In daily life, ordinary abusive terms achieve their intended effect; then why shouldn't the sacred, mantra-like words of the scriptures bear fruit? If you call a person a donkey, he becomes red with anger. If simple words have so much power, then why wouldn't the words of the scriptures, which are considered to be the form of God, have power? If scriptural words do not bear fruit, you must conclude that your faith is weak. One whose mind immediately feels the effect of words can grasp any subject. One who understands the meaning of the scriptures immediately upon hearing them should be considered most worthy.

**Gyan Chand:** *Even after study of the scriptures and satsang, the mind still runs after sensual pleasures. How can this be remedied?*

**Baba:** Even if the mind pursues sensual pleasures, it will not necessarily be tainted. Let the mind be drowned in the ocean of the inner Self just once. Afterward, regardless of how much it may be involved in worldly affairs, there will be no harm. It will never lose its equanimity. It is the nature of the mind to be constantly engaged in one subject or another. Therefore, keep the mind immersed in thoughts of God or the supreme Self. It is good to have an intellect that thinks and discriminates, but at the same time continue your sadhana. Spend time with the teachings of the saints; this is, in fact, true satsang.

Obtain the grace of the Guru and thereby become worthy of God's grace. The *turīya* state, described in the *Yoga Vāsishtha,* cannot be achieved without the Guru's grace. Whatever you were unable to achieve through the path of knowledge, obtain now through yogic discipline and meditation. The path of knowledge describes the world as unreal (*mithyā*). In yoga, however, it is not necessary to say that the world is unreal, because it reveals itself to be so through the seeker's own experience. One who has not achieved the *turīya* state remains a slave of *prakriti,* but *prakriti* becomes the slave of one who has attained that state. Just look. Bhagawan Nityananda established the village of Ganeshpuri in this desolate jungle without anyone's assistance, without appealing to or flattering anyone.

Divinity exists within everyone. I am always fresh, healthy, and happy despite a diet of a small quantity of simple food, because I have experienced my inner divinity. Although I am older than you, I appear younger, don't I? The source of this freshness is a place called *brahmānanda, sacchidānanda,* or *paramānanda* in which fear and sorrow are unknown. In comparison with this treasure, worldly wealth has no value. If you yearn to attain that state, remain in the company of saints. That is where the secret of attainment lies.

## *A Disciple Is Taught According to His Worthiness*

**Gyan Chand:** *Is it true that saints teach disciples differently according to their worthiness?*

**Baba:** Rainwater falls everywhere in the sea and water mixes with water, but only when a raindrop falls into an oyster during the *svāti* constellation is it transformed into a pearl. There are thousands of lecturers and they give discourses to millions of people, but for how many of them do the teachings bear fruit? Instead of giving or attending discourses, perform internal sadhana. Questioning is necessary, but along with it, contemplation is essential. You become like your object of constant contemplation. Ramakrishna Paramahamsa contemplated Hanuman and became like him. Similarly, one who contemplates Brahman becomes Brahman.

**Gyan Chand:** *I have heard that you don't give discourses, but you do say something if someone asks a question.*

**Baba:** This is not quite correct. If I feel like speaking, I speak; otherwise I remain silent. There is no fixed time or rule in this regard. Knowledge is not an ordinary subject, nor is it cheap. The limits of a discussion are automatically determined by the worth of the listener. Nowadays knowledge has been made a subject of discourses; hence, it does not bear fruit. Teachers have given countless discourses, but how many *jñānīs* have they produced? Knowledge arises only within a worthy seeker.

**Gyan Chand:** *Saint Jnaneshwar considers devotion (bhakti) and knowledge (jñāna) to be equal.*

**Baba:** Both are, in fact, one. Through devotion you obtain love; through knowledge you obtain bliss. What's the difference between these two? First make yourself worthy, then you will certainly attain God. There are many paths by which to attain Him, and among them the path of Guru's grace is the best.

**Gyan Chand:** *Neither Ramana Maharshi nor Lord Buddha had Gurus.*

**Baba:** How can one become a Guru without having been a disciple? Many seekers tell me that Ramana Maharshi is their Guru. To have become a Guru, he himself must have been someone's disciple, if not in this life, then in his past life. Lord Buddha had no Guru, and therefore he experienced only the void, which he expounded to others. He could only speak about that which he saw.

Shri Rama and Shri Krishna are accepted by all as incarnations of God, yet even they had Gurus. Shri Ramakrishna Paramahamsa had to seek the help of Totapuri. Even Matsyendranath has said that Adinath Parashiva was his Guru. Vasishtha also said that he attained knowledge from another. This is how it should be according to the scriptures. The Guru-disciple relationship is an eternal discipline to attain knowledge. It preserves propriety. Why destroy it? *Jñāneshvarī, Tukārām Gāthā,* and *Dāsbodha* were written by saints who had obtained the grace of the Guru. Even today, after the passage of so many years, these books are read in every house.

## Thursday, September 10, 1964

*Satish Moti, a college student in Secunderabad, comes now and then for Baba's darshan and has been at the ashram for the past four days.*

## The Importance of Leading a Regulated Life

**Satish:** *Baba, please give me some guidance for my life.*

**Baba:** Very well, listen. If you want to attain any happiness in this life, then first of all you must lead a regulated life. This means that you must arise, sleep, eat, and study punctually, and that you must stay away from bad habits and vices. At the same time, you must spend some time in meditation, quieting your mind. A controlled mind has such power that with it one can accomplish great works. When you need it, Truth reveals itself within you, giving you true guidance, and you acquire competence in your work.

A river that has been obstructed by a dam gushes forth with tremendous force when the dam is suddenly opened, washing away village after village. Such power arises because of the previous containment of water. Similarly, one accumulates a storehouse of power to execute future tasks by stopping the waste of one's mental powers through control of the mind. In this way, one acquires the strength to accomplish the most difficult work.

## Tuesday, September 15, 1964

*Today Shri Sheshrao Wankhede, the Minister for Industries in Maharashtra, his wife Shrimati Kusumtai, and the wife of Lieutenant General S. P. Thorat came to the ashram.*

## Seek Peace Where It Dwells

**Mrs. Thorat:** *Babaji, from my early childhood until now, I have received tender care and comfort. I have been married for thirty-two years. I have never undergone any difficulties either at my father's house or at my husband's. My husband is good to me. We have status and respect in the community. My sons are also well settled. Thus, I have every kind of happiness. I can expect nothing more from this world. In spite of all this, my mind is not at peace. I have read many books, I have read the Bhagavad Gītā, and have gone on pilgrimages. Still, I do not experience inner satisfaction. I wonder if I am unworthy of realizing God. Isn't it possible for spiritual and practical life to coexist?*

**Baba:** Every human being is a part of God and is thus worthy of knowledge of the Self and God-realization. Worldly life is not an obstacle to pursuing spiritual sadhana. On the contrary, it is helpful. God has created this world with love and for the sake of love, so how can it be an obstacle? This world is the embodiment of God. King Janaka ruled a great kingdom and the sage Yajnavalkya had two wives, and yet while living in the world they achieved realization of the Self; they became *jīvanmuktas.* As you can see, I am a *sannyāsī,* but can I escape the practicalities of daily life? In fact, while living in the world and performing your duties, you can remember and worship God.

**Mrs. Thorat:** *I have been trying to do just that, but even so, I have no peace of mind.*

**Baba:** After attaining all his worldly goals, man still has no peace, because lack of peace is inherent in the very nature of the things he achieves. He tries to find peace in that which is full of agitations, so how can he get peace? You want to go north and you are running toward the south. If you want to find peace, seek it where it dwells.

**Mrs. Thorat:** *I know that the short-lived, perishable objects of this* *world cannot give me inner satisfaction. Therefore, I try to sit for meditation every day, but within two or three minutes my mind becomes distracted and rushes out toward other subjects.*

**Baba:** Owing to constant contemplation of the objects and matters of the world, the mind assumes their forms again and again. For this reason, you cannot meditate on God for any length of time. Try to cultivate an increasing addiction to thoughts of God in your mind.

**Mrs. Thorat:** *I understand this, but I cannot seem to do it even after making an effort. What is the remedy for this?*

**Baba:** Satsang and Guru's grace are necessary. Through the grace of a Siddha Guru, meditation and contemplation on God occur spontaneously. He awakens the inner shakti of the seeker by his own spiritual power. By this means one attains inner satisfaction and peace.

## Wednesday, September 23, 1964

*Today Laresa Gahan, an American, asked Baba some questions about her difficulties in sadhana.*

### Isolation Is Not Necessary to Attain Peace

**Laresa:** *Baba, I would like to have a separate room so that I can remain in isolation. My peace is disturbed by the constant coming and going of people where I live.*

**Baba:** Peace cannot be obtained by sitting in a room behind closed doors. In fact, such seclusion sometimes has the opposite effect. By remaining in isolation, you develop tiger-like tendencies. If anyone disturbs a tiger in his cave, he will either leave the cave or attack the intruder. This is not the way to attain true peace. You must learn to remain peaceful and undisturbed in the midst of people.

Nityananda Baba first lived in a jungle. He would throw stones at anyone who went near him, but later on he lived among people and established a village. I, too, have established this ashram and live amid people. Town and jungle, isolation and mingling with people—being free from such dualistic ideas and being established in one's own Self in *nirvikalpa samādhi* is the true state.

**Laresa:** *I want to travel to remote places such as the Himalayas, Kashmir, Simla, and Darjeeling where I feel I would be able to overcome my restlessness and obtain some peace.*

**Baba:** You can certainly go wherever you like, but remember that by roaming about in this way, your mind will become more agitated; your restlessness will increase. One who cannot obtain peace here cannot obtain it elsewhere either. You may go anywhere, but your mind will accompany you. How can you escape it?

**Laresa:** *How can I know whether I have made any spiritual progress or not, and if I have progressed, how much?*

**Baba:** Your progress in spirituality can be judged by the following: a) how calm you can remain in trying and difficult circumstances; b) whether or not you are less disturbed than before by the pairs of opposites such as pleasure and pain, happiness and sorrow; and c) how much inner peace and satisfaction you experience in your heart.

## SUNDAY, SEPTEMBER 27, 1964

*Mr. Harshad and Mr. Ramnik, who are friends of Manilal Hingwala, a devotee of Nityananda Baba, came again for satsang today.*

# Choosing a Mantra for Japa

**Ramnik:** *Swamiji, I have been using the gāyatrī mantra for japa. Is this all right?*

**Baba:** Who gave it to you? Which mantra were you repeating previously?

**Ramnik:** *I obtained the gāyatrī mantra from a book. Prior to that, I was repeating the name of Krishna, but the man who gave me the book told me that the gāyatrī mantra has great power. Since then I have been using it for japa.*

**Baba:** All mantras possess similar powers. All mantras lead you to the same final achievement. If a person claims that a particular mantra is the most powerful, he says so merely to promote and propagate a particular *math* or sect. Here at this ashram, we are not engaged in any business. I recommend that people repeat the mantra that appeals to them most, the one that they have been accustomed to using. Both of you should read the biography of Ramakrishna Paramahamsa. Then you will understand the unity behind all religions and all mantras. It is being unfaithful to one's sadhana to give up one mantra and take up another one, and then take up a third one on someone else's advice. Why did you give up a short mantra and accept a long one? You can repeat Krishna's name ten times in the span of time that is required to chant the *gāyatrī mantra* only once. If you have to take a mantra, then take it from a *sadguru*, who has the authority to give initiation. Such a mantra is alive, or conscious, and will bear fruit immediately.

**Ramnik:** *While doing japa of the gāyatrī mantra, on what should the mind be concentrated? For example, while repeating Shiva's name, one thinks of Shiva; while repeating Krishna's name, one thinks of Krishna. In this way, who is the deity of the gāyatrī mantra?*

**Baba:** Every mantra has its own goal. While doing *japa* of any mantra, it is better to concentrate on the letters of the mantra. Gayatri is said to be a goddess. Thus, if you so desire, you can contemplate the goddess while repeating it. There is a particular technique for doing *japa* of the *gāyatrī mantra.* First, however, you must obtain thorough knowledge of this subject.

## *Knowledge Manifests Itself from Within; It Is Not Obtained from Books*

**Harshad:** *We have attended the discourses of scholars on several occasions, but we were unable to comprehend them. We also read books, but we cannot distinguish between truth and untruth.*

**Baba:** If liberation could be obtained by reading books all the scholars should be liberated, but in reality we find that this is not so. The knowledge contained in books is like a treasure buried underground; it is of no practical use to anyone. Do you think that knowledge is so cheap and so easily obtainable that just by listening to someone's discourse for two hours you can assimilate all the knowledge that he himself acquired after many years of *tapasyā* and scriptural study? The scriptures are absolutely true. Just because you cannot understand them does not mean that they are false. It is said:

> All scriptures are true, but our understanding is weak.[46]

If you want to know the real meaning of the scriptures, become addicted to singing God's name. Just as a drunkard cannot live without liquor, similarly, you should become restless without God's name. In this way, knowledge will manifest itself from within you.

*Barrister Nain came today for Baba's darshan.*

**Nain:** *Nowadays I am reading a book of questions and answers by Shri Aurobindo.*

**Baba:** He was a great thinker.

**Nain:** *He wanted to draw the shakti from above and disseminate it throughout the world. It is said that the Mother is now carrying out this work.*

**Baba:** The Mother has assumed the work which Aurobindo left incomplete. Now we will have to wait and see who will be capable of succeeding her. There must always be a disciple who is prepared to take on the work of his master, so that it may proceed without interruption. Shankaracharya, for example, established four *maths,* giving them such a firm and powerful foundation that even twelve hundred years later their stature is undiminished. Shri Ramakrishna transmitted such tremendous power to Vivekananda that through him thousands were transformed.

**Nain:** *Vivekananda propagated Hinduism very well.*

**Baba:** In actuality, Vivekananda propagated the Vedanta of Shankaracharya. In particular, he protested against the Hindu custom of untouchability; this is what made his impact so great. He proclaimed the equality of all men. He declared that everyone is worthy of attaining God. He imparted knowledge to orphans. He reformed the Hindu religion with a very broad outlook.

Shankaracharya was the protector of the religion and Vivekananda was its propagator.

**Nain:** *Swami Vivekananda had a short life span.*

**Baba:** Those who have been *yogabhrashta* always have short lives. Swami Vivekananda, Swami Rama Tirtha, Shri Shankaracharya, and Jnaneshwar Maharaj all departed at a young age.

*A group of seekers from Malad came to the ashram in the afternoon. Among them was a lawyer, Shri Chhantbar, who is a keen student of yoga and Vedanta. He had the following discussion with Baba.*

## The Self Is Always Complete

**Chhantbar:** *We are so small and God is so great. Our power is limited, while God's power is limitless. We are like a tiny well, while God is like the ocean. How can we convert the well into the ocean? I cannot even understand whether the individual soul is just a part of God or is completely God.*

**Baba:** As long as the individual soul considers himself to be a mere portion of God, he will remain as such. As soon as he gives up his limitations, he becomes perfect. For a well to become one with the ocean, it has to merge into the ocean; that is, when its limitation as a well is destroyed, it becomes the ocean, just as the space inside a pot becomes one with the total space as soon as the pot breaks. In reality, the space inside the pot is not different from the total space. It is one with the total space; it is not separate from it. Similarly, the individual Self is always complete.

**Chhantbar:** *How can the individual soul acquire the powers of God, enabling him to create a universe?*

**Baba:** The universe is already created. It is foolish to talk of creating it again. It is like building what is already built. It is true that Vishvamitra[47] demonstrated such power by creating another world. In fact, a separate world exists in every atom. You can think of innumerable universes because there is no limit to imagination.

God's world is only one and exists throughout the infinity of space, but in individual souls, imaginary worlds can be countless. What we mean by the world is the expanse of the five elements; that is, everything. The world of the individual soul is included in the world of God. The individual soul builds a house on the earth and thinks that he has created a world unto himself! The fact is that when the part becomes the whole, when the *jīva* becomes Shiva, when the space inside the pot merges into the total space, when the Self becomes one with Brahman, then no separate universes can be seen.

**Chhantbar:** *My intellect cannot conceive of anything beyond the idea that I am only a part of the Self.*

**Baba:** You will be able to understand the Truth only when your "pot" has been broken. In fact, your question itself is illogical because you are complete. The supreme Self is always in your possession, but it doesn't seem so owing to your ignorance. It is like searching everywhere for a diamond necklace that is around your neck. When you become aware that the necklace is around your own neck, would you say that you have found the lost necklace, or would you say that the necklace had never been lost?

The same thing is illustrated by the rope versus snake example[48] in Vedanta. There also, what did not exist disappears. Think about it yourself. In that example, was it the snake that was destroyed, or was it that which did not exist that was destroyed?

It is a matter of wonder that one who is already liberated becomes liberated. One who is already awake has to be awakened. If Consciousness never changes, then how can you undergo any change? You are what you are. Give up the thought that you are different from the supreme Self. You are already complete. Your wrong understanding that you are incomplete, caused by your ignorance of the Self, will vanish when you obtain the knowledge of the Self. Just as a disease caused by improper diet is cured through proper diet, similarly, ignorance is eliminated by knowledge.

## Wednesday, November 11, 1964

*A sannyāsī from Africa who has been in India for the past twelve years came to the ashram today.*

### Idol Worship

**Swami:** *What is your opinion of idol worship?*

**Baba:** One who has recognized God dwelling within the heart will see God even in a stone idol. One who cannot find God within will not be able to find Him outside either; that is, will not be able to see Him everywhere.

**Swami:** *What is your opinion about yajña?*

**Baba:** Your question is invalid. What doubt can there be about that which has been proven? What the seers, saints, Siddhas, and great beings have said and written cannot be doubted. What they wrote is based on their own direct experience. Patanjali wrote the *Yoga Sūtras* after practicing and experiencing yoga. Similarly, Narada wrote the *Bhakti Sūtras* after experiencing the bliss of *bhakti.* We accept their teachings as authoritative. Similarly, *yajña* as described in the scriptures is authentic. It is foolish to ask someone else's opinion about it. Our scriptures are absolutely true and should not be doubted.

## Thursday, December 3, 1964

*Today the two sisters of Shri Pravinbhai Modi of Secunderabad, Manjula and Vasanta, came to the ashram.*

**Manjula:** *Why is it that none of the work I undertake is ever successful?*

**Baba:** Divine help is essential for success in any work.

## *Contemplation on God Is the Only Means to Peace*

**Manjula:** *Despite my efforts to calm my mind, it does not remain steady and agitations persist.*

**Baba:** By contemplating God, the mind becomes quiet and concentrated. Contemplation of God is both a remedy and a blessing.

**Vasanta:** *Please give me knowledge. I am so deeply immersed in worldly life that I cannot find any time to worship God. I have five children and a husband to look after. We have an oil mill in Godhra and are materially prosperous, but I have not achieved anything in the realm of spirituality. My mind does not turn to God, nor do I have any opportunity to attend satsang.*

**Baba:** Remember God constantly. However large your family and fortune may be, they are not an obstacle to the remembrance of God. Many saints have attained God while living as householders.

**Vasanta:** *Whenever I try to think of God, other thoughts interfere and my mind becomes restless.*

**Baba:** Restlessness is the nature of the mind. It has become used to thinking about countless other subjects; therefore, it cannot suddenly become interested in God. However, with practice, the mind will get used to contemplation of God.

### FRIDAY, DECEMBER 11, 1964

*Today Shri Pravinbhai Modi's father and his uncle Shri Chimanlal Modi came with their families for Baba's darshan. Shri Chimanlal is highly educated, well versed in Vedanta, and widely respected in Hyderabad.*

# The Social Service of Saints

**Chimanlal:** *I once went to Tiruvannamalai. While there I asked Ramana Maharshi, "You have such great spiritual power. Why do you just sit in one place? Why don't you live among people and work for their upliftment? Many people would benefit from it." Ramana Maharshi replied, "Each individual does his own work in his own way."*

**Baba:** G. N. Vaidya, a famous lawyer from Bombay, asked me a similar question about Nityananda Baba. He went once for darshan, and when he arrived there was a long queue waiting and the front door was closed. At the appointed time, the door was opened. After Baba's darshan, the lawyer asked someone, "Why does Bhagawan Nityananda sit inside with the door closed? Why doesn't he come out?" That person replied, "I cannot answer such questions. Go see Swami Muktananda, who lives close by. He will clear up all your doubts." So then Shri Vaidya came to see me and we had the following conversation.

**Vaidya:** *People say that Bhagawan Nityananda possesses divine, mystical, and miraculous powers. If this is so, why doesn't he come out of seclusion and work among people for the reformation of society? Why doesn't he utilize his shakti to bring about a revolution in Hindu society? Why does he sit behind a closed door that is only opened at a certain time despite the long line of people seeking his darshan?*

**Baba:** What is your occupation?

**Vaidya:** *I am a lawyer.*

**Baba:** Do you go to court?

**Vaidya:** *Yes.*

**Baba:** Isn't there some kind of discipline in the court? Isn't there a rule stating that the court will open at a particular hour, and that a particular case will be heard on a certain day?

**Vaidya:** *Yes, of course. Without such a schedule, how could the work proceed smoothly?*

**Baba:** Then why are you so surprised by the discipline that is followed here by Bhagawan Nityananda? You should not find it so peculiar. How many people had gathered for his darshan?

**Vaidya:** *I guess there were about four thousand.*

**Baba:** What do you think? Did they all come for nothing, or is it possible that they benefited from Baba's darshan?

**Vaidya:** *After darshan I could see joy and satisfaction on their faces.*

**Baba:** Wouldn't you consider that to be the work of Nityananda Baba? Isn't he useful to the world without moving his arms and legs?

**Vaidya:** *Certainly he is.*

**Baba:** And one more thing: have you seen Bhagawan Nityananda's photo anywhere?

**Vaidya:** *Yes, I have seen his photo in many houses, hotels, and shops in Bombay.*

**Baba:** Isn't that also the work of Bhagawan Nityananda? You will find his photos being garlanded and worshiped with lights and incense in many shops in Bombay. In spite of living behind closed doors and without giving any discourses, he has created such a tremendous feeling of devotion in the lower strata of society. Do you think this is just an ordinary accomplishment? So many people have obtained happiness from him; so many miserable people have been relieved of their troubles. Isn't this social work? Do you consider social work to be going from one place to another arranging programs, going to courts and offices, holding meetings in parks, and giving lectures? Can such activities really be called social work? These days people consider work to be only that which they can actually perceive on a gross level.

There was once a Siddha named Pavahari Baba who used to remain in *samādhi* for six months at a time. One day a *sannyāsī* went for his darshan and asked him a question similar to yours: "Why don't you go out and work to uplift society?" Pavahari Baba replied, "Do you think great Siddha Gurus should be like postmen and go from door to door distributing their discourses, advice, and good wishes enclosed in envelopes?" Don't you see that God remains concealed, and yet carries on the work of the whole world? Doesn't the head of a large institution sit in his office and yet handle the management of the entire institution? In the same way, Siddhas do not have to wander about in order to carry out their work. Even in the solitude of an ashram, they keep on doing their divine work.

## *The Senses Acquire Power Through Control*

**Chimanlal:** *I have heard that a yogi's eyes and ears are very subtly tuned, that they can hear distant sounds and see faraway objects. Is this true?*

**Baba:** Yes, yogis acquire these powers through control of the senses. The subtlety of the senses increases in direct proportion to your degree of control over them, and that which is more subtle is more pervasive. Therefore, through control of the senses, sounds emanating from far-off places can be heard, remote objects can be seen, and distant odors can be smelled. It is also possible to know another person's thoughts. Similarly, the power and effectiveness of your words increases in direct proportion to the silence that you observe. This is known as omniscience.

In general, it has become the habit of most people to eat as much as is available, to talk as much as possible, to see and hear whatever they can, and then later on, their thoughts are completely occupied by these experiences. In this way, one completely exhausts one's energy. If one were to conserve it instead, one would be able to achieve higher goals. If you earn a thousand rupees, spend fifty, and save the rest, then after some time you can become wealthy. It is the same with energy. One's power is wasted by useless thoughts, but if the mind is made steady, its power increases and the intellect becomes subtle. Electricity is so subtle that it can pass through a thin filament, and yet its current is so powerful that it can burn a man.

On every path—whether *jñāna, bhakta,* or yoga—self-control is essential. As we turn within more and more, the senses become correspondingly subtler and more powerful, and the mind becomes one-pointed. A *jñānī* continually reflects, "Not this, not this," and goes deep inside, where finally only Brahman remains. Ramana Maharshi attained universal Consciousness through the mental inquiry "Who am I?" A devotee becomes Krishna by constantly repeating Krishna's name. A yogi achieves the realization of *So'ham* through meditation. In this manner, the goal and attainment of all paths is the same supreme bliss, just as in whatever business you have—factory, mill, or shop—the goal and achievement is money.

The main objective of every path is to control the *chitta vrittis* (thoughts). Steadiness of the mind yields great power. If an engineer were to build a dam across a small stream in the jungle some distance from its source, after a while so much water would be collected that, if allowed to flow, its torrential power could wash away many villages in its path. The same applies to our mental powers. Through concentration, the mind can be steadied at will, and thereby one gains unlimited power.

## Friday, December 25, 1964

*Shri Anand, who is a relative of Shrimati Gangaben Shah, a devotee of Baba, came to the ashram today. He is intensely interested in sadhana.*

## *Prāṇāyāma*

**Anand:** *What is the correct technique for doing prāṇāyāma?*

**Baba:** The aim of *prāṇāyāma* is to achieve equality between the *prāṇa* (exhalation) and *apāna* (inhalation). *Prāṇāyāma* must be learned from an expert. First he will measure your *prāṇa* and then recommend the appropriate length of time for practice. He will teach you how to equalize the *prāṇa* and *apāna.* The *prāṇa* and *apāna* can also be equalized through *japa,* and *prāṇāyāma* will take place spontaneously without any effort.

One technique of *prāṇāyāma* is to coordinate repetition of the mantra with each inhalation and exhalation. As you inhale, you repeat the mantra once, and when you exhale, you repeat it again. After practicing *japa* in this way for some time, the *prāṇa* and *apāna* become equalized. This is significant because unequal duration of inhalation and exhalation is the cause of mental unsteadiness. As soon as the *prāṇa* and *apāna* become equal, the seeker experiences great inner peace and contentment. He then understands that the mantra has begun to bear fruit for him.

*Prāṇāyāma* will also occur spontaneously as you keep steadying the flow of thoughts. Concentrate your mind on an idol or an image or even a black dot on a wall, or you can concentrate on the flame of a lamp, on *Om,* or on any other mantra. Any technique that is an aid to steadying the mind may be used. As soon as the mind becomes steady, *prāṇāyāma* takes place automatically.

These practices are not related to any particular sect. They are independent and are meant for everyone. Intelligent people do not waste time arguing about whether they are beneficial or not, but begin to practice them and attain their goal.

## *Contemplate the Witness of the Mind*

**Anand:** *Despite my best efforts to calm my mind, it remains agitated.*

**Baba:** Let it be agitated. It is the nature of the mind to be restless. Just as it is difficult to cool a fire, similarly, it is difficult to remove the restlessness of the mind. It is the nature of the mind to have a constantly changing flow of thoughts. From the scientific standpoint, purity or impurity of the mind is the same. We hear so many people saying, "Today such and such happened. He said this and that to me and I am feeling very upset." Next day the same people say, "Today I am experiencing great peace." The mind constantly alternates in this way between purity and impurity.

Have you ever contemplated the Witness who knows whether the mind has become pure or impure? Peace may be obtained by doing *prāṇāyāma,* but who knows this peace? Have you thought about this? This Knower, this Seer, has no connection with the mind, regardless of whether it is pure or impure, quiet or agitated. There is no loss or damage to Him if the mind is impure, nor any gain or profit for Him if the mind is pure. He watches the entire play from a distance, remaining aloof. Not knowing this truth, a person becomes miserable. Such an ignorant person will be unhappy even in the most favorable circumstances. A *jñānī* who knows the truth will always be happy even in the most adverse circumstances.

If you contemplate the Witness of the mind, then *prāṇāyāma* will take place spontaneously. Such contemplation has the power to free the mind from all anxieties and worries. Therefore, give up all other thoughts and contemplate the Seer. This Knower is ever pure. He knows all the states of the individual soul. He is the knower of the waking, dream, and deep-sleep states. The mind itself is just another object; it is not the Self. Concentration on the Seer of the mind is the highest type of meditation.

Choose any Siddha mantra and repeat it regularly. In this way, *prāṇāyāma* will occur spontaneously, and the mind will become peaceful. All mantras have the same effect. The shakti that pervades the entire world is only one. All deities are also one. Nonetheless, ignorant people love one and hate the others. God will never be pleased by such intolerance. Allah, Christ, and Shiva—all are one.

Concentrate on only one mantra. Sit in whichever *āsana* is most comfortable for you, such as *siddhāsana, padmāsana,* or *sukhāsana,* and do *japa.* The words of the mantra have tremendous power. No mantra is separate from God; the mantra is God in the form of sound. Only a person of highly developed discrimination can understand this. If you ask for salt, you will get only salt, not sugar. If ordinary words have this much effect, imagine what power must reside in a mantra! Let go of the mind; do not be concerned about its restlessness. One who understands the mind is known as *chaitanya,* a conscious being. Try to reach that state, which is the goal of human life.

Religious injunctions and proscriptions bind one only until one realizes the Truth. After attaining the goal, after realizing the Truth, one transcends the confines of religion.

# Chapter Four

# 1965

*Two months ago Harshad Panchal, a student, came to the ashram in a state of ecstatic devotion after having read an article about Baba in the Gujarati magazine Navneet. Baba gave him a banana to eat, and he calmed down. He returned today for Baba's darshan.*

## Seek God Within Yourself

**Harshad:** *I am now attending college regularly and studying. I am experiencing peace and can concentrate better on my studies.*

**Baba:** Very good. First complete your studies, then I will make friends with you. I like to make friends only with educated and learned people. This person sitting here is a successful engineer, that one is a doctor, that one is a lawyer, and they are all seekers. So practice spirituality, but at the same time manage the practical aspect of life with equal efficiency. Who told you that you can achieve God only by leaving the world?

**Harshad:** *May I sing a bhajan?*

**Baba:** Please do.

**Harshad:** *"My eyes are eager to see Hari; my eyes yearn to see the lotus-eyed one. Without seeing Him, I feel dejected day and night."*[1]

**Baba:** Without knowledge of the true nature of God, you will not be able to attain Him. First understand who God is, what His nature is, and where He dwells. Then try to see Him. Now I shall also sing a *bhajan.* Listen.

> Why are you seeking Ram in one jungle after another?
> He dwells right within you.[2]

This *bhajan* was composed by a great saint of Daulatabad named

Manpuri. He says that God is inside you; you need not go anywhere outside in search of Him. Make your mind steady and peaceful, and you will then understand this great truth.

**Harshad:** *I think that I must share whatever I attain with others.*

**Baba:** God is already attained by everyone. What do you mean by "I think"? Who are you? What is the validity of your thoughts? Are the Vedas, Vedanta, Narada, Vyasa, Patanjali, and Shankaracharya true, or are your words true? What they say is based on their direct experience. They first experienced themselves and then taught others. Therefore, we benefit from following their advice and teachings. We achieve nothing if we proceed according to our own thoughts and feelings. On the contrary, our minds become confused. So give up your singing and crying. First complete your studies and then pursue God-realization. Seeing you, I am reminded of the verse:

> Hearing that the fish remain thirsty while living in water,
> I feel like laughing.[3]

Here is another *bhajan (handing him a book entitled Āshram Bhajanāvalī)*. Read it aloud.

**Harshad:** *"If you really want to meet God, then meditate ceaselessly. Burn your ego and apply its ashes to your body."*[4]

**Baba:** This *bhajan* is by Mansur Mastana. He says the same thing I am saying to you. The teachings of those who have seen God are always similar. Read further.

**Harshad:** *"Throw away the prayer carpet, break the mālā, throw your books in the river. Hold the hands of angels, considering yourself their servant."*[5]

**Baba:** Angels, those who have realized God, have His authority to guide others. Mansur says not to rely on other things, but seek refuge in such beings. Do as they tell you. Give up the fancies of your own mind. Read further.

**Harshad:** *"Eat, drink, never neglect your Self. Revel in the intoxication of your own Self, burning your ego."* [6]

**Baba:** He says not to give up the routine of your daily life. Keep doing whatever you are doing. Therefore, you should complete your present engineering course. Continue your studies. A year and a half remains; complete it. Knowledge of the mundane world is essential for a monk. The scriptures also say this. Look at me. I am not only a monk, but also an Ayurvedic doctor, a farmer, and an engineer. I prepared the plans for all the ashram buildings. I am also adept at cooking. Don't give up your daily life. At the same time don't be negligent; don't consider whatever you fancy to be right. Don't get stuck in the mire of your own thoughts and beliefs. Don't perform worship according to your own will. The true path is to leave your own ideas and remain intoxicated, taking refuge in saints and sages. Read further.

**Harshad:** *"Let there be neither a mullah nor a brahmin; give up worship of duality. This is the command of the King of Kings. Ceaselessly proclaim 'I am Allah; I am God.'*

*"Mansur Mastana says, 'I have seen Him in the heart, and that is the tavern of the intoxicated ones. Enter into the midst of that tavern.'"* [7]

**Baba:** Mansur says that God is not outside; He is within you. I, too, have seen God within myself. He is to be worshiped within, not outside. It is God's command that you should keep repeating to yourself "I am God" and remain in the company of saints. You need not go anywhere in search of God. He will come searching for you. Have you read the life story of Chokhamela? If not, do read it. Whenever devotees would go on pilgrimage to Pandarpur, he would request them to "convey my *pranāms* to Pandarinath." He himself would never go to God. Ultimately, God had to come to him.

*For the past week Baba has been in Santa Cruz. Today a Parsi lady named Perin came for his darshan. When she met Baba two days ago, she experienced great peace. Perin has been worshiping Shri Krishna for several years, and wherever she goes, she carries a small idol of the child Krishna for daily worship. She was sitting deeply engrossed in thought when Baba asked her the following question.*

## God Loves Devotion, Not Caste

**Baba:** So, what did Bhagawan Krishna tell you?

**Perin:** *Bhagawan said, "Baba will take you to that place where you cannot go on your own."*

**Baba:** I also heard Him say this.

**Perin:** *I am not allowed in the sanctuary of the Radhakrishnan Temple here. I am told, "You are a Parsi, an outcaste." Therefore, I cannot have the darshan of God.*[8]

**Baba:** What is the need for you to go to such a temple? Will God be pleased only if you go to that temple? It is said, "Madhava is very fond of devotion." God is pleased by your devotion and love. He does not discriminate between caste and creed, the false divisions created by man. Devarishi Narada says in his *Bhakti Sūtras*:

> Distinctions of beauty, caste, education, family, wealth, or actions do not apply to *bhaktas*.[9]

Was the hunchback slave Kubja attractive? Was Sudama wealthy? Was Vyadha a man of good conduct? To which caste did Gajendra belong?[10] God became pleased with all these devotees only because of their intense devotion.

When you completely understand Krishna, you will realize that He is without attributes or form; He is ever pure and all pervading. Krishna is not this small idol the size of your finger. The following story will illustrate this truth.

Namdev was devoted to Lord Krishna for many years. Krishna would appear to him and talk with him. In spite of these exalted experiences, Gora Kumbhar, a great sage, tapped Namdev's head with a stick one day in front of a large gathering of saints, saying, "This pot is not yet properly baked." Namdev complained to Krishna, but Krishna said that Gora Kumbhar was right. Namdev recognized that his understanding was incomplete, and he accepted Vishoba Khechar as his Guru. Under his guidance, Namdev was able to realize the all-pervasive form of Krishna and become a perfect *jñānī*.

You should also remember that although Arjuna had known Krishna for many years, he did not know His true nature, he did not know that Krishna was an embodiment of the Lord. For this reason, Lord Krishna gave Arjuna the divine knowledge in the *Bhagavad Gītā*.

Shri Krishna's birth is described in the *Shrīmad Bhāgavata Purāna*, but can you say that Krishna only came into existence at that time? Vyadha shot Krishna with an arrow, but can you say that Krishna ceased to exist after that? Shri Krishna existed as the formless, attributeless supreme Self before His birth, He exists today, and He will continue to exist in the future. He is as He has been always and forever. In order to fulfill some purpose, Krishna manifested in a form. Do not cling obstinately to the idea that Krishna exists only in a photo, an idol, or a temple.

The attainment of liberation is not dependent upon membership in any particular caste. It is the priests of the various sects who place all these conditions on God-realization, saying that you can attain God only if you are a Jain or a Muslim, a Vaishnavite or a Christian, and so on. Isn't liberation possible apart from these sects? Love and devotion are quite sufficient for God-realization. A seeker may embrace any name of God according to his or her inclination. Whichever form of God you worship, the final achievement will be the same. One person will recommend that you go to Mecca, another one will advise you to go to Vrindavan, while a third one will say, "Go to Jerusalem," but God is not confined within any boundaries. Never forget this truth. Pushpadanta says, "The various paths are like many different rivers that merge into the sea and become one, losing their individual names and forms." Similarly, the supreme Self is beyond all sects. With this understanding, become intoxicated in the love and worship of God; become intoxicated with bliss.

## SUNDAY, JANUARY 17, 1965

*Chakrapani Ullal, a seeker and devotee of Baba, brought his friend Rasik Kadakia, who is a close devotee of Swami Chinmayananda, to the ashram. He discussed shaktipat with Baba.*

**Rasik:** *Shaktipat is not mentioned anywhere in Vedanta.*

**Baba:** In Vedanta you find such sentences as "Brahman is the One without a second" or "I am One; let Me become many," which indicate that That, which is without vibrations, has the power to create vibrations. The power that creates vibrations is shakti, and it is not separate from Brahman, the supreme Self. This shakti has such power that it can create many from one, and it can reabsorb the many back into one. This very power is the Sita of Rama, the Radha of Krishna, the *yogashakti* of a yogi, and the grace-bestowing power of a Guru. We must conclude that those who claim that shakti is not mentioned in Vedanta have not studied Vedanta thoroughly and have no experience in this matter.

Shaktipat is not a new science of the modern age. It is a *siddhavidyā* (science of the Siddhas) that has been described in the scriptures and handed down according to tradition from time immemorial. Read *Sadāchāra* of Shankaracharya or *Yoga Vāsishtha* or the books of saints like Jnaneshwar and Eknath. Read what Shri Shankaracharya says about the worship of Shri Chakra. His Guru, Gaudapadacharya, says, "The worthy disciple receives shaktipat by just one word from the Guru." Whatever is mentioned in the scriptures about initiation means shaktipat.

Even in our daily lives, we are aware of the impact our surroundings have on us. If there is melodious music, the listeners start swaying; if there is an atmosphere of excitement, people get excited. The same is true of the Guru's shakti. As soon as one comes into contact with the Guru, one starts undergoing mental and intellectual changes, and knowledge of the Truth begins to manifest spontaneously from within. Sanatkumara obtained knowledge from the silence of Guru Dakshinamurti. That was shaktipat. The meaning of the great Vedantic proclamations such as "That thou art" can be understood only by the Guru's grace. What Shri Ramakrishna received from Totapuri was shaktipat.

Some seekers follow a particular type of sadhana for many years, but when they find that they have not gained anything, they abandon their practice. This is not so with shaktipat *dīkshā*. The shakti will not leave you until you have completed your sadhana.

> Initiation, according to those who have true knowledge of the scriptures, is that by which one achieves union with Shiva, and the bondage of all karmas is destroyed.[11]

Shaktipat is not a religion of credit—it gives you immediate cash. It does not have to make any promises that if you perform this or that action with faith, you will someday find what you are seeking. An able Guru awakens a disciple's inner shakti and gives him an immediate experience of God. It is improper to conclude that shakti does not exist simply because one lacks the ability to give shaktipat. It is not a sign of intelligence to claim that there is no such thing as shaktipat because it is not mentioned in the *Bhagavad Gītā* or *Shrīmad Bhāgavatam.* Guruhood is not complete without the ability to give shaktipat. Guruhood is not attained merely on the basis of one's learning or skills as an orator. The Guru must be able to bestow grace (shaktipat) on the disciple, and he must also be able to control it. If something goes wrong, he should have the power to correct it.

Whether or not you believe in God, He does exist. Similarly, shaktipat *vidyā* exists whether or not you know anything about it. The Truth cannot be understood simply by listening to discourses on Vedanta. That does not mean, however, that you should give up listening to Vedanta. Listen to Vedanta, but at the same time do sadhana; contemplate what you have heard. To contemplate day and night after listening is implicit in the Vedantic teachings. Have you read *Aparokshānubhūti* by Shankaracharya?

**Rasik:** *Yes.*

**Baba:** You may remember that at the end of the book he describes the fifteen aspects of contemplation that he advises the seeker to practice repeatedly. Only in this way can the truth of Vedanta be grasped.

**Rasik:** *Can a person with an impure heart receive shaktipat initiation? Wouldn't it be harmful for one's kundalinī shakti to be awakened before one has attained purity?*

**Baba:** Every being is a part of God, thus everyone has the right to attain liberation. Everyone has some sort of impurity, but as soon as one receives shaktipat, the process of purification begins automatically.

**Rasik:** *What are the qualifications a disciple must possess in order to receive shaktipat?*

**Baba:** Love and devotion. The disciple's love for the Guru automatically attracts his shakti into the disciple. Shaktipat doesn't have to be done intentionally. If the disciple has true love in his heart for his Guru, then he is worthy of shaktipat initiation.

*Mr. Sarpotdar, who is a devotee of Rang Avadhut Maharaj, came with his family for darshan. He is the brother-in-law of Vasant Nigudkar, a longtime, sincere devotee of Baba.*

## *Natural Shaktipat*

**Sarpotdar:** *When the Guru gives shaktipat initiation, what is he actually doing?*

**Baba:** There are many types of initiation. Every Guru gives initiation in his own way. In shaktipat initiation, the shakti dwelling within the disciple is awakened. Truly speaking, this awakening need not be done consciously because simply by remaining in the Guru's company, the disciple's shakti is spontaneously awakened.

**Sarpotdar:** *What happens after that?*

**Baba:** This shakti remains active in the seeker, taking him further and further in his sadhana until he realizes God, until he becomes one with God. With the passage of time, the shakti increases in strength. Just as a seed, after being sown in the ground, automatically sprouts and grows into a tree bearing blossoms and fruit, Chiti Shakti continues to work within the disciple and ultimately merges with Shiva. Even before they merge, this Shakti is Shiva. Shiva and Shakti are not different. Shiva assumes the form of Shakti in order to achieve some purpose. In other words, Shakti is the active form of Shiva. In distinct form, this Shakti dwells in the *mūlādhāra chakra*, in the heart chakra, and in the five *prānas.* Actually, all forms of energy are one. This Shakti is no different from any other form of Shakti.

It is not essential for a Guru to formally bestow shaktipat in order to awaken this Shakti. Through the disciple's love and worship of the Guru, Shakti spontaneously and naturally starts doing Her work within him. Shakti has perfect understanding.

She knows exactly what She must do within each individual. This same Shakti is referred to in the *Devī Bhāgavatam* and the *Mārkandeya Purāna*, in which it is said:

> I bow to that Goddess, I salute that Goddess, I worship and pray to that Goddess who dwells in all beings in the form of Shakti.[12]

Just as a student must be worthy to learn a mundane subject from a teacher, a disciple must be worthy of receiving the Guru's grace through shaktipat initiation.

## TUESDAY, JANUARY 26, 1965

*A German couple from South Africa, Mark and Gita Obel, accompanied Nagin Pujara, a devotee of Baba, to the ashram. When they were at Ramanashram, Ma Talyarkhan had specifically advised them to meet Baba. Earlier this morning Baba had said, "Today some German yogis will be coming." Soon after their arrival they began asking Baba questions. Since it was Republic Day, a national holiday, the ashram was crowded with devotees, and they all gathered around to listen to the discussion.*

### *Yoga in Daily Life*

**Mark:** *Must the practice of yoga be pursued only in a specific place such as an ashram or a math, or can yogic sadhana be practiced anywhere?*

**Baba:** Yoga may be practiced anywhere and by anyone. This world was created by God through His yogic power; it is not different from yoga.

Shri Krishna, who expounded our famous religious scripture

the *Bhagavad Gītā,* was a great *yogeshvara* (lord of yoga). He explains in the *Gītā* that He created this world through the power of His *yogamāyā.* Thus, the very origin of this world is yoga.

Many people have mistaken notions about yoga and fear that it must be very difficult to practice. They believe that in order to pursue yoga one must grow a beard, live in a cave, and practice severe austerities, but yoga is something that can be understood and practiced by everyone. The truth is that everyone already practices yoga in daily life. Every day, you practice and live the various stages and aspects of yoga as described in Patanjali's *Yoga Sūtras.*

The first stage in yoga is *yama-niyama,* that is, disciplines that you ordinarily observe each day in one form or another. You arise at a regular hour in order to arrive at the office on time, you eat your meals and catch the train at a specified time. Offices, marketplaces, shops, courts, and schools all open and close at the appointed times. In this way, your daily life is already disciplined.

The next step in yoga is *āsana,* or posture. Don't you make use of posture in your daily life? Look, you have been sitting cross-legged, this man has been squatting for such a long time, and that man has been resting his chin on his arm, listening to me. I am sitting comfortably in this chair resting my feet on the floor. These are all *āsanas,* or postures.

*Prānāyāma* is another stage in yoga through which the *prāna* and *apāna* become equalized. This induces a steady mental state. *Pratyāhāra,* the withdrawal of the mind from the senses, and *dhyāna,* meditation, are also parts of yoga.

The meaning of meditation is concentration of the mind on a particular object. Is it possible for an engineer to plan the construction of a bridge without concentration? Watchmakers, mathematicians, and artists focus their minds on their respective subjects, thus achieving the mental concentration that enables them to be successful in their work. Meditation, or yoga, is always a part of daily life, but it is incomplete yoga, it is only about seventy-five percent complete.

In mundane activities, your mind is concentrated on

external objects, whereas the aim of spiritual practices is to transform the mind into non-mind. This is called yoga. Yesterday I met a doctor who told me that he can successfully carry out his research work only when his mind stops doing all other work. Such a thought-free state is called *samādhi* and can be easily achieved through the practice of yoga. Concentration, or meditation, is a state. The relief from tension obtained by swallowing tranquilizers can be achieved naturally without any drug through meditation.

**Mark:** *I am very thankful to you for explaining yoga so beautifully and using the comparison with everyday life. My second question is, we always know the purpose of our actions in worldly life, but what is the special purpose of yoga?*

**Baba:** The purpose of practicing yoga is to eliminate the agitations that constantly arise in the mind. The main purpose of yoga is to obtain profound peace, to put an end to all sorrow, and to enjoy permanent happiness and bliss.

## *The Yoga of Service to the Husband*

**Gita:** *Would it be a sin to leave one's husband for the practice of yoga sadhana with the goal of obtaining God-realization, or is a wife's only duty to serve her husband?*

**Baba:** There are strong bonds between husband and wife, father and son, God and devotee, and Guru and disciple. These relationships are not based on infatuation. For a disciple, no one is greater than the Guru. He would never leave his Guru. A devotee continues to worship God even after becoming a great saint. This is called *kshetra sannyāsa*, or one-pointed devotion. Similarly, the relationship between a husband and wife is permanent. Just as a disciple completely surrenders himself to his Guru, a wife should serve her husband with complete devotion and self-sacrifice. Selfless service and an attitude of devotion bring profound peace. This is the judgment of the ancient high court of saints and seers as revealed in the scriptures. The scriptures proclaim that a disciple who serves his Guru wholeheartedly might not do any sadhana, yet he will attain his goal. Similarly, *tapasyā* in the form of service and single-minded devotion to the husband definitely bears fruit.

There lived a great saint of high and noble character in Maharashtra named Tukaram. He said, "A woman who is faithful and devoted to her husband attains peace. Not only that, she achieves the power to command God Himself." Now you can decide for yourself the relative worth of other forms of *tapasyā* compared to the power acquired by a woman who faithfully serves her husband. In India a great book called *Chandīpātha*, which is a hymn to the goddess, is often recited by devotees. It has a prayer: "O Goddess, if You become pleased with me, grant me a wife of good character, whose nature is compatible with mine, so that under her influence I shall be able to cross over this ocean of birth and death."

Thus an ideal wife can also uplift her husband. This yoga of devotion to the husband has been bestowed on you naturally, and you have obtained the fruit of this *tapasyā* practiced over so many years. So do not worry, God is with you!

SATURDAY, JANUARY 30, 1965

*Shri Paramananda of Sri Lanka has been staying here for the past few days. This morning he and Albert Rudolph of America came for satsang with Baba.*

## The Effect of Shaktipat

**Rudolph:** *When does a seeker reach perfection?*

**Baba:** Man is born twice. His first birth takes place as a result of his father's seed. His second birth occurs when he receives the mantra from his Guru. As he progresses in his sadhana, he eventually achieves complete concentration and oneness with the mantra. By the power of the mantra, he becomes *ūrdhvaretas*; that is, his semen starts to flow upward. The fire of yoga converts this semen into *prāna shakti*. Through shaktipat, the Guru initiates a revolution in this *prāna shakti* within the disciple. This is his second birth. The Guru becomes father as well as mother. Just as a fertilized ovum develops into a child within the womb, the seed in the form of the mantra that is sown within the disciple develops steadily step by step. Just as a tree is formed from a germinated seed and bears flowers and fruit, similarly, a new identity is created within the disciple by which he achieves spiritual perfection. In order to reach this state, respect for and devotion to the Guru are absolutely essential. A disciple will become only as great as he considers his Guru to be.

**Rudolph:** *I am thinking of buying a house in New York. Will it be possible?*

**Baba:** The divine energy that pervades everything in this universe from the animate to the inanimate is also functioning through you. This energy is so powerful that with its help you can achieve anything you desire. However, for this you must possess an ever-increasing love and devotion for the Guru.

## THURSDAY, FEBRUARY 11, 1965

*Since morning, Baba has been sitting in the compound of a spacious bungalow called "Valley View" in Mahabaleshwar reading Pratyabhijñāhridayam, with a commentary by Shivanijayogi. Shri Yogendrabhai arrived and Baba began talking with him.*

# The Importance of the Shaivite Philosophy

**Baba:** What can I say, Trivediji; this book is really sublime! The science of Shiva-Shakti, shaktipat, is even superior to Vedanta. According to Vedanta, the world is not real, whereas in Shaivism, the world is not only said to be real but also filled with Consciousness.

**Yogendrabhai:** *Isn't it possible to explain the Truth in a few words? Is it necessary to read so many books to understand it? If it is, then those who have read the books should all be Siddhas because they have learned everything from the books.*

**Baba:** There is a great distinction between being merely learned and being a *jñānī*. Those who have read extensively and can give lectures are learned, while those who have realized God are *jñānīs*.

**Yogendrabhai:** *How can God-realization be achieved?*

**Baba:** Not everyone can attain God-realization. It is the result of many lifetimes of *tapasyā*. When Bhagawan Shri Krishna was born to Devaki, she told Narada with great pride, "You have been so devoted to Bhagawan, but He has taken birth in my womb." Narada replied, "I know the truth of the matter." Saying this, he covered her eyes with his hands and showed her several of her past lives. Then she understood that Krishna had been born to her because of intense *tapasyā* in previous lives.

In our ashram, some people receive shaktipat immediately upon arriving, while others stay for two or three years and yet remain unchanged. Your friend Bhaskarbhai Desai experienced the *khecharī mudrā* as soon as he came to the ashram. People vary in their worthiness to obtain knowledge.

**Yogendrabhai:** *What is the importance of the khecharī mudrā and other such yogic kriyās?*

**Baba:** All these *kriyās* lead to internal purification. The passage in the *sushumnā nādī* is cleared out, enabling the *prāna* to travel through it without obstruction to the *sahasrāra*. After becoming purified in this way, a seeker no longer experiences any pain or misery even though calamity or misfortune may occur. Such a seeker is contented and happy under all circumstances. Peace and contentment are not dependent on external circumstances, but on the inner state.

**Yogendrabhai:** *Can't this state be achieved through knowledge? Are yogic kriyās necessary in order to achieve this state?*

**Baba:** Even after obtaining knowledge, shaktipat is essential in order to preserve it.

**Yogendrabhai:** *Is there anything else that should be done to maintain the state of knowledge?*

**Baba:** Contemplate Shiva. Remember the name of God ceaselessly. Everything becomes possible with the Guru's grace. In fact without it, all other types of sadhana are nothing but various kinds of exercises.

### SATURDAY, FEBRUARY 20, 1965

*Gita and Mark Obel have been staying in the ashram since last Monday. They have satsang with Baba every day.*

## *Who Is the Experiencer of Pleasure and Pain?*

**Mark:** *Who experiences pleasure and pain, and how is it experienced?*

**Baba:** The same question is raised in Vedanta. The question is asked, "Who is the experiencer of pleasure and pain?" To say that pleasure and pain are experienced by the gross body is not true, because the gross body is composed of the five elements and is inert. And again, if it is claimed that the Self experiences pleasure and pain, that too is not correct, because the Self is not attached to anything. The nature of the Self is pure Consciousness, which never undergoes any change.

I shall explain to you through the following analogy who it is that experiences pleasure and pain. Heat a piece of iron in the fire. By contact with the fire, it becomes hot, its color becomes red, it melts and becomes a soft, flowing metal. On being removed from the fire, the iron again becomes solid and inert. The iron is the same as the gross body, the fire is the Self, and the flowing state is the feeling or experience of pleasure and pain.

The *sūryakānta* gem has such a unique property that when the sun's rays pass through it and strike a piece of cloth lying beneath it, the cloth will catch fire. The same gem, however, when removed from the sunlight, lacks the power to burn anything. Suppose this gem is lying in the sun and the sun's rays pass through it, and by chance an object lying near it starts burning. As a result, a fire breaks out and burns everything in the vicinity. Who is to be blamed for such a mishap, the sun or the gem? Who can be prosecuted and who declared guilty?

The gem cannot be blamed, because it is inert. The sun cannot be accused, because it does not burn anything with its rays and does not perform any action. The houses caught fire because of the contact between the sun and the gem. In Vedanta this phenomenon is called *pratibimbavāda*, or reflection. When Consciousness is reflected in the inert, gross body, the experiencer of pleasure and pain is created in the form of the *antahkarana* (the mind, subconscious mind, intellect, and ego).

## Wednesday, February 24, 1965

*Shri Jayakantbhai, a grandson of Sir Prabhashankar Patni, the former Chief Minister of Bhavnagar, has come to the ashram with his wife, Asha, for a one-week stay. In the evening everyone gathered in the satsang hall, and Jayakantbhai asked Baba the following question:*

## *Everyone Is Worthy of Practicing Sadhana*

**Jayakant:** *Can everyone practice yoga?*

**Baba:** Through *tapasyā* and good karmas, you can do anything, because you are a part of the supreme Self. However, one who has turned away from God through sins or bad actions cannot practice sadhana, just as a son born from someone else's seed cannot have the appearance or qualities of his father, nor can he act like him.

In the scriptures, one is given the understanding of one's true nature through the method of *pratyabhijñā*, or Self-recognition. Discover your true relationship with God just once and then see whether everything is possible or not, whether you understand everything or not.

One is born only from the seed of God, but one does not become His and therefore is miserable. The Lord says in the *Bhagavad Gītā*:

> O Son of Kunti! All the creatures born through any womb in this universe are born out of My *prakriti*, the supreme womb, and I am the father who casts the seed. I am the father of all the creatures in this universe.[13]

Due to the powerful effect of satsang and a holy place, all the glory that lies concealed within starts to shine forth. Think for yourself about the kinds of experiences you have been having since yesterday. The influence of the company one keeps is very great. The poet-saint Sundardas writes:

> You can get a father or a mother, a son or a brother, or a pleasing young woman. You can get a kingdom or elephants and horses, or all the precious possessions of

> this world that you desire. You can attain soc
> the heavens, the realm of Brahma or Vaikunth
> you can acquire any sort of comfort and pleasur
> could ever possibly desire, but it is extremely difficult to attain the company of a saint.[14]

**Asha:** *Is it imperative for one to undergo all the consequences of one's actions in previous lives?*

**Baba:** Some have to be undergone now, while others will bear fruit later. For example, Narada was cursed to endure poverty for seven lifetimes. A king who was also under a curse remained childless for three lifetimes. One must undergo the consequences of one's actions either in this lifetime or in a future one. There is no escape. Only realization of the Self has the power to burn all one's past karmas. Knowledge reduces all of one's karmas to ashes. It is said in the *Bhagavad Gītā*:

> O Arjuna! Just as a blazing fire reduces wood to ashes, similarly, the fire of knowledge burns all karmas.[15]

**Jayakant:** *Last Sunday when I was here, a gentleman whose son was lost came to ask for your blessings that he might be found. You assured the man that he would find his son, and immediately thereafter the boy was returned to him. Today this woman informed you that after you gave her a piece of fruit and blessed her, she was able to conceive a son. How do such things happen?*

**Baba:** I don't know anything about it. I said he would find his son and he found him. I might have given the woman a piece of fruit—at the moment I don't remember—and she conceived a son. Mudanna here had an ulcer, but he was cured simply by living in the ashram. Pure surroundings and good actions have tremendous power.

## *Is an Idol Conscious or Inert?*

**Devotee:** *Babaji, is an idol conscious or inert?*

**Baba:** Heed my words. A seeker desirous of liberation must not indulge in such idle discussions. Recently when I was in Mahabaleshwar, a spiritual camp was in progress that lasted four days. A certain gentleman gave a discourse each day. One evening two participants from the camp visited me. They told me that the lecturer was condemning idol worship, arguing that "an idol is inert, it is only stone or wood. Anyone who worships an idol is a fool. There is no reality in an idol. If you put it in fire, it will burn up without a trace." I told them, "First, put that man giving the discourse into the fire and see whether or not he burns up. If he is inert, he will burn up; if he is conscious, he will remain unaffected. After he emerges from the flames, if he retains consciousness and can still speak, then I will accept whatever he says."

It is characteristic of the common man to disrespect the scriptures, while it is characteristic of the *jñānīs* and saints to honor them.

## *True Religion*

**Devotee:** *Babaji, which is the true religion?*

**Baba:** There is only one religion, the rest are distinctions in the name of religion. If anyone were to say to God, "I am a Sikh," "I am a Christian," or "I am a Muslim," God would ask, "What is a Sikh? What is a Christian?" God does not differentiate between a Sikh, a Christian, or a Muslim. They are all similar human beings. Christianity was not created by Christ, but by his followers. Those who coerce others into changing their religion through outrageous means are merely exploiting others in the name of religion. From the perspective of a *jñānī* or a saint, all religions are identical.

Sit alone, meditate, and perceive That which arises from within. Everyone will experience the same inner vibration: "I am Brahman," or "I am That." In meditation, the feeling of being either a Christian or a Muslim will not arise. True religion is that wherein one experiences "I am the supreme Self" from within. As long as you maintain your sense of limited individuality, you will not achieve anything. The claim that one sect is superior to another is merely false vanity.

## Thursday, February 25, 1965

*This morning Jayakant and his wife, Asha, came to the satsang hall. Baba initiated the discussion.*

## *Renunciation of the World and Daily Activities Is Not Necessary*

**Baba:** You are a very well matched couple, as both of you are spiritually inclined. The life of such a couple is harmonious and free from strife. If only one of a pair is interested in spirituality, he or she will have to undergo some suffering. A judge of the high court used to come here often. His wife feared that he would turn into a *sannyāsī* one day, so she would always argue with him, trying to dissuade him from visiting the ashram. A professor's wife also used to come here despite her husband's disapproval, but after meeting me, he also developed feelings of love and devotion.

A spiritual seeker need not leave the world. Whatever you have to renounce can be renounced while living in the world. It is only a matter of changing your mental attitude. If one is incapable of doing this while living in the world, how will one be able to accomplish it by running away from the world? If one cannot renounce while living in one's own home, what will one be able to renounce by living in a jungle?

Shri Ramachandra and Shri Krishna did not give up the world. Both Saint Yajnavalkya and Saint Tukaram had two wives each, and had to look after their homes and families. Worldly life and spirituality are not incompatible. Understand this truth, worship and sing the glories of God with love, and continue to perform your worldly duties. In this way, you will attain happiness and peace.

## Friday, February 26, 1965

*This morning Gita and Mark Obel and five other devotees came to the ashram. Later in the afternoon they all gathered around Baba in the satsang hall.*

# *The Importance of the Guru*

**Gita:** *Why is it necessary to have a Guru on one's spiritual journey?*

**Baba:** In spirituality the Guru occupies the highest position. It is very difficult to obtain a Guru. Nonetheless, nothing is impossible in this world of God. As long as the sun, the moon, the stars, the Himalayas, and the Ganges endure, Gurus, *paramahamsas*, Siddhas, and great beings will continue to appear in this world. Their tradition will never be lost nor broken. Chandraloka, Indraloka, Siddhaloka—there are many such *lokas*, and numberless Siddhas dwell in such regions. One who has obtained the grace of the Guru and who follows the path shown by the Guru can have visions of these Siddhas. Such visions may not appear immediately after receiving the Guru's grace, but you will certainly see Siddhaloka before the final realization. Siddhas dwelling in Siddhaloka also give initiation. In order to obtain the knowledge of Brahman, it is essential to have a Guru in one form or another. Without the Guru's grace, one remains deprived of the supreme knowledge.

One must have devotion for the Guru to obtain his grace. You can understand its greatness from the famous example of Eklavya.

The devotion of Eknath Maharaj for his Guru, Janardan Swami, was also exemplary.

Once all the fellow devotees of Eknath Maharaj were about to set out on a pilgrimage, and they earnestly requested Eknath to accompany them. He declined, saying, "I am fully occupied in service to my Guru. Take this coin and offer it to the Ganges on my behalf." When the devotees reached Hardwar, they prayed and meditated according to the scriptural rites. Then they tossed Eknath's coin toward the Ganges, and Mother Ganga herself stretched out her hand to receive it. Beholding this amazing sight, the devotees were wonderstruck. Then they heard a voice saying, "Mother Ganga is always eager to accept any gift from one who considers his Guru to be the mantra, the center of pilgrimage, and God."

Perhaps a Guru may be found, but it is extremely difficult for a Guru to find a worthy disciple with correct understanding of the Guru principle. The fruits of worshiping the Guru will vary depending on whether you consider him to be mortal or divine. To think of anything besides the Guru is infidelity. The Guru is the essence of Brahma, Vishnu, and Mahesh. One who surrenders completely in body, mind, and speech to the Guru becomes the Guru himself. Just as after merging with the sea, the river itself becomes the sea, similarly, such a devotee does not remain separate from the Guru. One who remains separate from God cannot truly be called a devotee, and one who remains separate from the Guru cannot truly be called a disciple.

## Tuesday, March 2, 1965

*Prior to the departure of Gita and Mark Obel for South Africa today, everyone gathered in the satsang hall. A child who was playing happily in the hall suddenly started crying, and the next moment was laughing again. After a short while he became angry with his mother and started hitting her. Observing the child, Mark asked Baba the following question:*

## *The Eight-Petaled Heart Lotus*

**Mark:** *Why is this child's mind fluctuating so rapidly?*

**Baba:** The knowers of yoga speak of an eight-petaled lotus situated in the heart. Each petal has a different color and a distinctive quality—love, hatred, anger, fear, attachment, desire, compassion, and peace:

> There is an eight-petaled lotus in the heart. The *jīvātman* (individual soul) dwells at its center in a subtle form of light.[16]

The individual being keeps rotating over these petals, assuming the quality of the petal on which he dwells. As he wanders about on these petals, he indulges in such notions as "I am the doer, I am the enjoyer; I am happy, I am sorrowful; I am black, I am white." For example, when the individual soul dwells on the white petal, he is full of devotion and tends to be religious; when he dwells on the red petal, he becomes lazy and inactive.

You can understand this from your own experience. You may have noticed that sometimes when someone approaches you, you may feel love or anger toward that person for no apparent reason. Sometimes you feel sad and pessimistic without any cause. You have surely experienced the fluctuating states of your mind in this way. The aim of meditation is to disengage the individual soul from all these tendencies and make him steady in his own Self. When one becomes established in the center of the heart lotus, he experiences bliss and recognizes his true nature. Even a seeker who meditates regularly remains subject to mental instability until he attains perfection. Until then, he will vacillate between love and anger, dispassion and desire.

You should understand, however, that although the individual soul may be subject to changing moods and states according to the quality of the petal on which he dwells, in reality, these are not the essential qualities of the Self. The Self is beyond all qualities. Just as a person may be identified as the one wearing red clothes or the one wearing yellow clothes, in the same way, the qualities of the petals are superimposed on the Self, and then the person is said to be angry or kind, lazy or energetic, and so forth.

Further evidence to support the view that the individual soul is separate from all these attributes is that when he is experiencing one quality, he does not simultaneously experience any of the other ones. If all the qualities actually belonged to him, then he would possess them all at all times, but this is not the case. For example, when one is in a state of anger, he does not experience love. When one is in a mood of dispassion, he has no desires. These various experiences that the individual soul undergoes are the result of the merits and demerits he has earned by his own previous actions.

The essential nature of the Self is *sacchidānanda.* The true feeling arising from within him is "I am Brahman." "I am God, God is mine"—this is the individual soul's real inspiration. Have you understood this properly? I have explained it in this way just for your sake.

**Mark:** *You have explained it very clearly, and I am very happy to have learned all this.* (Addressing another devotee) *Kindly translate Baba's discourse into English and send it to my son in South Africa. It would definitely appeal to him. He is a well-known heart specialist there.*

**Gita:** *Baba, why does the individual soul keep rotating on those petals?*

**Baba:** In order to undergo the results of past actions. This is his nature.

## Thursday, March 4, 1965

*Draupadi Singh, a West Indian lady, has been staying in the ashram for seven weeks. She has studied yoga at many other ashrams in India during the past ten years. After meeting Baba and receiving his grace in the form of shaktipat, she finally feels satisfied. Baba gave her the book Pratyabhijñāhridayam, which she read twice, and today she discussed it with him.*

**Draupadi:** *Babaji, I read in Pratyabhijñāhridayam that Shiva Himself becomes the individual soul, but I do not understand how this transformation occurs. The ninth sūtra says, "By the contraction of shakti, that which is of the form of Consciousness is covered with impurities and becomes a samsārī (worldly soul)." What is the meaning of "the contraction of shakti"?*

**Baba:** Once in a while, in a transcendent state of bliss, don't you feel that you are Shiva? And again at other times, don't you feel that you are Draupadi? This is known as the contraction of shakti. This is the result of changes in attitude.

## Sunday, March 7, 1965

*This morning Shri Ishwarlal Barot came to the ashram accompanied by some Sindhi friends. They asked Baba a few questions.*

**Friend:** *I have been in India since the formation of Pakistan. I have been to many places in the country. During these travels, I have observed that the migrants from Pakistan may try any number of places, but they earn the best in Bombay. Why is that?*

**Baba:** It may appear to you that they earn very well in Bombay, but every person earns money according to his own destiny. What he is destined to have never goes wrong.

**Friend:** *I stayed for a month in the ashram of Shri Vinoba Bhave. While there, I noticed that about seventy-five percent of his devotees were government officers and ministers. Why should saints become entangled with ministers?*

**Baba:** In the olden days there were *rājagurus*, or Gurus to the kings. The kings consulted them regarding political and personal affairs. This was beneficial to both the king and his subjects. The royal Gurus were adept in all arts and sciences. They possessed the strength of *tapasyā.* Because of their selflessness and impartial outlook, they could recognize the truth in any situation and give the correct advice. Vinobaji is a saint and has faith in Brahman. What harm can there be in ministers seeking his company or advice?

**Friend:** *I have too much anger. How can I subdue it?*

**Baba:** Apply your faculties of reflection and discrimination each time anger arises, and it will automatically decrease.

## SUNDAY, MARCH 14, 1965

*This morning Shri Virendrakumar Jain, editor of Bharatī, the periodical of Bharatiya Vidya Bhavan, came to the ashram. He is also a well-known Hindi poet. He had a discussion with Baba in the satsang hall.*

**Virendrakumar:** *Since Shakti is formless and all-pervading, is it proper to see Her in the form of a gross body or to worship Her with attributes?*

**Baba:** This entire world is a manifestation of that formless, all-pervasive Shakti. It is said:

> The entire universe from Brahmaloka down to this earth is pervaded entirely by the supreme glory of Mother Shakti, who is eternal and free.[17]

The entire universe has been created by that Shakti. Can't She who has created rivers, mountains, trees, birds, and animals assume a form? It is a very simple matter for Her. Shakti is both with and without attributes. She is one and also many. She possesses the unique power of being able to convert one into many and many into one.

## *Material Enjoyments and Liberation*

**Virendrakumar:** *Lord Shiva is said to be the giver of both worldly enjoyments and liberation. How does he give material enjoyment?*

**Baba:** Lord Shiva is the giver of the fruits of action and He presides over all actions. Whatever actions you perform, whether good or bad, the Lord is the owner of all those actions. If you continuously act with this understanding, you will attain liberation, but if you do not have this understanding, you will attain only material enjoyments, the fruits of the mundane world. Whatever action you perform, do it for the sake of God. If you act with the understanding that Parashiva is the final reaper of the fruits of all actions, then you will attain liberation. The *Bhagavad Gītā* says:

> The wise, possessed of knowledge and action without desire for fruits, are freed from the bondage of birth and achieve liberation.[18]

The *Gītā* also says:

> Even the wise become confused about what is action and what is inaction.[19]

Many great beings tried to get rid of the fruits of action through renunciation, but the results would not leave them! Sai Baba of Shirdi, for example, was a great *tyāgī,* but today his *samādhi* shrine is worshiped. Lakhs (hundreds of thousands) of rupees are offered there, and it is covered with costly shawls and other valuable items. Similarly, the photograph of Nityananda Baba, a great *avadhūta,* is carried in procession in a silver palanquin. Siddharudha Swami of Hubli used to wear gold-embroidered clothes and a crown studded with diamonds and precious stones. If someone commented on it, he used to say, "I do it knowingly. Instead of my *samādhi* stone being polished (worshiped) after I am gone as is the case of other saints, I am polishing it myself."

Even great beings cannot escape their destiny. Some people criticize them for traveling in motorcars, living in palatial residences, and wearing costly, beautiful clothes, but what can they say when they see the *samādhi* shrines of the great *tyāgī* saints being adorned with silver and worshiped by devotees?

Knowledge is of two types, pure and impure. The awareness that "I am a gardener," "I am a potter," "I am forty years old," or "I have a family and children" is impure knowledge. To understand that "I am Shiva, I pervade this entire universe" is pure knowledge. With impure knowledge one remains a limited being, whereas after gaining pure knowledge one becomes Shiva. The *Shiva Sūtras* say:

> As soon as a seeker attains pure knowledge, he becomes a Siddha.[20]

Try to attain knowledge of the Self, discover the answer to the inquiry "Who am I?" In doing so, your environment or circumstances will not be an obstacle for you. Hanuman's attitude of being a servant to Rama did not prevent him from realizing "I am Rama."

The world is a drama. In a drama there are many characters, each played by a different actor. A skilled actor can bring out the character exactly as portrayed without forgetting who he really is. Similarly, while playing your part in this world, you must constantly be aware of your true nature. This true knowledge is the only source of happiness. You experience pleasure or pain according to your awareness. If you constantly remember "I am Shiva," you will be in bliss. Sanjaya, for example, was just a charioteer, but compared to the king, he was much happier.[21] Such is the power of knowledge of the Truth. This awareness is called pure knowledge. This knowledge brings you liberation.

Thoughts such as "I am the body" or "This is mine" belong to the ordinary mortal. The scriptures do not advocate contemplation on such thoughts, nor have the saints and seers uttered such statements; nonetheless, a person spends his entire life immersed only in such thoughts. The teaching of the Vedas, seers, and saints is *aham brahmāsmi*, "I am the Absolute." It is surprising that no one believes in this, no one has any respect for this idea. On the contrary, everyone believes in that which is false. Such is life in this world. One remembers only the experiences of one's mundane, day-to-day life. According to Vedanta, the world does not exist, and yet one experiences it. This is a matter of great wonder. All this confusion arises out of one's ignorance of our real nature. If someone does not address a doctor by his proper title, he feels insulted because he firmly believes in his identity as a doctor, and he constantly wants to be reminded and to remind others of his status. If someone is referred to by a wrong name, he takes the matter to court, because he identifies himself only with a particular name. This type of thinking or belief is ignorance, or impure knowledge. It brings about only mundane results, not liberation.

## Wednesday, March 17, 1965

*Today Shri Rasik Kadakia came to the ashram accompanied by some friends. While talking with him, Baba gave a beautiful discourse on japa.*

# The Importance of Japa in Sadhana

**Rasik:** *A learned āchārya who gives discourses has said that japa does not have an important place in sadhana.*

**Baba:** Those who do not consider *japa* to be important in sadhana are ignorant. Whatever the chosen method, the aim of sadhana is to make the mind one-pointed, and *japa* is a simple and easy method. Although *japa* loses its significance after liberation is attained, it carries great importance during the period of sadhana. Whether or not you do *japa,* it is automatically going on within you. You are alive by virtue of this *japa.* When you realize this *japa,* you become liberated. In *Sadāchāra,* Shankaracharya says:

> Within every being the *japa* of *So'ham* is constantly vibrating. When this *japa* is realized, one attains liberation.[22]

One must actually do *japa* in order to understand its importance. What can one who does not understand *japa* tell others about it? Only those who have attained *nirvikalpa samādhi* by means of *japa* sadhana can make a judgment in this matter. If you were to attain *nirvikalpa* meditation, you would understand this for yourself. The vibration of letters is called *japa.* It is the theory of *Spanda Shāstra* that the first thought wave, or vibration, arises in that state in which the mind is *nirvikalpa* (thought-free) and *niramaya* (completely still). *Spanda* is that *savikalpa* (with thought) state[23] through which the mind passes before it enters *nirvikalpa samādhi.* A verse in the Upanishads says:

> I am One; let Me become many.[24]

Here "I" signifies the *nirvikalpa* state and "many" signifies vibrations. The *ham* of *aham* has created this entire universe. This vibration is its root cause. The scriptures describe God as both with and without attributes:

> Before the creation, God existed in the form of letters.[25]

The *Bhagavad Gītā* says:

> Among the various types of *yajñas,* I am *japa yajña.*[26]

Namdev says:

> The Name is my own abode, full of Consciousness.[27]

Great beings such as Prahlad, Dhruva, and Vasishtha crossed over this ocean of birth and death through the constant remembrance of God's name. Saint Tulsidas says:

> Shuka, Sanaka, and other Siddhas, sages, and yogis attained the bliss of Brahman by singing God's holy name.[28]

According to all four Vedas, remembrance of God's name is the most effective means of sadhana in all four *yugas.* In the present Kali Yuga, there is no better path than the name of God.

The sadhana of repeating God's name is advocated by all the sects of Hinduism and by Christianity and Sufism as well. All seekers vouch for it regardless of whether they are *jñānīs, bhaktas,* or yogis. The *Yoga Sūtras* say:

> One should repeat the mantra and contemplate its meaning.[29]

In the words of Tukaram Maharaj, the taste of God's name is so delectable that it can cause even a *jñānī's* mouth to water. Mahatma Laldas says:

> Fools do not understand how sweet and nectarean the name of Rama is. The intelligent and the wise drink this nectar. Its sweetness is beyond compare.[30]

The following verse is from Saint Dadu:

> Sweet is the name of Ram, and rare
>     are the wise and the holy who taste its nectar.
> Drinking its love, they glide into eternity.
> It is the resting place of the enlightened,

Of the seeker and the yogi,
Of the faithful wife and the one who controls his senses.
Beyond vision and imagination is its perennial flow.
It is this nectar that kept Namdev, Pipa, and Raidas
    intoxicated day and night.
Never tiring, Kabir was always athirst for more of its love.
Whoever has drunk this sweet nectar has drowned in it.
Sweetness mingled with sweetness.
Ah, how can Dadu describe it![31]

Many saints have sung the glories of *japa*. How can anyone say that the repetition of God's name is of secondary importance?

Shri Adi Shankaracharya, in his commentary on the *Vishnu Sahasranāma*, writes that if any error is made in following the scriptural injunctions and rites during the performance of a *yajña*, it remains incomplete. In order to complete it, he advises chanting God's name three times by chanting *Om*. Such is the power of God's name. *Japa* sadhana is very important and most auspicious under all conditions, at all times, and for all people.

One further point is that the practice of *japa* sadhana is very simple and straightforward and has no special requirements. In *dhyāna yoga*, or meditation, for example, a proper place and observance of certain rules are essential requirements. In *jñāna yoga*, a Guru and books are needed. In *japa* sadhana, nothing external is required. It can be practiced at any place and time without any prior preparation. It can be practiced by everyone—children, the elderly, the virtuous, and sinners. Both the one who chants God's name and the one who hears it derive the same bliss.

**Ratilal:** *How can this bliss be obtained? I chant the Vishnu Sahasranāma, but I don't derive any joy from it.*

**Baba:** Chant with one-pointed faith, and you will begin to experience the joy in it. The nature of God is nectarean; it is natural to feel an attraction toward Him.

**Ratilal:** *Perhaps I don't understand the meaning of the chant, and therefore I do not experience joy in it.*

**Baba:** Even if you do not understand it, continue to chant it. You will certainly attain the fruit, just as surely as you would be burned by stepping, even unknowingly, on hot coals.

In the study of Vedanta, fifteen steps must be ascended one by one in order to obtain knowledge. Yoga has eight stages. But the remembrance of God's name is always one and the same, right from the beginning until the end.

That which is beyond words is achieved through words. The *ajapa* state is achieved by doing *japa.* The name of God signifies the *nirvikalpa* state. To obtain that state, take refuge in God's name. Tukaram Maharaj says, "If you have God's name on your tongue, realization will be in your palm." The essence of this entire discussion is contained in that one sentence.

**Rasik:** *The āchārya to whom I referred claims that he speaks from his own experience.*

**Baba:** Everyone's experience is different. Which of them can be considered true? If you were approached by two people who had had opposite experiences, how would you decide whose was true? And if both of these experiences were contrary to the scriptures, would you accept the scriptures or these experiences as true? To assert the truth of anything, three types of evidence are required: one, scriptural statement, two, the Guru's words, and three, personal experience. Where these three coincide, that alone is truth.

## *Give Up Attachment to the Mind*

**Madhubhai:** *How can the mind be quieted?*

**Baba:** The mind is like the wind—sometimes steady, sometimes agitated. To say "My mind is agitated" is like saying "My horse is sick." What is the relationship between you and the horse? Your feeling of my-ness for the horse is what causes you to worry and feel sorrowful. A farmer develops attachment for a bull, saying, "This is my bull." When the bull dies, he starts crying. He could have said, without crying, "The bull is dead. Bury it in the pit." You can maintain a similar detachment toward your own mind.

**Madhubhai:** *How can the stream of thoughts be stopped?*

**Baba:** Stop paying attention to what the mind is doing. Give up identifying with the mind as your mind. Vedanta asserts that the less you identify with the mind, the quieter it becomes. Give up the company of the mind. The resident of a house can stay in it with an attitude of either "the house is mine" or "the house is not mine."

Observe from where the waves of thoughts arise and where they subside. Watch the pulsations of the mind; see where they go. You can either flow with them or stand apart from them. Understand that the one who watches the mind is different from the mind. Attachment or identification with the mind is only ignorance. The best way to destroy this ignorance is to give up saying "my mind."

The truth is that the mind is the means by which you enjoy the painful or pleasant fruits of your past actions. It is for this reason that God has created this entity called the mind. Sometimes the mind is happy, sometimes sorrowful. Just as we immediately feel happy if someone praises us and angry if someone criticizes us, our virtuous and bad actions also immediately affect our minds.

The mind is not different from Chiti; it is Consciousness in a subtle form. It is Chiti alone who takes the form of the mind, *chitta* (subconscious mind), and speech. In the *Bhagavad Gītā*, the Lord says:

> Among all the senses, I am the mind.[32]

By doing *japa* ceaselessly, the mind assumes the form of God; it is not destroyed. God dwells within you in your mind. What can you do to that which is the dwelling place of God Himself? Because the mind is the abode of God, the name of Rama fills it with peace. If God Himself is Arjuna's charioteer, how can that chariot be stopped? Now, you tell me: should we try to control the mind, or should we install God within it and transmute it into the form of God?

**Madhubhai:** *A swami used to advise concentration on the sound of Shri Rām, Jay Rām.*

**Baba:** This is also a means of sadhana. When the Name finally dissolves into silence, the seeker experiences the *nirvikalpa* state.

## Thursday, March 18, 1965

*Mr. Anthony Brook, a friend of Gita Obel, arrived at five o'clock this evening after spending two months at Pondicherry. He has also visited Ramanashram. His grandfather was king of the State of Sarawak in Malaysia, and Anthony fought against the British, who ultimately captured the state. He has now become a pacifist, engaging himself in the work of world peace. In the evening when all the devotees gathered together, he had a very interesting discussion with Baba.*

## On the Spiritual Awakening of the World

**Anthony:** *I feel that the spiritual awakening of the world will accelerate tremendously in the coming three years. God is manifesting Himself in order to hasten this awakening. The consciousness of the world is being awakened, seemingly by the descent of Consciousness from above. Do you agree with me?*

**Baba:** Just as space is all-pervading, similarly, Chiti Shakti is also all-pervading. It is not that She dwells in one place and not in another, or that She exists to a greater extent in one place than another. Furthermore, whenever the world needs a savior, there is a great being ready to perform that function. Therefore, it is not that someone particularly descends from above. The Lord says in the *Bhagavad Gītā*:

> O Bharata! Whenever righteousness is in peril and unrighteousness takes a strong hold, I incarnate myself into this world.[33]

**Anthony:** *I feel that God has incarnated in several places in order to bring about a spiritual awakening.*

**Baba:** You have this perception according to your own thoughts and ideas, because an awakening is taking place within your own mind. Your consciousness is expanding each day, and so you are seeing God everywhere.

**Anthony:** *Yes, what you say is true. In* 1951, *I experienced everything as God for seven days.*

**Baba:** The final state is attained when this experience becomes firmly established.

**Anthony:** *I pray that you will help me become established in that state through the grace of your shakti.*

**Baba:** It is already becoming firm.

## Friday, March 19, 1965

*Anthony planned to return home today, so when Baba was seated, Anthony and several other devotees gathered around.*

**Baba:** Did you have a good meditation last night?

**Anthony:** *I couldn't sit continuously so it was not real meditation, but I did experience a kind of joy arising from within.*

**Baba:** Everyone meditates for this experience of joy. The real attainment is to experience this joy without having to sit for meditation.

**Anthony:** *The Buddhists say we must become desireless, but desirelessness creates a state of void. I do not have any other desires except a desire for liberation that is so intense that I can't get rid of it despite my best efforts. Is this kind of desire an obstacle to spiritual progress?*

**Baba:** According to Vedanta, one who has such a desire is said to be in a divine state. An intense longing for liberation coupled with renunciation of all worldly desires is also a sadhana. Besides, isn't the striving for desirelessness also a type of desire?

## Religious Sects

**Anthony:** *Babaji, on my way back to Malaysia, I will visit several countries where I plan to continue meeting with saints and leaders and members of various institutions. What would you like me to tell these people? Do you have any message for them? In this atomic age when disharmony prevails everywhere, I want to make an effort to establish peace in the world by conveying to everyone that we are all one.*

**Baba:** Wherever you go, tell people to live with self-control and to develop love for one another. Spread the message of universal brotherhood. Universal brotherhood is true religion. Our ashram emblem says *paraspara devo bhāva*, "See God in each other."

Inner peace is lacking in the lives of many. In the name of God, people have established narrow sects, and in order to increase their membership, they have offered others various tempting inducements. Any religion that attracts members with the help of such enticements cannot have much truth in it. Even wars have been waged in the name of religion. Isn't it uncivilized for men to kill each other? Even in the jungle, tigers do not prey on one another. In the olden days, those who engaged in such atrocities were called *rākshasas* (demons). I call such people modern *rākshasas.* Look what ultimately became of Stalin. Even his dead body was dug up and thrown away like trash. His photos and everything else that might serve as a reminder of him were destroyed. The state of those who follow religious sects is somewhat similar. It is outrageous for some religious sectarians to lure the poor and ignorant by feeding and clothing them, educating and nursing them, and converting them to their own religion. Yet such persons consider themselves to be civilized, cultured, and progressive when, in fact, they are worse than the wild beasts of the jungle. The fact is that everyone wants to spread his own religion to the greatest possible extent.

There was once a prostitute who became rich trading on her youth and beauty. As she approached old age, however, she decided to devote the remainder of her life to gaining some knowledge of religion and thereby obtain peace. She decided to give away all her wealth in charity. Hearing of this, leaders from many different religions and sects went running to advise her. The woman tried to learn from all of them, but after hearing so many contradictory discourses, she became confused and could not decide which of the many religions was true.

A poet from Karnataka has written that there is only one heaven and one hell for all the religions, not separate ones catering to Hindus, Muslims, Jains, Buddhists, and Christians. Then how did so many religions and sects come into existence in this world?

God is beyond religion. Therefore, teach people to live a life of self-control with a feeling of universal brotherhood. This is my message.

*Present this evening were Dr. Pratap Shroff, his sister Malti, and an elderly seeker who often comes for satsang.*

**Seeker:** *Can one achieve the attributeless Brahman through the worship of God with form?*

**Baba:** It is the attributeless that manifests as a form with attributes. Tukaram Maharaj writes from his own experience:

> While meditating on God's name and form, I reached the attributeless Absolute.[34]

**Seeker:** *Is this world true or false?*

**Baba:** The world is real for some and unreal for others. Because the world exists only on the basis of the triad of knower, known, and knowledge, it is unreal for a person who is asleep. If even one of these three factors is absent, the world will cease to be. The *Vivartavāda* of Vedanta is meant to explain that the world is unreal.

**Seeker:** *Yes, but in the example of the snake and the rope, the rope does exist. How can you say that the rope is unreal?*

**Baba:** The supreme Brahman (symbolized by the rope in the analogy) is also true. The world appears to exist because of That. The snake also exists in the rope. Where was the snake in the beginning? In the rope. Where was it seen? In the rope. Where did it vanish? Into the rope. The snake is a form of the rope. Before its manifestation, this world existed in Brahman, it remains Brahman when it appears or manifests, and it merges back into Brahman at the time of dissolution. Therefore, a *jñānī* sees this world as a form of Brahman, who is its material cause.

**Seeker:** *Then why do we have experiences of pleasure and pain?*

**Baba:** Pleasure and pain will certainly be experienced as long as we remain individual souls.

**Seeker:** *Can we again meet the Self-realized saints after they give up their bodies?*

**Baba:** After they have completely merged with the all-pervasive Brahman, how can they meet you? However, saints who have transcended their bodies can certainly meet you.

**Seeker:** *Despite an intense desire to do sadhana, I can't do it. My surroundings are not conducive to spiritual practice. What should I do?*

**Baba:** Let the surroundings remain as they are. Without thinking about them, continue your efforts.

**Seeker:** *This way, when will I reach the final state?*

**Baba:** Why do you want a promise as to when and at what time you will attain the goal? What does it matter if it comes to you after two or ten more births? Since you have already lived millions of lives without attaining anything, why should you worry if there are ten or twelve more lives? Don't become disheartened. Efforts in this direction never go to waste. Everything will take place according to your destiny.

**Seeker:** *Can't destiny be changed?*

**Baba:** Destiny is our own creation. For a wise man, undergoing one's destiny or changing it are both one and the same. Nevertheless, destiny can be changed by very intense efforts, as the sage Markandeya demonstrated.[35]

**Seeker:** *Despite my best efforts, my mind keeps pursuing me.*

**Baba:** This is a state of the mind. It is so because you are engrossed in the world. You should live peacefully in your old age like a true *sannyāsī.* The four *āshramas* described in our scriptures have great significance. They were conceived after profound contemplation. Give up your attachment to your children and worldly objects; they can never give your mind happiness. More than anything else, the mind is the greatest cause of pain. For this reason, the scriptures advise a person to give up his life as a householder after a specified time and to enter into the *vanaprastha āshrama*, followed by the *sannyāsa āshrama.*

Eat whatever you receive and sleep wherever a place is available to you. Sing the glories of God constantly. In this way, you will at least attain a better birth next time.

**Seeker:** *Can we get a birth according to our own wishes?*

**Baba:** You get a birth according to your desires. Birth is according to the desire that is most powerful.

**Seeker:** *Do yogis have a desire for any particular type of birth?*

**Baba:** The only desire of yogis or seekers is to attain liberation. They yearn for the *nirvikalpa* bliss, not for another birth and to again become entangled in the snares of this world.

**Seeker:** *But if everyone were to have such a desire, the world would come to an end.*

**Baba:** That's God's problem; why should you worry about it? Rid your mind of all thoughts. Entrust the burden of this world to God. It is His job to keep it going.

Someone once asked Swami Rama Tirtha, "Can we become the supreme Brahman?" He replied, "I have already become the supreme Brahman." The question was then raised, "Can you do anything you wish?" He replied, "Yes, I can do anything."

"Can you create another world?"

"Yes, certainly I can, but please tell me where it is to be created. Show me a place where no creation yet exists, and then I can certainly create a new world there. But right from the sky down to the sea and the earth, God has already created the world."

**Malti:** *With what material has God created this world?*

**Baba:** God does not require any material to create the world. He has created it out of His own Self. The world that requires some other material for creation is a human being's creation, for example, a house, a garden, a road, or a car.

God created this world by His will alone. He thought, "I am One, let Me become many," and the world came into being. This power also exists in man, although in a smaller proportion. Man's creation is dependent upon action, whereas God's creation does not require any action. The *Bhagavad Gītā* says:

> The seven great sages of old and the four Manus are of My nature and born of My mind, and from them are born all these creatures in the world.[36]

## Tuesday, March 23, 1965

*Miss Mina Sarpotdar, a lecturer in Ancient Hindu Culture at Siddhartha College, has been staying at the ashram for the past five days. Her family members are devotees of Shri Rang Avadhut of Nareshwar, who was brought up by Mina's grandfather in Godhra. This morning Mina had the following discussion with Baba:*

### The True Nature of Devotion and Meditation

**Mina:** *Baba, I want to have bhakti.*

**Baba:** Do you know what the real nature of *bhakti* is? Read Narada's *Bhakti Sūtras* thoroughly at least three times if you want to understand the real meaning of *bhakti.* Narada says:

> One who has *bhakti* is intoxicated with bliss. He is peaceful, knowing that he has achieved his goal. He has no desire for sensual pleasures; hence, he becomes the supreme Brahman.[37]

Knowledge (*jñāna*), devotion (*bhakti*), and yoga are, in essence, the same. To see God everywhere is *bhakti.* To become steady in meditation without any mental vibration is also *bhakti.*

**Mina:** *I sit for meditation, but I can't enter into samādhi. I remain fully aware of my surroundings and know, for example, if someone arrives, if someone is talking—whatever is happening around me.*

**Baba:** You may become fully immersed in meditation, but the Knower within you remains ever present. The Self is the Knower; it is omniscient. It will naturally know everything. It knows not only what is happening here in the vicinity, but also what is happening in Delhi or Mathura. This power of knowing will not vanish, because it is not a faculty of the gross body; it belongs to the Knower who dwells within the body.

It is the mind that attains *samādhi*, not the Knower of the mind. When the mind becomes steady, when it becomes peaceful even in the midst of activity, that is meditation. To sit behind a closed door controlling the senses alone is *jada*, or inert, *samādhi*.

## SUNDAY, APRIL 4, 1965

*This morning some devotees gathered in the satsang hall. One devotee asked Baba a question.*

**Devotee:** *Since the mind can never be without thoughts, then what thoughts are best?*

**Baba:** Think of the Self. Truly speaking, the only real existence is the *nirvikalpa* state. Thinking of the Self is a means to drive away all other thoughts. It is like removing one thorn with another thorn, and afterward throwing both of them away.

You do experience the *nirvikalpa* state, or a state devoid of thoughts, when you are overcome with anger or struck with wonder. Suddenly, for a fraction of a second, the waves of the mind are absolutely still.

## Monday, April 5, 1965

*In the evening, a woman presented Baba with a book by a famous poet. Baba accepted the book and then spoke about two different kinds of poets.*

### *Divinely Inspired Poets and Ordinary Poets*

**Baba:** There are two types of poets. Some are inspired by God. Others create through their own effort. A divinely inspired poet is one who becomes a poet by the blessing or grace of God. His language emerges as a natural impulse from within and is, therefore, pregnant with meaning. It uplifts the mind of the reader. His work becomes immortal as, for example, *Jñāneshvarī*, the *abhangas* of Tukaram, and *Dāsbodha* by Samartha Ramdas.

The other type of poet turns and twists the words, somehow making them fit into a particular metrical form. Such poems are easily forgotten; the words never touch our hearts.

## Tuesday, April 13, 1965

*This morning Yogacharya Hansraj Yadav came from the Santa Cruz Yoga Institute. Under instructions from the Government of India, he is preparing a systematic report on the condition of all the yoga centers in India. He brought an official questionnaire with him, which he used as the basis of his discussion with Baba about the ashram.*

# The Religion of Yoga

**Yadav:** *Who was the founder of your institution?*

**Baba:** Bhagawan Patanjali. Our knowledge has been handed down to us according to tradition.

**Yadav:** *Which religion or philosophy do you teach or follow?*

**Baba:** Yoga is an aspect of religion. We do not need any other religion. The purpose of Sankhya philosophy is to obtain the knowledge of the supreme Self. *Bhakti* arises from an intense desire to attain God. Meditation is an effort in that direction. Therefore, yoga includes all the religious paths.

**Yadav:** *How is the financial aspect of this institution managed?*

**Baba:** A yogi does not expect any wealth. He lives according to his destiny. Yoga is complete in itself; it is powerful and independent. It can fulfill whatever is required on its own.

**Yadav:** *Are there any specific sources of income for your institution?*

**Baba:** Yes, we have many—the hearts of the devotees. Our wealth is the faith of the devotees.

**Yadav:** *What are the necessary qualifications for being admitted to your institution?*

**Baba:** An intense desire for yoga sadhana. Since every man is an inseparable part of God, it is his birthright to practice yoga, and that is his basic qualification.

**Yadav:** *Can yoga be taught to all or only to a select few?*

**Baba:** It can be taught to everyone. In a way, all the creatures in this world are yogis, because they all observe some discipline in their daily lives. They sit in a particular posture and that is *āsana.* They concentrate on their work and that is *dhyāna,* or meditation. So, knowingly or unknowingly, every individual is qualified to practice yoga.

**Yadav:** *Should the science of yoga be kept secret?*

**Baba:** What is the necessity of keeping it secret? If yoga is taught openly, everyone will benefit, everyone will become inspired. What in yoga needs to be concealed? In books such as Patanjali's *Yoga Sūtras* and *Hathayoga Pradīpikā,* yoga has been clearly explained. Only one who wants to be accorded unjustified importance will speak of concealing it.

**Yadav:** *Do you feel that the traditional methods of yogic practice need to be changed in any way?*

**Baba:** The saints and seers who originally conceived the science of yoga were neither ignorant nor imperfect. Whatever they have expounded is perfect. To change their teachings would amount to considering them imperfect, and such consideration is sheer foolishness.

**Yadav:** *Would you like to suggest any improvements in the manner in which yoga is being taught at present?*

**Baba:** He who wants to teach yoga must himself attain the final stage, the experience of *nirvikalpa samādhi.* After he has obtained the fruit of yogic sadhana, he should then transform the hearts of others by his own shakti, giving them the experience of peace and bliss. Dry or fruitless yoga is of no use.

**Yadav:** *Do you know of any book or individual who has made an innovative or basic contribution in the field of yoga?*

**Baba:** There are the lives of many yogis of the past and, in modern times, there are our experiences. What more is necessary? *Jñāneshvarī* is an excellent book on yoga. Patanjali's *Yogadarshana* is a complete book with no scope for enlargement or improvement.

**Yadav:** *Are you doing any research on yoga?*

**Baba:** There is no need for any new research on yoga, because the science of yoga is perfect as it has been handed down to us.

**Yadav:** *What are you doing in order to spread your work?*

**Baba:** Our work does not require publicity in newspapers, because the changes in seekers who have obtained inner peace automatically spread the fame of our work.

**Yadav:** *Do you have any suggestions as to how the government should spend its resources on propagating yoga so that it will be beneficial to the nation?*

**Baba:** Cultivating a feeling of universal brotherhood is for the real welfare of the people. Without this, nothing else can really benefit them. People's welfare certainly cannot be achieved simply with the help of money.

**Yadav:** *Do you agree with the viewpoint that yoga should be included in the regular school curriculum as a part of physical education?*

**Baba:** Yoga is not physical education; it is a spiritual subject. Nevertheless, the study of yoga certainly improves one's physical well-being.

**Yadav:** *Do you agree that yoga is a method of curing diseases?*

**Baba:** It is a great mistake to associate yoga with disease. There is an independent science called Ayurveda for the treatment of disease.

**Yadav:** *How many sick people are treated here through yoga?*

**Baba:** We do not do anything particularly for healing diseases; however, the purification of the *nāḍīs* through yoga automatically cures any disease a seeker may have.

**Yadav:** *How many patients have been cured here so far?*

**Baba:** We have not kept any statistical data. Nonetheless, many people have benefited. Bhagawan Nityananda cured innumerable patients. For him it was a very simple matter.

**Yadav:** *What medicines do you use for patients?*

**Baba:** Yoga itself is the perfect medicine. The physical rejuvenation brought about by yoga creates the internal medicine.

**Yadav:** *What diseases can be cured by yoga?*

**Baba:** The worst disease—birth and death—is completely cured by yoga.

**Yadav:** *By what means do you teach yoga here?*

**Baba:** We do not require any means other than the practice of yoga.

**Yadav:** *How many assistants do you have to help you in your work?*

**Baba:** A yogi is absolutely independent. He does not require anyone's help.

**Yadav:** *How much time is required for the study of yoga at your institution?*

**Baba:** Yoga has to be practiced regularly until one reaches perfection.

**Yadav:** *How many students are here?*

**Baba:** This question applies to ordinary schools, not an ashram. We are not concerned about numbers, so we do not count how many seekers have joined the institution, nor do we maintain any register for this purpose.

**Yadav:** *What are the age limits for gaining admission as a student? Are classes segregated according to age groups?*

**Baba:** We do not have any age limitations here. Children and the elderly, men and women, all can practice yoga. The time at which a person arrives here is the proper time for him or her to begin the practice of yoga, and everyone is in the same class. We do not segregate seekers into different classes.

**Yadav:** *By what method do you judge who has made progress in yogic sadhana and who is lagging behind?*

**Baba:** A yogi is able to judge this for himself. A Guru who is not hungry for disciples can judge their progress by himself. We do not have any instruments to measure the progress of yoga students, nor do we hold any examinations for them.

**Yadav:** *Can the students of your institution help in propagating the knowledge of yoga?*

**Baba:** Any seeker who has himself reached perfection in yoga will certainly be able to impart his knowledge to others.

## Saturday, April 17, 1965

*During the summer, the ashram is especially crowded with devotees. Tomorrow is the Sunday holiday, and many devotees have come today to spend the weekend. Since Baba's room could not accommodate everyone for satsang, people moved to the ashram lobby. Baba came and sat in their midst. Among the devotees were Virendrakumar Jain and Amrita Bharati, a Sanskrit professor and poetess. The discussion began on the simple nature of Dr. Brahma Prakash, a director of the Atomic Energy Commission and a devotee. Baba then spoke of the similar nature of Professor Bhagwat of Ruia College and described his first meeting with him.*

**Baba:** About eight or nine years ago, Professor Bhagwat came for Nityananda Baba's darshan. He was actually a professor of philosophy, but he was also very knowledgeable in chemistry. He could tell the composition of a sample of earth or ore just by holding it in his hand. He felt, however, that his abilities were not sufficiently appreciated in India, and that he was not receiving the necessary financial assistance to use his talents effectively.

Therefore, he was thinking of emigrating to Russia, hoping that he would receive a better salary and adequate facilities for his chemistry experiments.

Before making his final decision to go, however, he came to Ganeshpuri to seek the advice of Nityananda Baba, but Baba would not give him an answer. Professor Bhagwat then became confused and did not know what course to take. When he again began to ask Baba, someone advised him to seek an answer to his problem from Swami Muktananda, so he came to the Gavdevi Ashram (now Gurudev Siddha Peeth).

In those days, the ashram consisted of only three rooms. The compound walls were not even built. When Professor Bhagwat arrived, I was sitting alone on a stone wall....

## *The Law of Destiny*

**Bhagwat:** *I have been told that a certain swami lives here. Is this his place?*

**Baba:** Yes, it is.

**Bhagwat:** *Is he here?*

**Baba:** Yes.

**Bhagwat:** *I want to see him.*

**Baba:** What is his name?

**Bhagwat:** *Swami Muktananda.*

**Baba:** Everyone calls me by that name.

Professor Bhagwat was completely surprised. He couldn't believe that he had been speaking to Swami Muktananda, but I reassured him and he sat down and narrated his story from beginning to end.

**Baba:** What kind of work are you doing now?

**Bhagwat:** *Sir, I am a professor of philosophy.*

**Baba:** Have you studied this subject merely to teach it to students, or have you studied it for your own benefit as well?

**Bhagwat:** *For my benefit also.*

**Baba:** You may be aware of the law of destiny as explained in our philosophy. Do you accept it?

**Bhagwat:** *Certainly I do.*

**Baba:** Then can you tell me how your difficulties that cannot be overcome in India will be resolved in Russia? Don't you know that everyone's destiny follows him? It cannot be changed. You may live anywhere, you may go to Russia or you may remain in India, but you will only get that which is written in your destiny. Therefore, the duty of a wise man is to remain content wherever he is.

Professor Bhagwat was at last satisfied; his mind became peaceful. He gave up the idea of going to Russia. He knew how to make brass out of copper and other metals. He had a great desire to make gold out of these metals, but that technique is kept secret and is written in a code that can only be deciphered by one who has received the grace of God. Our seers and saints had knowledge not only of the Self, but also about Ayurveda, chemistry, and botany. But ultimately, such knowledge is of no use. This body may be protected and maintained even for thousands of years, but at last a day will come when you will have to leave it.

## *After Merging with Brahman, No Trace of a Siddha's Individuality Remains, Even in Subtle Form*

**Virendrakumar:** *Baba, Tukaram Maharaj is said to have ascended to Vaikuntha in his gross body. How is that possible?*

**Baba:** His devotees may have seen him depart in that form, but where the body is of no use, what could be the point of retaining it? If one can see without eyes, why should one have eyes at all? In the state of complete liberation, neither the gross nor the subtle body is of any use. For a great soul to remain even in the subtle body, let alone in the gross body, is a state of imperfection.

**Virendrakumar:** *Some Siddhas and great beings give darshan even after they have departed from the gross body. How is that possible?*

**Baba:** It does not mean that they exist in the subtle body. The subtle body is also a kind of bondage. If the gross body can be compared to iron handcuffs, the subtle body can be compared to gold handcuffs—but they are both still bindings. If anyone were to say that Nityananda Baba still exists here in a subtle body, it would indicate imperfection in his Siddhahood. You tell me, is the space inside a pot greater, or is the total space greater? Is a drop greater, or is the ocean greater? Why should you want to limit the limitless?

*Chaitanya* has great powers. It can assume any form it chooses. All the forms in the world are God's, so it is a very simple matter for Him to assume the form of Rama, Krishna, or any Siddha or great being. Whatever you see in this world is Consciousness, and it can appear before a devotee in any form according to his faith.

**Virendrakumar:** *Some people claim that a certain sannyāsī is an incarnation of some other saint. Is that true?*

**Baba:** According to the *Bhāgavata Purāna*, there have been only ten incarnations. Whenever a Siddha or a great being comes to this earth for any special purpose, he leaves as soon as his work is completed. Some individuals attain Siddhahood after practicing austerities over many lifetimes. As soon as they have exhausted their *prārabdha karma* (karma that must bear fruit in their current lifetime), they drop their bodies. They do not have to be incarnated again and again, nor is there even any possibility of their being reincarnated.

## The Cosmos Created by God Cannot Be Changed

**Virendrakumar:** *Is it true that after achieving oneness with the universal Self, who is even beyond the mind, we will be capable of effecting changes in the gross world?*

**Baba:** Perhaps such possibilities are discussed, but has anyone ever demonstrated this? Are there any examples of such feats related in the scriptures? On the other hand, we have many examples of individuals attaining Siddhahood that we can see for ourselves. The first is only wishful thinking while the second is a reality. To ensnare devotees and disciples by making false promises for the future is to capitalize on their hopes while to give them a direct, immediate experience is an actual proof in the present.

This cosmos, which has been created by God's will, cannot be changed in any way. No one can transgress the limits set by God. God created everything systematically. Without God's direct order, no one can interfere in His creation. Even a judge must proceed according to the law. The same principle applies to saints. Jnaneshwar was a Siddha with such extraordinary powers that he made a buffalo recite the Vedas and a brick wall move. He had the power of infusing Consciousness into inert or lifeless objects. Even so, he did not attempt to make any changes in this cosmos created by God.

**Amrita Bharati:** *Everyone has really enjoyed today's question-and-answer session.*

**Baba:** If one question is answered, another one will arise. There is no end to it. What is the use of asking so many questions?

**Amrita Bharati:** *If the questions and answers give us joy, why shouldn't we ask questions?*

**Baba:** Because that joy which is dependent on any outside source is artificial. The bliss that arises independently of anything else is the only true bliss.

*Many devotees have come to the ashram over the three-day holiday. Rasik Kadakia and some friends were among them, and today they had an interesting satsang with Baba.*

**Rasik:** *Which sadhana must be practiced to attain God?*

**Baba:** You may do any sadhana that you choose, but it must be a complete one. The sadhana of the Siddhas is complete; therefore, it is advisable to follow the path trodden by them. Yoga, *jñāna*, and *bhakti* are all complete sadhanas created by our seers, who showed these paths to others only after practicing them themselves and attaining perfection.

Give up insisting that only one particular type of sadhana is correct. Follow whichever path you like best, and your sadhana will then be very easy. It is not necessary to follow all the paths simultaneously. In fact, to do so would only increase the likelihood of mental confusion. If you can make the mind thought-free, you will attain the Truth. This thought-free state can be achieved by any of the paths. The ultimate aim of all paths of sadhana is the same, so follow any one path.

Each path includes the other types of sadhana to some extent. For example, in *japa*, or constant remembrance of God, yoga and *jñāna* (knowledge) are included. The posture that you adopt becomes an *āsana*, which is a part of yoga. What is *japa*? To know how to practice it and what its aims and objectives are is *jñāna*. Therefore, *japa*, the repetition of God's name, automatically includes yoga and *jñāna*. The vision of oneness obtained through *bhakti*, the mature, subtle *prajñā* attained through the study of Vedanta, and the *nirvikalpa* state achieved by the practice of yoga are all one and the same. When you achieve perfection in any one type of sadhana, you will have reached the final perfection.

**Rasik:** *What should one think of while doing japa?*

**Baba:** Concentrate your mind on either aspect of God, with form or without form, according to your preference. Even if you think of God as having form and attributes, you will ultimately reach the formless, attributeless Brahman.

The means and the end of *japa* are the same, whereas in other paths they are separate. In yoga, the practice of the eight steps[38] is the means leading to the goal of *nirvikalpa samādhi.* In Vedanta, the means is contemplation on the Self leading to attainment of the *turīya* state. In *japa* sadhana, the aim is to attain the *ajapa* state in which *japa* takes place automatically without any effort or attention.

## *The Mantra Received from the Guru*

**Rasik:** *Which mantra should be used for japa?*

**Baba:** It should be a Siddha mantra, a mantra that Siddhas have used for *japa.* It is best to take a mantra from one who has himself done *japa* with it. Such a mantra is alive, or conscious, and therefore yields better results.

Before doing *japa* of any mantra, one must have a thorough knowledge of it. Such knowledge can be obtained only by taking refuge in a being who knows and has directly experienced that mantra. Without knowledge of the mantra, one cannot appreciate its value.

A Guru once gave the mantra *Shrī Rāma* to his devoted disciple, telling him to keep it secret. The disciple was very pleased and started doing *japa.* The next day he went to bathe in the Ganges, where he came across several other people loudly chanting the same mantra, *Shrī Rāma.* Immediately a doubt arose: "If so many people already know this mantra, what is the need for secrecy? Why did my Guru attach so much importance to this mantra?" Even after pondering this matter for a long time, the disciple could not resolve his doubt. At last, he went back to his Guru and explained his doubt. The Guru told him, "I shall reply to your question later. First, I want you to do something for me." The Guru then handed him a clear, sparkling bead, telling him to ascertain its worth in the bazaar. He ordered, "Go and only ask its price, don't sell it."

The obedient disciple immediately went to the bazaar. First, he asked a vegetable vendor the price of the bead. The vendor replied, "I'll give you two eggplants in exchange for this glass bead." Next, he went to a goldsmith who said, "This is a topaz. I'll pay you one hundred rupees for it." Now the disciple's curiosity was aroused, so he stopped next at a diamond dealer. The dealer exclaimed, "This is a precious gem. It is the biggest diamond I have ever seen. I'll pay you one hundred thousand rupees for it." Finally, the disciple went to the largest diamond dealer in the area, who examined the bead with awe. He said, "O brother, this gem is invaluable! Even if the entire wealth of the country were paid for it, it would not be enough. I would advise you not to sell it." The disciple, being intelligent, immediately understood why his Guru had sent him to find out what the value of the gem was. His doubt cleared up. He returned and fell at the Guru's feet, begging his forgiveness for having raised a doubt about the mantra.

So you see, he who does not know the worth of something cannot appreciate its real value. Even if you already know the mantra that the Guru gives you, it is always more powerful when it is received directly from him.

Mantra *japa* must be done with total faith and love. Repeat it with a concentrated mind and lose yourself in it. A mantra is the sound-form of God and has tremendous power. Look how much power there is in ordinary words. On August 15, 1947, Lord Mountbatten declared, "From today onward, India is a free nation." These words brought about a complete transformation in India. Insulting words immediately create anger in our minds. The sages did not create bad or insulting words, they cannot be found in the scriptures, nor does anyone perform any recitation or repetition of them. Even so, you can see what a powerful effect they have. If even trivial words have such power, then you can imagine the infinite power in God's name. Forget about yourselves and merge with the mantra.

You may choose any path, you may adopt any means of sadhana, but the one basic requirement is that you must completely lose yourself in it. A saint has said:

> You cannot attain God as long as you have not given up the notion of "I" and "mine." One who aspires to a higher state must first give up his own identity.[39]

Radha became so engrossed in Shri Krishna that, as a poet describes it:

> By constantly repeating "Krishna, Krishna," Radha herself became Krishna and began asking her friends, "Where has Radha gone?"[40]

Follow whichever path you prefer, but become one with it. Then you may stay anywhere or you may go anywhere. All external circumstances will appear the same to you. You will see God everywhere, and eventually you will experience that you yourself are God.

Faith has tremendous power. Always contemplate "I am the supreme Brahman" while following the path you like—*bhakti*, meditation, *japa*, or *jñāna*—and you are bound to attain the final goal, the supreme Self. In the *Bhagavad Gītā*, the Lord says:

> An eternal part of Me lives as creatures of the world.[41]

In order to return to our origin, we have to retrace the path by which we came. We have lost our way in the jungle of such thoughts and ideas as "I am so-and-so, my name is such-and-such, I belong to such-and-such a family." We have to turn back and retrace the same steps that led us astray. Our name, family, lineage, home—none of these is different from the supreme Self. Give up the wrong path of limited thinking—"I am so-and-so"—and return to the correct path, *aham brahmāsmi*, "I am the Absolute." This is the essence of all the scriptures.

# See the World as a Form of Brahman

**Rasik:** *A learned professor is currently in Bombay giving discourses to large audiences. He does not believe in idol worship. He teaches that when you see a beautiful idol, you should only observe it without allowing any thoughts about it to arise in the mind.*

**Baba:** By this he means that one should not contemplate its name or form, doesn't he?

**Rasik:** *Yes, the mind should be emptied.*

**Baba:** Instead of having any thoughts about the world, it would be better to perceive it as a form of Brahman. It is the formless that has assumed form. Instead of breaking the idol into pieces to discover that it is made of clay, it would be better to see the clay in the form of the idol. Instead of separating every single thread from a cloth to discover that it is cotton, it would be better to see cotton in the texture, color, and appearance of the cloth.

You should have the vision of the goldsmith, not that of his customer. For the customer, a ring, bangle, and necklace are all different. He evaluates them according to their design and craftsmanship, whereas the goldsmith sees them only as different forms of gold. He sees only how much gold they contain. Similarly, the world can be perceived in two different ways. One viewpoint corresponds to that of the customer, the other to that of the goldsmith. Even after gold has been transformed into a bangle or a ring, it still remains gold. In the same way, Brahman pervades every form of this world.

The vision of a scholar differs from that of a realized being who has experienced the universal Self. You should learn to have the vision of the realized being. See the supreme Brahman everywhere, and try to accept both pleasure and pain with equanimity.

*Today Draupadi asked some questions at satsang.*

## *Riches and Poverty*

**Draupadi:** *Babaji, an Indian swami recently visited America where people asked him, "You give big lectures here, but what is the condition of your own country? How does your philosophy help your poor people?" Swamiji replied, "It makes them wiser."*

**Baba:** If I had been in his place, I would have replied, "Our philosophy enables a man to experience riches even amidst poverty." It is said:

> Knowledge makes a pauper rich, a beggar a king, and a king an emperor. It destroys all sins. It creates dispassion. It makes the ignorant learned, and it makes the learned unconquerable.[42]

**Draupadi:** *But philosophy is not noticeable among the poor. Vivekananda once said, "First give them enough to eat and drink, and then talk to them about philosophy."*

**Baba:** Learn to fully observe and study all aspects of any given situation. Study Vedanta completely. Then you will understand the truth.

Who says that philosophy is nonexistent in the lives of the poor people of our country? In fact, many of our philosophers have lived like ascetics. After seeing this ashram, you may feel that philosophy can spring up only where there is wealth, but that is not so. Saint Kabir was an ordinary weaver. Swami Narasimha of Pandharpur used to wear only a loincloth. He would cover himself with an old, torn blanket and sleep in any available place. He would eat only when offered food. Nonetheless, his inner experience was "I am the Lord of this universe." Another saint,

Bapu Mai, used to wear a ragged loincloth. He would save any alms received during the day and in the evening throw the entire amount into the Chandrabhaga River. Wasn't this an indication of his wealth? Ramakrishna Paramahamsa was also poor, and what wealth did his disciple Vivekananda have? There was never enough food in the house to feed his family. What about Ramana Maharshi? Even Nityananda Baba lived in poverty. There was wealth around him only after he settled down in Ganeshpuri.

Speak to those who are offering their services in this ashram. Many of them come from poor families, but ask them about their present state of mind. Ask them if they suffer from even a slight feeling of poverty. Our philosophy can be realized even amidst material poverty.

SUNDAY, MAY 23, 1965

## *The Mind*

**Kadakia:** *Babaji, can the mind be known by the mind?*

**Baba:** Just as the sun is seen by its own light and it also illuminates the world, the mind can be known by the mind. The mind perceives others and can also perceive itself.

**Kadakia:** *Can the mind be known with the help of yoga?*

**Baba:** Yes, just as a singer who sings with a concentrated mind immediately knows when the rhythm or melody is off, one who meditates or chants with a concentrated mind remains aware of his own mind and notices its every activity.

Why are you chasing the mind? What do you hope to achieve by controlling the mind? Let it do whatever it wants to do. Consider what your aim is. You want to achieve God, don't you? Then obtain knowledge about God. After that, you will understand that you have nothing to do with the mind. Give up thinking about the mind for now.

**Kadakia:** *Many devotees sincerely do sadhana and have exalted experiences. Then why are their minds still so full of thoughts, both good and bad, and why do they still have so much doubt and confusion?*

**Baba:** An ordinary man's mind is constantly immersed in the affairs of this world. Often he is not even aware of his mind. The awareness of the mind arises in the company of saints. The thoughts were there before, but as the mind becomes quiet, the thoughts become more noticeable. Before becoming completely quiet, the mind appears to be more agitated.

**Kadakia:** *How can the ego be eliminated?*

**Baba:** There is only one remedy for all such diseases: seek refuge in God. This entire universe came into being through the expansion of the universal "I." The entire universe is a form of God. There is this difference between our "I" and the "I" of Brahman: if anyone insults us, our anger is aroused, whereas the vibration of the universal "I" created this entire universe.

Make an effort to achieve contentment and peace of mind. This is possible with practice. Your mind can attain satisfaction and contentment because these qualities already exist in it. Contentment destroys ego.

**Kadakia:** *Why does a person become disturbed in adversity despite having faith and devotion?*

**Baba:** This happens because one expects something in return for one's devotion. Have devotion without any expectations.

*Bhimsen Chadha, a devotee of Baba, and his sister Mrs. Kailash Pratap have come from Delhi to spend a few days in the ashram. This morning they had satsang with Baba.*

## *The Gītā Expounds a Synthesis of Paths*

**Bhimsen:** *In some places the Bhagavad Gītā advises a seeker to become a yogi and in other places to become a bhakta. Which is the true path, yoga or bhakti?*

**Baba:** If we do not understand the real meaning of the scriptures, they can act like a boomerang. You have understood just the opposite of the intended meaning, and thus your thinking is misdirected. Learn to synthesize the scriptural verses into a unified whole, and then you will be able to understand each one in its proper perspective.

**Bhimsen:** *Even the power to do this is obtained by the grace of God, isn't it?*

**Baba:** One must also learn to think and discriminate for oneself. Krishna has expounded both *bhakti* and yoga in the *Gītā*, but to whom were the teachings given? To the same person or to different people? They were given only to Arjuna. This indicates that the same seeker has to incorporate both of these paths. Each sadhana automatically includes the other sadhanas. Yoga, *bhakti*, and *jñāna* are not different from one another. It is incorrect to conclude that the *Gītā* gives different teachings in different chapters. Some say the *Gītā* prescribes karma yoga, some say it advises the practice of *rāja yoga*, some say it advocates *jñāna yoga*, while others say it teaches the path of *bhakti*. The truth is that we have to synthesize all of these paths to progress in sadhana and attain God.

**Kailash:** *My mind does not turn toward spirituality. Should I consider this to be God's will? Can we seek God only if He desires it?*

**Baba:** If you want to follow this line of reasoning, then why not apply it in other fields as well? For example, why did you put so much effort into building your house? You should have sat with folded hands saying, "If God so wishes, He will build a house for me." On the contrary, you took so much trouble to draw up the plans, carefully considering each step that had to be taken. You decided to buy land from the government and to take a loan from a bank. You planned how to build the house with the minimum expense while ensuring the maximum possible return in terms of rent, and also to make it useful for you in your old age and for your children later on. In this way, you thought out every detail very carefully before building the house. Isn't that so?

Just as you plan ahead in your mundane affairs, you must give some thought to your spiritual life. Contemplate who you are, where you have come from, where you will go after death, and what the source of true happiness is. Also consider who God is and how you can attain Him. Contemplate these points. Why don't you determine to obtain an experience of God-realization and make a wholehearted effort in that direction?

**Bhimsen:** *Should we consider all saints as the same or different?*

**Baba:** All saints are the same. Despite being in different times and in different places, they all do the same work, just as one tax collector goes and another takes his place and also does the same work. Even different tax collectors in different places do the same work. It is the same with saints.

## Friday, May 28, 1965

*D. M. Parulekar is a lawyer famous throughout Maharashtra for his expertise in land revenue law. During the time of Bhagawan Nityananda, he often came to Ganeshpuri, and on many occasions he also had satsang with Baba Muktananda. Today he has taken time out from his busy schedule to come to the ashram.*

## *The Greatness of Nāma Japa, Repetition of the Lord's Name*

**Parulekar:** *Baba, from time to time the thoughts you express are very original, and I wish to collect them and keep them with me.*

**Baba:** Thoughts are like waves arising on the surface of the sea. Many ripples arise each moment. Which of these are you going to collect?

**Parulekar:** *This is true, but permit me to gather those thought-waves that create joy and inspire the mind, so that they can be preserved.*

**Baba:** I have no objection to it.

**Parulekar:** *Tukaram Maharaj says, "O Vithoba, Your name is the essence, the final essence. Your name is the real essence." Many other saints have also sung in a similar way about the greatness of God's name. Why is remembrance of God's name considered to be the very essence of God?*

**Baba:** You can see the play of the Lord of this universe in God's name, you can see the play of Brahman. The Name is the complete and pure form of God.

**Parulekar:** *How can one realize this?*

**Baba:** This can be understood when you no longer have to make any effort to do *japa* of God's name, when *japa* starts going on automatically in your heart.

**Parulekar:** *How can one know when japa is arising automatically in the heart?*

**Baba:** The inhalation and exhalation that result from the functioning of *prāna* and *apāna* in the body is the naturally occurring internal *japa*. This is the *So'ham japa*. That supreme Self, which pervades every minute atom in this universe, sports in every body as Consciousness in the form of *So'ham*. Tukaram Maharaj says:

> This body is Pandari, Vitthal is my Self, all this is the play of Panduranga.[43]

People think God is somewhere outside themselves, but this is a great illusion. God is within and very close to them. Sundardas says:

> It is with deep frustration that I say my confusion has not come to an end. Such a long time has elapsed, and yet I have still not seen my own Self. O Sundar, forget that you are confused. Once that feeling of confusion goes, only the Self will remain.[44]

The musk deer searches everywhere for the precious musk that is actually within its own navel. It wanders here and there vainly seeking that which it already possesses and ultimately dies of exhaustion. Man, too, because of his own ignorance, has forgotten the Self dwelling within him. There is no difference between him and the musk deer.

**Parulekar:** *What is the cause of a human being's confusion?*

**Baba:** One's confusion or misapprehension is caused by the three *gunas* of *prakriti*. The *Bhagavad Gītā* says:

> O Arjuna, the three *gunas*, or qualities—*sattva, rajas*, and *tamas*—born of *prakriti*, bind the immortal Self to this perishable gross body in which it dwells.[45]

**Parulekar:** *How can this confusion be eliminated?*

**Baba:** By transcending the three *gunas*.

**Parulekar:** *How can that be done?*

**Baba:** It is for this purpose that the saints have given us the simple means of chanting the name of God. They have said, "This mantra *Hare Rāma* is very easy, repeat it constantly." Without devotion to God, life is a waste. Jnaneshwar Maharaj says:

> Without the head, a body becomes a corpse. A river is a terrible chasm without water. Life without Hari is worthless—like the sky without the sun and moon.[46]

The *Bhagavad Gītā* says:

> O Arjuna, I am easily attainable by that steadfast yogi who ceaselessly remembers Me with a one-pointed mind.[47]

In the present time when life is so full of hustle and bustle, only the seeker who keeps firm faith in God and constantly remembers Him can attain God-realization. Saint Tulsidas says:

> Without singing God's name, you cannot swim across the ocean of this world. There can be no doubt about this.[48]

The remembrance of God's name that occurs naturally with each inhalation and exhalation is the best. Kabir says:

> As long as *prāna* is dwelling in this pot (the gross body), continue to chant the name of Rama.[49]

As long as *chaitanya* is dwelling within this body, let your remembrance of God's name be like a steady stream of oil flowing from one vessel to another. The saints have always advised seekers to chant God's name with each incoming breath and each outgoing breath. If you breathe out without chanting God's name, that breath has gone to waste. But remember one thing—if you repeat His name mechanically without any love or devotion in your heart, its spiritual value is zero. In fact, the love in the devotee's heart is considered to be more important than the actual chanting of God's name. Saint Tulsidas says:

> The devotee who repeats God's name naturally and with love enjoys happiness and also sanctifies his dwelling place.[50]

**Parulekar:** *Are there different types of nāma japa?*

**Baba:** Yes, there are three main types. The first is verbal or *vaikharī japa*, which is done by chanting with the tongue in a low voice. The second type is *upāmshu japa*, which is done with the movement of the tongue and lips, but the sound is inaudible. The third is *mānasa japa*, or mental *japa*, which is subtle and done only in the mind. Even more subtle and superior to that is the *ajapa-japa* that goes on constantly within you day and night. It is said:

> Sit quietly in seclusion without any thoughts. Watch attentively. Then what do you discover? You discover the following words: *So'ham, So'ham.*[51]

**Parulekar:** *Why are there these different types of japa?*

**Baba:** Because of the varying degrees of worthiness of different seekers. Each one is given the type of *japa* that he is capable of doing. Seekers differ in their worthiness, and they are advised accordingly to observe the sadhana or spiritual discipline that suits them.

**Parulekar:** *Yes, I understand, but I still have one doubt. If the Name is a form of God, why is it necessary to receive it from a Guru? Isn't it possible to attain God by repeating any mantra that one selects for himself?*

**Baba:** A mantra that has not been imparted by a Guru lacks the power to grant God-realization. A mantra received from the Guru is called a mantra with seed. It has been sown with the seed of shakti, which has the power to carry one to God-realization.

**Parulekar:** *By what means does the Guru impart the mantra?*

**Baba:** The *sadguru* has realized the Self; he is an embodiment of the supreme Self. He enters into the disciple through his ears in the form of the mantra and infuses divine energy into his body. A mantra given by the Guru is charged with divine energy and takes the seeker along the path to God-realization.

**Parulekar:** *But in the modern world, how can a seeker find a real sadguru? Many sincere seekers have had bitter experiences at the hands of impostors posing under the guise of saints and sannyāsīs. As a result, many people are hesitant to accept anyone as a Guru. The mind, however, cannot rest in peace until a Guru is found. In such circumstances, how can a real Guru be recognized?*

**Baba:** One obtains a Guru as a result of merits earned in previous lives and also by pursuing sadhana sincerely in this lifetime. One must continue one's sadhana and attend satsang with saints. By persisting in such practices, one will certainly be able to recognize a real Guru for oneself.

**Parulekar:** *What are the signs of a true Guru?*

**Baba:** A true Guru is beyond any signs. No one is fit to become a Guru until he has totally merged himself with the supreme Self. A true Guru is beyond any attributes or signs. The only sign is his being established in the *nirvikalpa* state.

**Parulekar:** *Please tell me something more about the Guru.*

**Baba:** The Guru is like a potmaker. Just as a potter shapes the clay, the Guru lays the foundation for his disciple's spiritual life in a systematic way. The Guru is the doctor who cures the disease of transmigration from birth to death and death to birth. He uproots all the undesirable characteristics from his disciple, such as the six inner enemies (lust, anger, pride, jealousy, ignorance, and greed), all kinds of sorrows, agitations, and also physical illnesses. Not only this, but he also nourishes the disciple with the nectar of love, consolidates his faith and devotion, and strengthens his knowledge. Just as a skillful boatman easily ferries his passengers across a river, a *sadguru* takes his disciple safely across this sea of painful transmigratory existence and sets him on the opposite bank of supreme bliss.

*Dr. Jivanlal Amin, a professor of ancient Indian culture at a college in Khambat, has come today after hearing about the glories of Baba and the ashram while in Pondicherry. He is a sincere seeker with a keen interest in spirituality and he asked Baba many questions.*

## *Have Faith in the Inner Self*

**Amin:** *It is my personal experience that a seeker does not feel satisfied until his sadhana is properly guided by a Guru. What should he do until he meets a true and able spiritual teacher? How can he make progress on his own in sadhana?*

**Baba:** Even though the individual soul is a part of the universal Soul, he considers himself to be limited. This is his ignorance. Since the individual soul is not different from God, he has the capacity to know everything, cognize everything, so until he receives guidance from a Guru, he must surrender himself completely to his own inner Self and concentrate his mind on God.

He must keep faith in the inner Self, because it possesses divine shakti. Consider, for example, the dream state. This state is neither true nor false. Since it rests in the Self, it cannot be said to be false. A simple, straightforward old man named Mudanna lives and works in the ashram. He had a vision in a dream which revealed that Bhagawan Nityananda was going to leave his body within two days, and that's what happened. Everyone has the power to know and understand the truth. An individual may not be aware of this inner power, but this shakti is ever present, lying dormant in his Self.

Tukaram Maharaj received mantra initiation in a dream. The *antarātman* (inner Self) exists in every human being. The great Vedantic statement *aham brahmāsmi*, "I am the Absolute," is true. If a dream turns out to be false, it is due to some limitation of the mind superimposed on the Self.

**Amin:** *What attitude should one have toward whatever is seen or heard during meditation?*

**Baba:** It is just a mental play; it is like watching a movie. You should use these experiences to cultivate the attitude of being a witness of the mind.

**Amin:** *I have heard that many seekers meet their Guru in his bodily form and receive instructions despite being miles away from him. Is this possible?*

**Baba:** Such experiences are necessary as long as a disciple has not completely merged with his Guru. A seeker will get such experiences from time to time according to his needs.

**Amin:** *How can sadhana be made easy?*

**Baba:** Whichever sadhana you do will be easy if it is according to your liking. The aim of every kind of sadhana is the same, but for sadhana to become simple and effortless, it must come directly from the Guru. A man who used to teach yoga once came here. He was suffering from a severe headache despite having tried many remedies to alleviate it. I told him to stop doing *japa.* He followed my advice and his trouble soon vanished. He had not understood that the headache was caused by the vibration of the mantra in his head.

Many obstacles may arise like this in a self-prescribed sadhana because of limitations in your understanding. It is most improper for such imperfect seekers to become gurus. It is harmful for both the guru and the disciple. How can such a guru understand others when he doesn't even understand himself? Only one who knows oneself can also know others.

*In today's discussion, Baba explained the secret of mantra to Kailash Pratap.*

## *The Secret of Mantra*

**Kailash:** *Which mantra should I use for japa, the one I am already using or the one you have given me?*

**Baba:** Which mantra are you now using?

**Kailash:** *A swami gave me his Guru's name as a mantra.*

**Baba:** The term "Guru mantra" does not mean the mantra of the Guru's name, but the mantra that is received from the Guru. The Guru gives that mantra to others by which he himself has achieved liberation. This is called the Guru mantra. I give to others the mantra that enabled me to become Shiva. I would not give my Guru's name as a mantra, such as *Om Namo Nityānanda*, nor would I ever advise anyone to meditate on my form. I tell everyone to meditate on his own inner Self.

Just as one king can easily meet another king or one rich man can make friends with another rich man, you can attain Shiva by becoming like Shiva yourself. This means that you will attain God when you realize "I am God." The four great statements of Vedanta[52] proclaim the same vision.

You should remember That which is our root cause. Remembrance of this root cause is the real mantra. The mantra is that which enables you to realize your own true nature. Only that mantra is called a Siddha mantra or *chaitanya* mantra which unites the seeker with the deity of the mantra. The mantra, repeater of the mantra, and the mantra deity are all one. The *Shiva Sūtra Vimarshinī* says:

> If the mantra and the seeker who repeats it remain separate, it will never bear any fruit.[53]

This is the secret of mantra. The *Mahānirvāna Tantra* says:

> The seeker who does not know the meaning of the mantra and does not understand that it is conscious will not attain any result, even after repeating it a million times.[54]

## SATURDAY, JUNE 5, 1965

*A group of devotees who come to the ashram regularly on Saturday was sitting with Baba in the satsang hall. Barrister Nain was also present.*

**Nain:** *Baba, what is the special feature of kundalinī yoga?*

**Baba:** The yoga in which all yogas are automatically included is called *kundalinī yoga, mahāyoga*, or *gurukripā*. It can be obtained only by the grace of a Siddha Guru. Its special feature is that it enables one to reach the supreme Self quickly and easily, whereas to perfect the eight stages set forth in Patanjali's *Yoga Sūtras* takes a very long time.

**Nain:** *In order to obtain perfection in this yoga, is it necessary to be a sthitaprajña (one who is established in steady wisdom unaffected by the pairs of opposites)?*

**Baba:** No, it is not necessary to be a *sthitaprajña* right from the beginning, but after taking up this path, a seeker acquires these qualities naturally.

*Anthony Brook arrived at eight thirty this morning for a ten-day stay. Around* 10:00 *A.M. Baba met the devotees who had gathered in the satsang hall. Anthony asked Baba some questions.*

## *Transcend the Pairs of Opposites*

**Anthony:** *It seems that divine Consciousness is about to descend upon earth. What would you say about this?*

**Baba:** When cunning and cruelty become dominant in the world, divine Consciousness has to make itself felt; God has to assume a form in order to manifest on earth. For example, the Lord had to appear on earth in the form of Rama to vanquish the cruel *rākshasa* Ravana; He had to come as Krishna to destroy the evil Kamsa. People turn toward God when life becomes unbearable for them. They remember God after undergoing extreme misery, poverty, and hardship.

**Anthony:** *When will such an incarnation come? I personally feel that the time is not too far away. Do you also feel that a time will come when misery and upheaval will cease to exist in this world?*

**Baba:** Yes, certainly such a time will come. The life of the world is like a wheel. The pairs of opposites always exist within it. Pleasure and pain, wealth and poverty, love and hatred, day and night keep rotating like the spokes of a wheel. After one, its opposite is sure to follow. Thus after misery, happiness will certainly return to this world.

There was once a great saint who had a peculiar habit. Whenever his devotees would talk about their pleasure or pain, the saint would reply, "This, too, will not last." If someone said to him, "My wife has run away, my sons do not obey me, I have no money, and I am undergoing very bad times," he would always respond, "This, too, will not last." If anyone were to say,

"Maharaj, I am very happy. Due to God's grace, I hav two lakh (200,000) rupees," he would also tell him, ' will not last."

A reading of the Puranas gives one the feeling that exist when everybody was happy. Today it appears as if nothing but misery and sorrow prevail everywhere, but it is this very misery and pain that compel God to come to the earth. If you read the life stories of saints and great beings, you will notice that it was only after undergoing tremendous suffering that they turned toward God and ultimately attained Him.

Knowing this, a wise, discriminating person must go beyond the opposites of pleasure and pain, and understand the Truth. This world is a play of God; it is His own sport. God makes use of people like Ravana as His reason for incarnating on earth. The world proceeds according to the will of God. Understanding this, a wise, intelligent person of discrimination will consider it to be all the same whether death comes from an atom bomb explosion, a gunshot, a disease, or the natural deterioration of a body that has reached the end of its life span. A wise person never sees disharmony anywhere in the world.

## Wednesday, June 9, 1965

*Anthony came to the satsang hall at seven this morning. Shortly thereafter, Baba arrived and their discussion resumed.*

### *Penetrate to the Root Cause of Thoughts*

**Anthony:** *This morning while sitting in the veranda of your meditation room, my body became perfectly still and I felt as if my mind had become absolutely peaceful.*

**Baba:** This is precisely the experience of the awakening of *kundalinī*. To have a peaceful mind is an exalted experience. It is not necessary to have only certain types of experiences due to the awakening of *kundalinī*. A variety of experiences may occur. Steadiness of mind, peace, and bliss are some of the most significant experiences.

**Anthony:** *But at other times when I sit for meditation, my mind keeps wandering here and there. What should I do to keep it under control?*

**Baba:** An excellent method is to watch where the mind goes. Discover who watches the mind and remain steady in Him.

Clouds in the sky keep assuming different shapes and sizes, and then disperse. Where do they go? No one knows. They are born in the sky and dissolve back into the sky. Waves in the sea arise on the surface of the water and again subside. In the same way, thoughts come up and vanish again. Try to discover from where these thoughts arise; understand their origin. The source from which they originate is the Self. This Self has no connection with the mind. It only functions as the Witness. The Self is uninvolved and untainted. Just as the sea and the sky remain unaffected despite the waves or clouds arising within them, similarly, our inner Self always remains unaffected despite the thoughts in the mind.

Therefore, maintain Witness-consciousness; establish yourself in Him who is the Witness of all thoughts. When you become steady in Him, the desire to cling to your thoughts will cease and you will understand that all this is a play of the inner Self. That witness state is the abode of God, the source of the light of Truth.

Vedanta describes the four states of the individual soul: the waking, dream, deep-sleep, and *turīya* states. Upon attaining the fourth state, *turīya*, pleasure and pain lose their effect and the world appears to be only a dream. Then you experience, "I am the Absolute." Just as man experiences his body from head to toe as "I am this," God experiences this entire universe as "I am this; this is My body." After God-realization you too will feel, "I am not only this body, but I am this entire world." Then you will be unaware of either pleasure or pain anywhere in this world.

## The Function of Saints

If the son of a rich man were to start feeling impoverished, and if he were to complain to you, "I am very poor," you would naturally explain to him, "Your belief is wrong. You are the son of a wealthy man. You have plenty of money. How can you be poor?" The function of a saint in relation to ordinary people is similar. Saints are here to explain: "You are not an individual soul; you are Shiva." In other words, they are here to make human beings aware of their real nature, and so dissolve their individuality and merge it into the totality, just as a drop merges into the ocean.

**Anthony:** *Your words are absolutely true. People cling to their individuality so tenaciously that they will not give it up for any price. God is always ready with outstretched arms to embrace them.*

**Baba:** Yes, that is so. I shall tell you about Gurudev Bhagawan Nityananda. It would be very difficult to find another great *avadhūta* like him in this world. He was a great being, a great Siddha. His main work was to make man transcend his jivahood and become established in the awareness of his Shivahood. Thousands of people used to come to him, but I hardly saw one among them who prayed to attain Shivahood. On the other hand, I saw many, nay, innumerable people asking for such mundane things as sons, money, business, or employment, or to be cured from disease.

This reminds me of a story. There was a shepherd named Ramzan who used to take his sheep to graze in the jungle every day. While tending them, he would eat whatever he could cook for himself. One day the king of that area was hunting in the jungle and lost his way. While wandering about he came across Ramzan. The king was hungry, so he asked Ramzan for some food. Even though the food that Ramzan served him was not properly cooked, it tasted delicious to the famished king, and he was very pleased with Ramzan. Before departing, the king gave him a note and told him, "Whenever you are in need of anything, come to me."

Ramzan's son was to be married, so a few days later he went to the city to sell some sheep, and then he went to see the king. The king welcomed him warmly and served him a meal of several delicious dishes. Then the king reminded him, "You can ask for anything you want." Ramzan liked to chew tobacco so he asked for some lime to mix with it. All that the wretched fellow asked for was lime! He was not even aware of the king's infinite wealth and power. Similarly, very few people knew about the divine power of Gurudev.

**Anthony:** *Can man be turned toward God by seeing miracles performed?*

**Baba:** This world is full of the miracles of God: the sun and moon rise and set at fixed times; the seasons come in rotation; birds fly in the sky and fish live in water; from a small drop of semen, a beautiful, adult human body consisting of bones, muscles, flesh, and blood is formed. Aren't these miracles? When such great wonders already exist, the display of some trivial miracle is like holding a candle before the sun. I don't mean to say that miracles are false. The mind can acquire almost limitless power through concentration. To perform miracles is not something great. But what is the purpose of such things? It is more likely that worldly-minded people would follow a wrong path because of such miracles. It is not the function of saints to perform miracles.

## *The Source of True Happiness*

**Anthony:** *Last night while meditating, I felt something happening behind my mouth and nose, and there was also a loud noise.*

**Baba:** This was caused by your *prāna* moving along the

*sushumnā.* Listen, it sounded like this, didn't it? *(Baba demonstrated the kriyā.)*

**Anthony:** *Yes, it was exactly like that.*

**Baba:** This *kriyā* clears the *sushumnā* channel, enabling the *prāna* to travel toward the *sahasrāra.* Opening the disciple's *sushumnā* is the Guru's main function. This is the true miracle, not those worthless magic shows that are put on merely to entertain others. Whatever is to be gained is gained through the *sushumnā.* True happiness is experienced when the *prāna* dwells in the *sushumnā.* That is Chiti Shakti, the elixir of life. It is because of this Chiti Shakti that the body is alive, beautiful, and attractive. If you were to cut away a piece of the body's flesh and put it aside, it would soon start stinking. The body becomes ugly when this Chiti Shakti leaves it at the time of death. Even the dead person's near and dear ones are anxious to remove his corpse from the house. This is the quality and effect of that shakti. It is verily the omnipresent God dwelling inside and outside us.

This wonderful shakti dwells in the *sushumnā.* It is this power that sees through the eyes, smells through the nose, and hears through the ears. It is with this shakti that we perform all our activities and work in this world.

According to the Yoga Shastras, the body contains seventy-two million *nādīs.* Just as a tree is kept alive by water and supported by the earth, the body is supported and given life (*chaitanya*) by the *prāna shakti,* which keeps moving through these *nādīs.* This verily is *kundalinī shakti,* which is the pranic energy as well as the knowing faculty. It pervades every inch of the body down to the smallest cell; it energizes the entire body. Just as a king's power extends throughout his kingdom even though he himself remains seated on the throne, *kundalinī shakti* pervades the entire body in the form of *prāna.*

This Kundalini, this Chiti Shakti, is either turned outward or turned inward. When turned outward, She causes one to perform worldly activities; when She turns inward, She turns one toward God.

When a seeker's Shakti is awakened by the grace of the Guru, She makes him or her indrawn and gives the experience of knowledge and bliss. As She travels up the *sushumnā* toward the *sahasrāra*, the seeker has various kinds of experiences. There was a time when I did not believe in the existence of Svargaloka (heaven) and Chandraloka (realm of the moon). I considered happiness as heaven and suffering as hell, but when I actually saw Chandraloka and Siddhaloka in meditation, I had to admit that, just as this earth exists, other worlds also exist in this universe. A seeker may experience flowers being showered on his or her head. At that time, the golden lotus that falls from Siddhaloka may also be seen, indicating that the seeker has become a Siddha.

After attaining that state, one certainly experiences happiness in pleasurable experiences, but one also experiences happiness in painful and adverse circumstances. No desire for attaining anything remains. Even so, wealth and *riddhi-siddhis* come to a Siddha on their own. Just as ordinary people go to a saint and he becomes their support, *riddhi-siddhis* go to a saint and beg him for powers. The *siddhis* are ever at the command of the Siddhas to fulfill their work.

The main goal of human life is to become merged in the *sahasrāra*. Then one understands that this world will always remain the same as it is now. The Guru's main function is to enable a seeker to achieve this state. No one can ever snatch away this wealth bestowed by the Guru. You may have all the pleasures of worldly life, but if you do not have this spiritual wealth, you are poor and miserable.

## *The Greatness of Man*

**Anthony:** *How can one come to understand that a human being is great?*

**Baba:** Everyone sees one's own reflection in the world. A virtuous person sees virtue everywhere, while a wicked person sees vice everywhere. Hence, if one considers himself to be God, one will certainly have an experience of God. Once you have realized God, you will easily understand that the *jīvātman*, or the individual soul, is the same as *vishvātman*, or the universal Soul.

Again and again we remember our essential nature. It is for this reason that a person constantly desires to be happier and greater than others. It is God who is searching for God, but the individual does not know this truth. Because our true state is Godhood, we experience *Shivo'ham*, "I am Shiva," *So'ham*, "I am That," or *ana'l-haqq*, "I am God," in meditation. All realized beings proclaim the same truth that your true identity is "I am the Absolute."

A Sufi saint says, "When I had some understanding, I realized I am not this body; I am that light which has expanded in the form of this universe." Therefore, you must always maintain the understanding "I belong to Him, He is mine, I am He, and He exists in everyone." It is that God principle alone that exists everywhere in this world, pervading everything equally. Nowhere is it bigger or smaller, more or less, better or worse. It is That which exists in brooks and rivers, in the sky and the mountains, in stones and grass, in birds and animals, and also in human beings. It can take innumerable different forms. We call this principle Parabrahman. Just as a tree grows out of a seed, this world evolves out of Parabrahman.

Just as the tree is in the seed in a subtle form, the world is in Parabrahman and His qualities are seen in the world. The nature of Parabrahman is *sacchidānanda*; therefore, this world also manifests these three qualities. Every individual has this divine essence.

The principle "See God in each other" states the same truth. Everyone should behave toward others keeping this fully in mind. If this were imbibed by everyone, there would be no more wars, unrest, or chaos. Just as a father has a feeling of "my"-ness toward his sons and grandsons, God has a feeling of "my"-ness toward this world. For Him, all are equal. And just as a father does not like his sons to fight among themselves, God does not like us to fight among ourselves. God is pained by wars; therefore, we must resolve our differences and live together peacefully in this world.

**Anthony:** *Can God experience pain?*

**Baba:** This is only a manner of speaking. From the viewpoint of the individual, it can be expressed in this way. Pain, hardship, and sorrow cannot even come near the state of Godhood.

**Anthony:** *How can one develop the attitude of seeing God in others?*

**Baba:** This can be achieved by expanding and developing your inner shakti, because everything is within you. A human being is great, but out of ignorance he considers himself small. He wastes a lot of valuable time in pursuing many useless sense pleasures. He does not understand that human life is a very precious gift. If a person were to try sincerely, he could attain a state in which he could have whatever he wished.

**Anthony:** *If a great leader were to start spreading the message "See God in each other," would it achieve the same result?*

**Baba:** Yes. In a way, we are already practicing this. For example, when we meet someone, we greet him with folded hands saying, "*Namo Nārāyan,*" "*Shalom Aleichem,*" or we shake hands and say, "Good morning." What is the meaning behind these greetings? When you visit someone's home, he rises and welcomes you and honors you by offering water, tea, and snacks. To some extent, this is a practical application of the motto "See God in each other," but we do not perceive it as such. If you propagate this message, it would certainly be implemented by some, and an appreciation for it would be nurtured in others.

THURSDAY, JUNE 10, 1965

## *The Four States of the Individual Soul*

**Anthony:** *Last night I slept soundly. I was not even aware of falling* *asleep. When I woke up in the morning, I felt that I had just gone to sleep and awakened again. Was it all right for me to have slept, or should I have controlled sleep and sat for meditation?*

**Baba:** What did you experience in sleep?

**Anthony:** *I was not aware of anything, and I had no experience except a feeling of happiness and contentment. In the morning I felt quite refreshed.*

**Baba:** From this, it is clear that true happiness is where there are no activities and that is right within you. Happiness lies in detachment, not in involvement. To explain it, I'll give you an example.

A businessman spends his entire day attending to his business and making money. By evening, he is exhausted and returns home. He finishes his dinner, removes his expensive clothes, and gets ready for bed. At that time, if his secretary comes to discuss even a transaction involving two lakhs (200,000) rupees, the businessman would say, "I am not prepared to listen to anything now." Without even talking to his wife and children, he falls fast asleep. When he gets up in the morning, he feels refreshed. Then he calls his secretary and happily resumes his business.

What does this example illustrate? It illustrates that happiness is in that state in which there are no activities or thoughts regarding one's family, children, business, costly clothes, ornaments, or money; that is, in a state of detachment. A patient asks a doctor for a medicine to help him sleep, because without sleep he feels unwell. The first question a doctor asks a patient is whether or not he slept well the previous night. This indicates that there is great happiness in sleep, which is a state free from worries and thoughts.

To understand this, one must have knowledge of the four states of the individual soul: waking, dream, deep sleep, and *turīya.* In the waking state, the individual soul enjoys the external world with the help of the nineteen instruments: the five organs of action, the five organs of knowledge, the five *prānas*, and the four aspects of the *antahkarana*, which are mind, intellect, subconscious mind, and ego. The individual soul who enjoys the waking state is the size of the gross body. His color is red; his dwelling place is in the eyes. In meditation, he is seen in the form of a red light. The *Māndūkya Upanishad* refers to the individual soul in this state as *vaishvānara.*

In the dream state, the individual soul experiences the subtle world with a subtle body the size of a thumb. His color is white and his dwelling place is in the heart. In meditation, he is seen as a thumb-sized white light. The individual soul in this state is known as *taijasa.*

In the deep-sleep state, the individual soul experiences happiness in the causal body, which is the size of a fingertip. His color is black and he dwells between the eyebrows. In meditation, he is seen in the form of a small black light. The individual soul in this state is known as *prajñā.*

After these, the last, or fourth state, is called *turīya.* In this state, supreme bliss is experienced. It is seen in meditation as a small blue dot, which is the supracausal body. Its dwelling place is the *sahasrāra.* In meditation, yogis see it as a shining Blue Pearl, which appears and disappears. Sometimes it is also seen with the eyes open. In fact, what is within is seen outside. This Blue Pearl is verily Parabrahman as well as Kundalini. The Self is realized within this Blue Pearl. It is your true form.

These four bodies of the individual soul are seen in the form of lights during meditation. Bhartrihari says:

> Blessed are those who meditate in mountain caves and see these lights.[55]

As you go from one body into the next, from one state into the next, your happiness keeps increasing. Compared to the waking and dream states, there is more happiness in deep sleep, and the bliss experienced in the *turīya* state is greater still; it cannot be described in words. This is absolutely true. Everyone can experience it, and today you had such an experience. Isn't that so?

The fulfillment of human life lies in obtaining this bliss. In its absence, birds and beasts are superior to human beings. How beautiful the peacock is! The *chakora* bird drinks only the nectar of moonlight, and it is difficult to find anything comparable to the sweet, melodious tune of the cuckoo. The elephant has the strength of a hundred men. A person looks attractive and vibrant only after obtaining inner bliss. Gurudev Nityananda used to wear only a loincloth; even so, his devotees found him so attractive that they would gaze at him for hours and still their hunger for the sight of him could not be satisfied. What attracted them was the inner bliss that radiated from him in all directions.

Many people ask me, "Can we also achieve that state? Would it be possible for us to do sadhana?" I tell them, it is easier to become God than to become a doctor or an engineer, because to become a doctor, you have to fill yourself with everything from outside, whereas God is already within you. You have to attain what is already attained. Then knowledge becomes complete and perfect. After obtaining That, nothing else remains to be obtained. Ask any doctor, "Have you mastered all the knowledge available in your field?" He will reply, "I still have a lot more to learn. There is no end to it." On the other hand, after knowing God, nothing else remains to be known.

## FRIDAY, JUNE 11, 1965

*This morning at nine o'clock, the devotees gathered in the hall for satsang with Baba.*

**Anthony:** *Babaji, will such a time come when the medium of language will become unnecessary and people will be able to communicate automatically through the mind?*

**Baba:** In ancient times it was so, and such a time can also come again. There is a place in the heart where you can obtain knowledge of all the objects in this world. By being in that place, one can see all other countries and all other worlds while sitting right here.

## *Give Up the Temptation for Siddhis*

**Anthony:** *Can we also know about the pleasure and pain of others?*

**Baba:** Yes, we can know that, too. The mind has such power. An unusual story about a painter appeared in a publication called *Imprint.* While painting on the second floor of a building, he fell and remained unconscious for two or three days. When he regained consciousness, he had acquired the power to know everything about others. He told everything about whoever came before him. This incident demonstrates that the mind does possess such powers.

But I ask you, what do you gain from knowing about the pleasure and pain of others? True happiness and bliss are beyond such *siddhis.* One who wants to reach Delhi quickly will not stop off at any of the small intervening stations en route but will go directly to Delhi. Similarly, the seeker whose aim is God-realization will be indifferent to trivial *siddhis.*

It is not difficult to know the thoughts of others or to perform magic. Magic can be done by mental concentration; it is the creation of the mind. It has no connection with your sadhana for liberation, because God is beyond the realm of the mind. God has created this entire universe by the will power of His mind. Therefore, since we are a part of the very same God, what can be beyond the capabilities of our minds? Actually, it is like creating a world of the mind within the outer world.

What is the use of creating another magical world of wonders within this world? Both of these worlds are limited and perishable. God is eternal, changeless, and uninvolved in any worldly activities. Matsyendranath taught his disciple Gorakhnath:

> A person may learn to vanish and reappear, he may travel in an instant to places of pilgrimage like Mathura and Kashi, he may walk on water, whatever he says may come

true, still he is not a perfect being; he cannot be called the Guru's son (disciple).[56]

A person may display any number of wonderful phenomena; he may make the impossible possible; even so, if he has not merged with Brahman, he is still imperfect.

It is easy to learn how to perform magic, but it requires a lot of effort to attain the *nirvikalpa* state. There will be no real peace until the mind is free of all thoughts. One who wants to achieve permanent peace must give up the desire for insignificant *siddhis* and go far beyond them. One has to achieve the kind of high *siddhi* by which Prahlad made the Lord manifest in the form of Narasimha (the man-lion, Vishnu in His fourth incarnation), and by which the *gopīs* made Him dance within the compounds of their houses.

If you attach importance to the outer world, it will constantly be reflected in your mind, where it will create agitations. By giving importance to the world, your mind acquires the qualities of the world. So drive away all thoughts from the mind. Make it void.

*At half-past three in the afternoon, the devotees again assembled in the hall. Also present were Professor Jivanji Amin from Cambay and Virendrakumar Jain.*

**Amin:** *While pursuing meditation, how long does it take for a seeker's desires to be completely destroyed?*

**Baba:** It takes time for desires to be completely eradicated. Sometimes during meditation, desires become even stronger, and one may see hell or a naked man or woman.

**Amin:** *Yes, I asked this question because I see such things.*

**Baba:** This is a good sign. It indicates that your sadhana is progressing very well. Sometimes your sexual desire may become intense. This happens because the impressions and desires of many past lives lying dormant in the *sushumnā* gain strength and are activated. After this, you will see lights of red, white, black, and blue, and then you will see the Blue Pearl. You will have the darshan of gods, goddesses, and Gurudev. Such phenomena are seen in the *tandra* state, which is between waking and deep sleep. In this state you feel as if you are asleep, but internal *kriyās* are taking place.

The sadhana of shaktipat belongs to the *siddhamārga* (the path of the Siddhas). The seeker's shakti is awakened by the grace of a Siddha. After that, sadhana progresses automatically and the seeker has many experiences. This is not a topic for discussion, discourse, or philosophy. It can be understood only through personal experience. You can be sure that anyone who poses as a Guru and tries to guide others without knowing anything about this is not a realized being.

> Without knowledge of the red, white, black, and blue lights (seen in meditation), the illiterate and the learned are equal.[57]

**Amin:** *I am no longer getting the same kind of meditation as when I first came here.*

**Baba:** That state will return slowly. Early in your sadhana, you may have an experience of *samādhi*, the *nirvikalpa* state, or realization of Truth. Later on, as you continue your sadhana, this state recurs at the appropriate time and eventually remains steadily and permanently with you.

## *The State of Jīvanmukti*

**Virendrakumar:** *What is the state known as jīvanmukti?*

**Baba:** That person who performs all activities while knowing in his heart of hearts that all the world is like a dream is called a *jīvanmukta* (realized being). The poet-saint Sundardas expresses this in verse form:

> Outwardly, he performs his worldly activities; inwardly, it is all a dream to him.[58]

Such beings are free from the restrictions of rules and regulations. Rituals, rites, injunctions, and prohibitions are meant for those who are living in ignorance. They are similar to the codes of law that are intended to regulate the activities of the common people. But the one who has realized the Truth transcends all such limitations. It is said, "Codes (of conduct) can howl like jackals in the forest only till the mighty lion of Vedanta starts to roar."

For those who have not realized the Truth, scriptural injunctions and prohibitions are necessary. After realization, they become superfluous. The remainder of a *jīvanmukta's* life unfolds according to destiny. It is said in *Vichāra Sāgara*:

> A dry leaf is blown along with wind, going wherever the wind carries it. A *jīvanmukta* acts in this world in the same way.[59]

This means that the actions of a *jīvanmukta* are like roasted seeds, which do not sprout or bear fruit. Such a being is seen to be acting in the world, but does not have to undergo the fruits of his actions.

The scriptures do not mention anything about the *jīvanmukta's* way of life. We perceive and know the world by name, form, and the qualities of objects, whereas the *jīvanmukta* perceives it according to its reality. A saint named Shukadevji once lived in Icchalkunjeri, a town in Karnataka. One day the tribal jungle dwellers fed him fish and gave him wine to drink. As a result of this incident, the townspeople became very critical of him. Finally, a *jñānī* admonished them, saying, "Saints are beyond all these things. Put some shit in front of him and see what he does with it." The townspeople did as he suggested, and the saint ate the shit as well! So a *jīvanmukta* may live in any way, he may eat and drink anything, but his mind is always steady and indifferent.

The *jīvanmuktas'* ways of living are varied. One may live in poverty and act like a simpleton, while another may live like a king with pomp and show. The *Vichāra Sāgara* says:

> Some move about in chariots or on elephants and stroll in gardens, some lack even footwear and wander barefoot. Some wear different clothes, sleep in beautiful beds, and enjoy the best of everything in the world, while others wander with empty stomachs in mountains and caves and sleep on stones. Thousands of devotees flock to them and worship them, while some worldly people consider them degraded and condemn them.[60]

There was a *rāja yoga* saint named Amritrai who lived like a king. He sat on a silver swing and slept on a silk mattress in a canopied bed. He ate rich food from silver plates and had many servants. But he used to preach to others, "Why do you want to gather wealth? Why do you need a bungalow to live in? Why do you crave rich and tasty food? It is better to beg for food. It is better to live in a hut and wear rags!"

Upon hearing this, one *sādhu* got enraged. He challenged Amritrai, saying, "Why are you entangled in all this? If you really believe what you say, come along with me. We will go on foot and beg for our food, eating whatever we get." Amritrai immediately agreed to go with him, and they set out on a pilgrimage.

The next day as they were passing through a jungle, the *sādhu* told Amritrai to sit under a tree while he went to fetch some water. Nearby, a king had set up his camp. When it was time for the king to have his meal, he ordered his servants to go out and find a saint and invite him for lunch. The servants came across Amritrai and brought him to the king. The king seated him on a silk mattress, supported him with pillows, and served him delicious food on a silver plate, while the queen sat beside him and fanned him. At this point, the *sādhu* arrived on the scene in search of Amritrai. He was stunned to find him again surrounded by luxury, and he prostrated at his feet.

The moral of this story is that no one can escape his destiny. The inner state of a *jīvanmukta*, however, is unchanging in all situations and circumstances. One who sees everything as Brahman cannot be bound by any karma, nor can the actions of such a being be limited by such factors as time and place.

SATURDAY, JUNE 12, 1965

## *Repaying One's Debt to the Guru*

**Anthony:** *Baba, you have given me so much and you want to give me more, but how can I become worthy of receiving your grace?*

**Baba:** The debt you incur by receiving something from the Guru can be repaid only by achieving oneness with the Guru. The scriptures say that the devotee and the Lord, the disciple and the Guru, the means and the object of sadhana are inseparable; they are one. When the disciple is completely merged with the Guru, the devotee with the Lord, or the means of sadhana with its object, then Truth is attained. Then one feels, "O Lord! You are me and I am You. It is You who pervades everywhere." After this, the disciple's sense of separate existence, or the idea of "I"-ness and "my"-ness, vanishes. As long as "I"-ness and "my"-ness remain, there is a separate existence. As long as a drop identifies with its drop-ness, it remains a drop, but when it identifies with and merges into the ocean, it becomes the ocean itself. When a person experiences "I am everywhere," then the sun, the moon, and the stars rise and set within him. Rama Tirtha says:

> The wind is blowing within me, within me, within me.
> The river is flowing within me, within me, within me.[61]

Sundardas says:

> Although there are trees of different varieties and names, the forest is one. Although there are lakes, wells, and rivers, water is always the same. Although there are

> different sources of light such as a candle flame and a lamp, the light is the same. O Sundar! Get rid of the idea of differences. It is Brahman alone who is manifesting as the play of this world.[62]

This is the truth. After realizing this, one feels that one is the Lord of the entire world. Whatever is seen in the world is the Self. The Upanishads proclaim, "Thou art That." The world has emerged from the supreme Self.

**Anthony:** *Has the human body also come out of the Self?*

**Baba:** Yes. You will understand this when you know what the body is. One's body is formed from the semen of his father. Semen is formed from food. Thus the body is said to consist of food.

> Beings are born out of food, those who are born grow by food, and into food they merge.[63]

Food comes out of the earth. Food is earth, so the body is also earth. The body, which consists of food, comes out of the earth, grows on the earth, and in the end, it is either buried in the earth or its burnt ashes return to the earth.

Earth has emerged from water. To understand this, fill a glass with water and leave it undisturbed. After a while, you will find that some particles of earth have settled to the bottom. Water is the cause, and earth is the effect. Water, in turn, has emerged from fire. The summer heat forms clouds that produce rain. Also, when it is hot, we perspire. Fire has taken birth from air. The damp clothes we hang outside are dried by the element of fire in the air. Where there is space, there is air. Wherever there is space in the body, there is also air. This is everyone's experience. This space is ether. Air emerges from ether, and ether arises from the Self.

> Ether was born from the Self.[64]

The Self is the root cause of everything. The sequence is from the Self to ether, air, fire, water, earth, food, and then the gross body. The same steps are retraced and everything returns to the Self. Therefore, the entire world is full of Consciousness. One is a realized being who understands, "I pervade the entire world in the form of Consciousness."

The world appears to you according to your own outlook. Sundardas says:

> If you are given to differentiating, duality is what you will see.
> But if you look at it as a unity, all This is only One.
> When you look at the sun, it is one whole blaze.
> But if you look at its rays, their colors are so many.[65]

If you have the outlook that the world is Brahman, you will see Brahman everywhere. This entire world of objects, mundane activities, science, and politics—everything is full of Consciousness. Nothing but Consciousness exists. This entire world is its play. Sundardas says:

> The one who sees is Brahman,
> the one who hears is Brahman,
> the speech coming from the tongue is Brahman.
> The earth, water, fire, air, ether,
> and all creatures are Brahman.
> The beginning, the middle,
> and the end are all Brahman.
> Understand without a doubt
> that everything is Brahman.
> O Sundar, the *jñānī* understands
> that the knower, known, and knowledge
> are all verily Brahman.[66]

If you maintain this vision of the world, you will see Swami Muktananda everywhere. You yourself will also become That. True religion is to understand things as they are in reality, and non-religion is to understand the opposite. If a person understands that he himself is the all-pervading supreme Brahman, that truly is religion, but if he feels "I am so-and-so and this is mine," then that is non-religion. To make distinctions between one human being and another is also contrary to religion. A seeker who maintains a divisive attitude achieves nothing in this world or in the next world.

> One who sees many in this world goes from death to death.[67]

**Anthony:** *It is true that one must attain unity with the Guru, but isn't it also true that one must keep a respectful distance from him?*

**Baba:** Cut through the separateness and attain oneness, but at the same time, worship the Guru as if he were separate. You should have a feeling of oneness in your heart, but outwardly you have to maintain some distance. You should not, for example, go and sit on the Guru's chair just because you feel that you are one with him. You must have the humility and modesty of a disciple in your daily behavior. With respect to the gross body, you should behave as his servant, while at the same time understanding that your Self is not different from the Guru. This is true worship of the Guru.

## Bestowing Grace on a Multitude of People

**Anthony:** *Can grace be bestowed on many people gathered together?*

**Baba:** Yes, certainly, but all cannot receive grace that way. Not everyone is worthy of receiving it. Just as a student must first pass his high school examinations before he can enter college, similarly, a person must be worthy before he is able to receive grace.

**Anthony:** *Since the last World War, the entire world has been filled with sorrow and pain. Will this pain purify the world and bring about a transformation?*

**Baba:** For the world to be purified and transformed, God Himself must will it. Only God possesses the power to influence the mind of the people and bring about a mass transformation.

Such work is dependent on God's will and is carried out by an incarnation of God.

## Sunday, June 13, 1965

*The devotees gathered in the ashram courtyard at ten o'clock this morning.*

**Anthony:** *How can one understand that God is manifest everywhere in the world?*

**Baba:** This cannot be understood until you have achieved Self-realization. Until then, you must have faith in the words of the scriptures. You will understand the truth for yourself at the proper time. For example, when a six-year-old boy asks his father "How do you grow a moustache?" his father will reply, "When you are sixteen years old, you will find out for yourself." Similarly, when you achieve God-realization, your understanding will be: "This entire world is my play." As long as your mind is turned outward, absorbed in the activities of the world, you will not be able to comprehend this secret.

**Anthony:** *Baba, when will an era of righteousness dawn in this world?*

**Baba:** We can speak of one era with respect to the individual and another with respect to the world as a whole. With respect to the individual, a period of righteousness has begun when a person turns toward God. Nothing can be said about such an era with regard to the world as a whole.

After realizing the Truth, such questions will not arise at all. Our present question-and-answer session is taking place only in a dream. Whatever you are saying now is in that dream. After the true awakening and divine realization, you will have no more questions.

# The Waking and Dream States Are Both False

**Anthony:** *Can the Truth be understood only after Brahman has awakened from His dream?*

**Baba:** Brahman is always awake. It is you who are dreaming, so it is you who must wake up. In this connection, listen to a story about Ashtavakra and King Janaka.

King Janaka once dreamed that another king had attacked his kingdom, defeated him, and banished him from his former domain. After this happened, he wandered unknown and uncared for, with nothing to eat or drink. Nearing the point of starvation, he went into a cornfield and began to eat an ear of corn. The farmer, seeing the trespasser, went running up to him and started beating him. As soon as the farmer struck him with his wooden stick, King Janaka awoke. He immediately saw that he was lying on his usual soft, scented bed with a retinue of servants fanning him. He again closed his eyes and saw the same scene: the corn, the farmer, and the stick. Thus, he was seeing two entirely different scenes, one with his eyes closed and another with his eyes open. The king was perplexed by these two contradictory appearances and started wondering which of the two was true. Was the dream true or was the waking state true? The king could not decide for himself, so he assembled all the learned scholars, sages, and saints of his kingdom and asked them, "Is this true or is that true?" but nobody could answer him. The king got annoyed. Considering them to be wise and learned, he had supported them for such a long time, and yet none among them could answer his question. Finally, he put all of them under arrest.

One of the imprisoned scholars had a son who was about sixteen or seventeen years old. The son was ugly, and everyone called him Ashtavakra, meaning that his body was bent in eight places. He was a great *jñānī*. Hearing of his father's predicament, he went to the king's court to get him released. When Ashtavakra arrived, everyone started laughing at him. Standing in the center of the court, Ashtavakra also started laughing heartily. The king asked him, "Why are you laughing? We have a reason to laugh, but I don't see any reason for your laughter. Can you answer my question?"

Ashtavakra replied, "First, you tell me the reason for your laughter, then I shall tell you the reason for mine."

The king said, "I laughed because a crooked, lame fellow like you has come to answer the question that has baffled even great learned scholars. Now, tell me, why did you laugh?"

Ashtavakra said, "I have heard that King Janaka is a great *jñānī*, but now I find that you are a *jñānī* not of the Self but only of the flesh. You do not see the Self; you see only the gross body. That is why I laughed." Hearing this, the king and his entire court became silent.

Ashtavakra then told the king, "I have come here to answer your question on behalf of my father. Ask me the question." The king related the whole story and asked him which was true, this or that. Ashtavakra replied, "Just as this is false, that is also false. Like the dream, the waking state is also unreal. The state in which we are dwelling appears to be true while it lasts; however, when we enter the next state, the one we have just left appears to have been false. In the waking state, the dream state appears to be false, while in the dream state, the waking state does not exist. The waking state is also just a long dream. Come out of the waking and dream states and enter into the *turīya* state. Only then will you understand what the Truth is."

## TUESDAY, JUNE 15, 1965

*Today's satsang started at about ten o'clock in the morning.*

**Anthony:** *Baba, can you tell me how many and what kinds of previous births I have had?*

**Baba:** I could tell you about your past lives, but you would think it was purely my imagination. How could you determine whether what I told you was true or false? What proof would you have? Give up such futile inquiries. What is gained by knowing your previous lives? On the contrary, sometimes such knowledge is painful. Instead of knowing about your past five, ten, or fifteen lives, attain realization and recognize yourself as the supreme Self. Then you yourself will be able to know about all your previous lives. Sometimes during meditation, you may see your past lives like a movie. I once saw in meditation that I had been a king in one of my past lives.

WEDNESDAY, JUNE 16, 1965

## *Marriage Is Not Opposed to God-Realization*

**Anthony:** *Is the world an obstacle on the path to Self-realization?*

**Baba:** This world was created by God. How can it be contrary to Him? If the relationship between husband and wife is proper, it will not become an obstacle to one's sadhana, but deviation from one's dharma is harmful. Attachment is the obstacle for a seeker, not the world.

**Anthony:** *If a man wants to realize God, can he still marry?*

**Baba:** One who really wants to attain God does not need anything of this world. Why should one who wants to drink nectar drink from brooks or rivers? We have created the institution of marriage to provide love, happiness, and bliss, but when bliss manifests independently from within, what is the necessity of seeking it outside?

**Anthony:** *What about the responsibilities of a man who is already married?*

**Baba:** Marriage is not opposed to God-realization. After marriage, the husband and wife have responsibilities toward each other and toward the children, but you must not think that the entire burden is to be carried by you alone. God, who has created this world, looks after all beings. Everyone must live out their destiny. However, you should not think that there is no one besides you to take care of others. So many women in this world have lost their husbands, so many men have lost their wives, many fathers have no sons, and many sons have no fathers. So many infants lose their mothers soon after birth. Nonetheless, they all go on living. Everyone's life goes according to their destiny.

**Anthony:** *Is it true that a celibate progresses faster on the path to realization?*

**Baba:** A celibate can concentrate better and also develops greater powers of comprehension. For this reason, the scriptures advise students to observe celibacy during the period of their education.

**Anthony:** *I would like to bring my family here, but they are independent. I can't compel them.*

**Baba:** Quite true. Spirituality is not for everyone. Very few tread the path of sadhana. In the *Bhagavad Gītā*, Lord Krishna tells Arjuna:

> Only one in a thousand will make the effort to realize the Self.[68]

In those days, one in a thousand may have been available, but in the present times such a person can scarcely be found even among ten thousand. Not everyone can tread the path to Self-realization. It is essential that the person be worthy of it.

**Anthony:** *America and England have made valuable contributions to the material progress of the world. Will they be able to make any contributions in the field of spirituality?*

**Baba:** They will be able to accomplish something in the field of spirituality only after turning away from materialism.

**Anthony:** *My daughter has a keen interest in the material world.*

**Baba:** It sometimes happens that a person with a keen interest in the material world turns toward spirituality and develops an equally keen interest in and love for God.

**Anthony:** *One of my friends in England has asked for your blessings. What shall I tell him?*

**Baba:** Tell him to remain intoxicated in devotion to God. No harm can befall one who makes friends with God. The *Bhagavad Gītā* says:

> Wherever Lord Krishna, the Lord of yoga, and Arjuna, the wielder of the bow, are, I know that prosperity, victory, glory, and righteousness abide there.[69]

## FRIDAY, JUNE 18, 1965

*Anthony again had satsang with Baba this evening.*

**Anthony:** *Would you explain the importance of Guru Purnima?*

**Baba:** One's own feeling is more important than the particular day, time, or object. In the daily life of Indian culture, certain days such as the full-moon day, the new-moon day, certain weekdays, and days of the lunar cycle are associated with God. Among these are Guru Purnima, Sharad Purnima, Shravan Purnima, Vatasavitri, and Holi. In India, you will see that even trees such as the pipal, banyan, *ashoka*, and *tulsī* are worshiped as gods and goddesses. Wherever you go in India, you will find many temples. Such is our Indian culture. All this may appear meaningless to you, but this religion was not established by fools. It is the great Truth that we have inherited from our ancient, all-knowing saints and seers. This religion was established after deep contemplation. By living this religion, one sees God everywhere. God is omnipresent. He exists in rivers, seas, mountains, trees, leaves, everything. Therefore, we worship all these things. This it eventually takes a person from the outer world toward his own inner world; it makes the mind indrawn and gives one a clear experience that God dwells within him as well.

## Saturday, June 19, 1965

*Since Anthony planned to leave today, satsang took place early in the morning.*

**Anthony:** *Doesn't God ever get tired of creating such a vast universe?*

**Baba:** God never gets tired. From your viewpoint, the universe appears immense, but for God it is like a game. He creates this entire universe in a fraction of a second. We are so entangled in the mundane world that we cannot comprehend this. After the final realization, you too will feel that the universe is quite small.

## *Two Types of Divine Incarnations*

**Anthony:** *Who would be considered an incarnation of God?*

**Baba:** He who comes to this earth to perform some special work that cannot be carried out by any ordinary mortal is called an incarnation. There are no obstacles in his work, and even if obstacles do arise, he overcomes them successfully because his shakti can never be defeated. He doesn't have to beg for help or depend upon anyone else to fulfill his mission. He has the capacity "to do, to undo, or to do otherwise." Some wicked beings may try to harass him, but they can never defeat him. An incarnation has the power to rule over all. No one can rule over him.

There are two types of incarnations. The first are special incarnations of God such as Rama, Krishna, and Narasimha. The alled messengers of God. Lord Vyasa and a are said to have been God's messengers.

e, Buddhism became widespread in India. It was a who counteracted its influence and reestablished gion from Kanyakumari to the Himalayas with no t but that of his *yogadanda.*[70] Even while the great Sufi saint Mansur Mastana was being hanged, he kept proclaiming to the very end, "*Anā'l-haqq*, I am God." Shams Tabrizi was condemned by his enemies, who decided to remove his skin, but he himself stripped the skin off his body and threw it at them. Such great beings have achieved oneness with God and are never defeated at the hands of this world. No sorrow can touch them, as they are always intoxicated with supreme bliss. Jnaneshwar endured harassment by so many people, but he did not yield. When the bullet was fired at Gandhiji, he did not cry "O God, save me! I am dying!" The last words he uttered were "O Rama."

Mirabai drank poison without any harm. Prahlad, a staunch devotee of God, saw God everywhere: in fire, in the sea, and even in poison. His father made many attempts to kill him, but they all failed. God Himself had to manifest for such a sincere devotee. If a devotee of God possesses so much power, you can imagine how much power must reside in an incarnation of God Himself.

**Anthony:** *Some incarnations of the Lord such as Shri Rama, Shri Krishna, and Buddha were kings. Can God's messengers also be kings?*

**Baba:** Saints and yogis are considered to be kings. For this reason they are called *rāja yogis.* The king wields his external power while the yogi uses his divine inner power. The king sits on a lion-shaped throne while the yogi sits on a lion skin, because the lion is recognized as the king of beasts. The lion is not a cruel beast; it never preys on anyone without a reason.

**Anthony:** *Can animals subsequently obtain human birth?*

**Baba:** If a person performs cruel actions, the next birth will be as an animal, but the Self remains the same. The Self never changes. By observing the behavior of some animals, we easily conclude that they were human beings in their prev life. Those animals who live with and enjoy the company of human beings obtain a human birth in their next life. Some animals seem to be more intelligent than humans. The Queen of Jhansi's horse was able to recognize her enemy immediately. Such animals are very close to being human. Either they have been human beings in their previous life, or they are going to have a human body in their next birth.

## *The Self Has No Birth*

**Anthony:** *What is the Self? What are its attributes? How is it born?*

**Baba:** The Self is the Self. There is nothing similar to it in this world that I could point to for the sake of comparison. The Self is never born and never dies. When man does not even understand such a simple matter as how and when the body contracts disease, then how can he understand such a great mystery as the Self? The Self is all-pervading. It is without birth and death. It is only from our perspective that it appears to be born and to die. The relationship between the Self and the body can be compared to that between the body and the clothes worn on it. You may change your clothes, but your body remains as it is; it does not change. Similarly, the Self remains as it is; it is only the body that changes. This means that it is the body that is born and the body that dies.

The subject you want to discuss is extremely profound. This science is even more abstruse than that of atomic energy or aeronautics. In order to understand it, you must study Vedanta. After such study, you will consider your initial questions to be like those asked by children.

According to the Vedantic philosophy of nondualism, the Self is only one, even though there are many bodies. Although we see as many suns as the number of mirrors we place in the rays of the sun, the sun remains only one and is unaffected by its reflections. We cannot destroy it by breaking the mirrors. The sun remains as it is. This is known as the principle of *bimba prati-bimba*, original object and its reflection. You may think you are seeing many selves, but the truth is that the Self is only one. The Self is as it is. It never undergoes any change.

By what power does this body function? From where does this power come? Who experiences pleasure and pain? After pondering these questions, you will understand that the Self is beyond the body, mind, intellect, and even the subconscious mind. The body is gross; it is inert. It derives consciousness from the Self, and then it perceives objects through the sense organs. It sees with the eyes, hears with the ears, and speaks with the tongue. Although the Self pervades the entire body, it is not attached to it. It remains ever pure and God-like. It neither takes birth nor does it die.

**Anthony:** *Can one understand this through meditation?*

**Baba:** Along with meditation, you must practice contemplation. You must combine meditation and knowledge, then it becomes easier to understand the Truth.

## Wednesday, June 30, 1965

*Today a Parsi woman named Daulat Dalal came to the ashram to invite Baba to the annual function of a yoga school she attends.*

**Daulat:** *Since our Guru became a paramahamsa two years ago, he is not able to leave the ashram. All the ashram's teaching work is done by Mataji.*

**Baba:** Who told you that a *paramahamsa* cannot go out anywhere? The scriptures say that a *paramahamsa* is beyond rules and regulations as to what he should and should not do. There is nothing that he must or must not do. What kind of sadhana are you doing?

**Daulat:** *I am practicing concentration on chidākāsha (the space of Consciousness).*

**Baba:** How?

**Daulat:** *Our Guru has initiated us and taught us chidākāsha dhāranā (concentration on chidākāsha). We concentrate our minds on the tip of the nose, and take our meditation from the ājñā chakra to the sahasrāra. From there, we take the meditation through the sushumnā to the mūlādhāra, passing through the anāhata, manipūra, and other chakras on the way. We also call this practice kriyā yoga.*

**Baba:** Initiation is a divine act by which the disciple's deficiencies and imperfections are removed, and he is taken to perfection. Imperfection means ignorance, or limitation. Perfection means Godhood, or knowledge. Just as a patient's blood is automatically purified when the doctor administers an injection, similarly, the Guru makes the shakti flow through the disciple, initiating a spontaneous process of purification. The body contracts disease through indiscriminate conduct and regains health through proper conduct. An impure disciple becomes pure by the touch of the Guru. True *kriyā yoga* is that in which *kriyās* take place spontaneously without any special effort.

## SATURDAY, JULY 3, 1965

*A young seeker named Mohan who is from a new ashram near Bombay has been staying here for the past few days. His guru has initiated him into brahmachārya and given him saffron clothes. Currently he is interested in investigating other ashrams for himself.*

# A True Disciple Can Recognize a True Guru

**Mohan:** *How can one recognize a true Guru?*

**Baba:** If you possess true discipleship, you will be able to recognize a true Guru. How many years have you been staying at your ashram?

**Mohan:** *Two and a half years.*

**Baba:** How much have you changed during that time?

**Mohan:** *How can I judge for myself how much I have changed?*

**Baba:** Recognize him to be a Guru by staying in whose company, even for a short while, you notice some change or transformation in yourself. Know him to be a Guru who can change you by taking you to a new and higher state from the one in which you first went to him. Do not think that your inner state has changed just because you are wearing these saffron clothes. Your life changes when you take to true discipleship. Nothing happens just by dressing like a *sannyāsī.* What did you do for two and a half years in the ashram?

**Mohan:** *I studied Vedanta. I read books on Vedanta such as Āmabodha, Vivekachūdāmani, and others.*

**Baba:** Can you explain the Vedantic teachings to me? Which sadhana is indicated in Vedanta for Self-realization?

**Mohan:** *How can I explain it just like that? Kindly tell me.*

**Baba:** There is no means for attaining the Self, because Vedanta says that the Self is always with you. We have to liberate that which is already liberated; we have to attain that which is already attained.

*Yesterday Dr. Brahma Prakash and his wife came to the ashram. Dr. Brahma Prakash is a director of the Bhabha Atomic Research Centre at Trombay.*

## Knowledge of the Truth Resolves All Doubts

**Brahma Prakash:** *Swamiji, please explain to me when, how, and by whom this world was created.*

**Baba:** God created this world. He willed "I am One, let Me become many," and the world came into existence. He is both the efficient and material cause of this world. Just as a spider spins its web from the secretion of its own saliva and later withdraws it back into itself, this world has emerged from God and will ultimately merge back into God.

Don't ponder over when, how, and for what reason this world came into being. Try to get liberated from it. I shall give you an analogy. Once, two men with a desire to eat mangoes entered a mango orchard. According to the rules of the place, no one was allowed to stay in the orchard after twelve noon. One of the men immediately climbed up a tree and ate as many mangoes as he could. The other man started looking around the orchard, analyzing the different kinds of mangoes growing there, their breed, shape, place of origin, the age of the trees, and so on. He became so involved in his inquiry that soon the allotted time came to an end, and he had to leave the orchard without having eaten even one mango. Recognize God and attain Him before your time is up. Then all your questions will be automatically answered. Become God yourself, and then you will feel that this entire world is your own.

**Brahma Prakash:** *How can one recognize God?*

**Baba:** There are four different means of gaining knowledge of a particular subject. They are: one, direct perception; two, inference; three, scriptural statements; and four, statements of reliable people. To accept the statement of an expert in a certain subject about which we ourselves are ignorant is trustworthy evidence. For example, I would accept completely any statement you make about atomic energy, because I believe that you know the subject thoroughly. Similarly, you should accept whatever I say with regard to spirituality, because that is my area of expertise.

At the moment of birth, you did not know who your mother or your father was. As you grew up and gained understanding, you came to know from the statements of your parents and others that a particular person was your mother and a particular person was your father. You accepted what you were told; you simply had to believe it. Similarly, you should accept the statements of Mother Shruti (the scriptures) and all the saints that your true Father is the supreme Self.

> O man! Don't you remember? You are a part of Brahman. Your family and ancestors are Brahman. Your descendants will also be Brahman.[71]

You must believe in the words of Mother Shruti. Only the Mother can tell you who your true Father is.

You can also know about God by direct experience, but you will first have to spend a few years doing sadhana, just as one has to spend several years of systematic study to become a scientist or a doctor. If you invite me to see your laboratory, I will certainly come and see everything directly for myself. Likewise, I am inviting you to come to my laboratory (the ashram). Like you, I am an expert in my subject, and I shall give you a direct experience of it.

According to Vedantic teachings, the world was never created; it exists only because of our delusion. Just as in darkness a rope may appear to be a snake, the mind superimposes the world on Parabrahman (the supreme Reality). The world appears to be real before acquiring true knowledge. After gaining true understanding, it is seen as false. When the roaming mind becomes still, the Truth can be understood. The world exists for the ignorant because it is visible to the gross eyes, but when the subtle eyes of a *jñānī* are opened, the gross world vanishes for him. How then can he answer any questions with regard to that world?

Once a man was sleeping on a chair beside Swami Rama Tirtha. The man saw a tiger with two horns in a dream, and he woke up screaming with terror. He asked Swamiji, "Where did the tiger with two horns go?" Of course, Swamiji had not seen the tiger, so what reply could he give? If two people are on the same level, then a real discussion can take place between them; otherwise, their dialogue is like the conversation between persons listening to two different radio stations. If one were to ask the other, "Which raga is this?" the other one would reply, "What raga are you talking about? I'm listening to the news."

Take another example. The experience of a crow is opposite to that of an owl. The crow sees the sun while the owl does not. What then can they say to each other about the sun? If they try to say anything, they will only start quarreling. It is better if they don't open a discussion at all. If the owl became a crow, or if the crow became an owl, then they could have a meaningful discussion.

Everyone experiences the three states of waking, dream, and deep sleep. There is a higher fourth state beyond these three known as *turīya.* It is the state of Self-realization. After entering that state, this world appears like a dream. Try to achieve the *turīya* state by realizing the Self. Then all your questions will be answered.

## FRIDAY, SEPTEMBER 3, 1965

*Rasik Kadakia arrived this morning with some friends.*

**Rasik:** *Can yogis take on the destiny of others?*

**Baba:** Yes, yogis possess such power, but in general they would not do so, because it is not in harmony with the laws of destiny.

The one who performs an action must undergo its consequences. If one person is guilty, does the judge give the punishment to someone else?

## SUNDAY, SEPTEMBER 26, 1965

*Recently Ram Chadda has been reading the English translation of Jñāneshvarī. At eight-thirty this morning, he approached Baba with the book. Many other devotees were also present.*

### The Greatness of Jnaneshwar Maharaj

**Chadda:** *Babaji, I am amazed by Jnaneshwar Maharaj's ability to write a wonderful book like Jñāneshvarī at the young age of fifteen.*

**Baba:** I, too, used to wonder how a young boy could expound such profound knowledge. From a literary standpoint, the language and poetry excels even that of Sanskrit works. It is a very beautiful book.

Omniscience is a state, and Jnaneshwar Maharaj was omniscient. I'll tell you how I came to believe this. One of the *Shiva Sūtras* says "Knowledge is bondage." The *Shiva Sūtras* is a book about Kashmir Shaivism. Seven or eight hundred years ago, the *Shiva Sūtras* was available only in the form of a handwritten manuscript. In those days there was no possibility of its being printed, and Jnaneshwar never went to Kashmir. It was not possible for a fifteen-year-old boy to make such a journey. Nevertheless, it is obvious from the books written by him that he knew about the *Shiva Sūtras.* For example, he says in *Amritānubhava*: "Lord Shiva says in His *Shiva Sūtras* that knowledge is bondage." How could Jnaneshwar have come to know about this *sūtra*? This indicates that he was omniscient. He also writes about shaktipat in the sixth chapter of *Jñāneshvarī.*

Jnaneshwar was a supremely powerful yogi. His teachings uplifted even Changdev, who was by far his elder. Changdev had an amazing control over tigers and snakes, but don't we see this even in the circus today? Jnaneshwar, on the other hand, had the power to infuse life into inert objects. He made a wall move. His greatness was such that even old people addressed him as Guru Maharaj. He took live *samādhi.*

Jnaneshwar's *Chāngdev Pasashthī* contains the highest philosophy. While writing *Jñāneshvarī,* he had to contain himself within the framework of the original verses of the *Bhagavad Gītā,* but he had no such restrictions while writing *Pasashthī,* in which his writing is even more profound than Vedanta.

# Chapter Five

# 1966

*At today's satsang, Hariyantlal Sonawala, his wife, Pushpa, Suryakant Jhaveri, and Vasuben Mapara were present.*

## *Do Not Renounce Family Life; Renounce the Idea of "I" and "Mine"*

**Hariyantlal:** *Babaji, please give some advice to those of us who lead a family life, so that we may progress in spirituality while at the same time attending to our family responsibilities.*

**Baba:** What is worldly life? Man and wife, children, home, and business do not constitute worldly life. The worldly life consists of ideas of "I" and "mine" and "you" and "yours." That is the world. As long as there are vibrations of the world in the mind, pleasure and pain—which arise as a reaction to these vibrations—will persist. So learn to forget the world. The world exists only because of the mind. Mentally give it up. There is happiness only in mental renunciation. This is proved by our own direct experience. At night you put aside all your costly belongings such as expensive clothes, the latest wristwatch imported from Germany, and ornaments. You give them up and then go to sleep. At that time, you forget all those things. Not only that, you forget about your business too. Only after doing so can you fall into a deep sleep where you experience peace and happiness. When you wake up, you feel refreshed. This common experience proves that man finds happiness not in thinking about the world, but in forgetting it. Achieve such a thought-free state of mind in the waking state too. Practice detachment; that is where true happiness lies.

To attain God, it is not necessary to give up anything outwardly. Even if you want to renounce, you will not be able to unless it is your destiny. You cannot escape from your destiny by running away from it, nor can you get something not destined by asking for it. Therefore, let the world remain as it is. Just try to forget it and go within. Sit quietly and meditate, reflect on the Self, try to become God yourself. See the God who dwells within you, know and understand Him. Learn to properly use the objects, situations, and events of this world.

I would advise you to set aside some time each day for contemplation of God, just as you reserve some time for eating, drinking, sleeping, going to clubs, dramas, and movies. If you practice this regularly, after a while you will experience that its pleasant effect remains with you throughout the day. The remembrance of God's name is so powerful that it enables a person to himself become God. This does not happen in worldly life. No one becomes an engineer or a doctor simply by remembering the name of an engineer or a doctor!

Try to cultivate faith and an attitude of surrender to God. Insure yourself with God so that, when the need arises, He will be there to protect you. Insurance policies are taken out for financial protection against unforeseen accidents and damage. A wealthy man once insured himself for a huge sum. When someone threatened to murder him, his insurance company made prompt arrangements for his protection. Therefore, keep in mind the Lord's words:

> Give up all other dharmas and seek refuge in Me alone.[1]

Insure yourself with God and He will say:

> Grieve not; I shall liberate you from all sins and defects.[2]

## WEDNESDAY, JANUARY 12, 1966

*Today Dr. Vora and some other devotees were sitting with Baba.*

## A Seeker's Experiences During Meditation Are His Own

**Dr. Vora:** *I don't have any experiences during meditation. Won't you give me some?*

**Baba:** Many people tell me the same thing. Put aside the thought of experiences; sit quietly for meditation.

A seeker's experiences are his own. Saints and sages are only an apparent cause. You experience your own Self; I don't give experiences to anyone. The light is within you; it is neither in Vaikuntha nor in heaven. You will see it right within yourself. Whatever is in God is also in you. God pervades your body just as the seven elements do. You can certainly experience this, but you must make a devoted effort. That which you want to realize is within you. I can see that. If you cannot, what can I do about it? I can only show you the path—you have to walk on it and do sadhana. Whether you have experiences or not is a matter of your own good fortune. See, this woman started having experiences as soon as she arrived here. One more point: What is an experience? A seeker must know the exact meaning of experience, because many times it so happens that a seeker has experiences but does not recognize them as such.

### SUNDAY, FEBRUARY 6, 1966

*Yesterday a Frenchman named Manuel Densil came to the ashram with Ram Chadda. During today's satsang, he asked Baba some questions.*

**Manuel:** *Is it true that beings living in other worlds have progressed further than beings in this world?*

**Baba:** Yes. It is true that beings in Siddhaloka and Indraloka have many *riddhis* and *siddhis*. They have the power to curse and to bless. Compared to man, those beings are stronger, more energetic, and more brilliant. They enjoy eternal youth without any disease, misery, or disappointment, but as soon as their merits are exhausted, they have to come back to this earth.

Remember, though, that compared to the infinite universal Being, all other worlds are limited and imperfect. Whatever can be measured is considered to be ultimately limited. Just as India, America, and England are limited in size, these other worlds also have boundaries, or limits. In the end, they are limited, and it is said, "Whatever is limited is perishable."

**Manuel:** *What is your opinion about flying saucers?*

**Baba:** Have you seen them?

**Manuel:** *A pit created by the descent of one can be seen in Mexico.*

**Baba:** The aircraft of other worlds are mantra aircrafts. They do not need any gasoline, engines, or pilots, but are operated by the mind. This means that they are mental instruments.

**Manuel:** *Yes, I remember having read something like that somewhere.*

**Baba:** Before you read any book, try to find out about the background of its author. The writings of our saints and sages don't contain even a trace of fiction. They had no reason to write anything false. They had no desires or ambitions and lived simple lives full of *tapasyā*. In modern times, books are written to earn money and fame or for propaganda; it was not so in those days. Therefore, the saints and sages had no reason to write anything false. Due to the power of their *tapasyā*, true knowledge was awakened in them. They wrote with the help of supramental powers. Their writings are not based on dry research, poetic imagination, or bookish learning. The sages came to know of the existence of Chandraloka and Suryaloka (the realms of the moon and the sun). Not only that, but they had a direct experience of these

realms during meditation. It was only then that they ac‹
their existence and told others about them.

Sometimes we also have the experience of seeing som
in a dream that later comes true. There is a place within us, by reaching which nothing remains unknown. The scriptures are based on knowledge obtained from this source.

**Manuel:** *Is it true that there are some great beings in the Himalayas who are not visible, but who sometimes come down and move in society?*

**Baba:** Such great beings are not only in the Himalayas, but also at other Siddha *pīthas* such as Shri Shailam, Tibet, and Girnar. They can take up a subtle body and go wherever they want. Their bodies can move about anywhere without any difficulty because they cannot be obstructed by any object, nor can they be burnt by fire. They do not have the limitations of modern airplanes.

**Manuel:** *Is it true that beings from the planet Venus come here?*

**Baba:** Venus is a world of Siddhas. The beings living there have the power to come here. If you do spiritual sadhana, you will also be able to see them during the higher stages of meditation.

**Manuel:** *Perhaps you have also come here from some such world.*

**Baba:** No, I belong to this very world.

**Manuel:** *Are there men in the Himalayas known as abominable snowmen?*

**Baba:** Have you seen them?

**Manuel:** *No, but there are frequent reports of their large footprints, which are visible in the snow.*

**Baba:** This is only an inference. There are Siddhas in the Himalayas who are taller than us. In our Puranas, it is mentioned that *yakshas* (demigods) whose height exceeds ours live in the Himalayas.

**Manuel:** *Is it true that man is constantly evolving?*

**Baba:** Yes, this evolution has been going on for ages. The true evolution of a man is his inner, or spiritual, progress. The inner awakening can occur at any time. Man is always worthy of aspiring to be liberated.

**Manuel:** *I am not talking about spiritual evolution. I am referring to the theory of evolution proposed by Darwin, according to which man has evolved from the ape.*

**Baba:** His theory is based entirely on inference, isn't it? The truth of any statement can be proved in one of two ways, either by seeing it directly through experimentation and research or by experiencing it during the higher stages of meditation.

**Manuel:** *Can I also have experiences like other seekers?*

**Baba:** If you become like those people who have experiences, then you can also have experiences. They have intense devotion, faith, and an earnest desire to know God. If you want to experience the cold of the Himalayas, you must go there; you cannot know it by sitting here. In the same way, if you want to have experiences, you must become worthy by preparing a fertile ground for them.

**Manuel:** *There is a seeker who initially had many experiences during meditation, but now he has none.*

**Baba:** It is not that a seeker must have experiences continuously. If you have them constantly, it is just like witnessing a drama or a movie.

**Manuel:** *A friend of mine, who is a doctor, went to see Anandamayi Ma and he had some wonderful experiences.*

**Baba:** Saints and great beings are not interested in performing magic. The power dwelling within them automatically influences a seeker, enabling him to start having some inner experiences. Such experiences are not within our control, but depend on the inner Shakti. This Shakti is independent and works according to Her own wishes.

## Sunday, February 13, 1966

*This morning all the devotees were gathered in the satsang hall. Ram Chadda asked Baba a question.*

# *Who Is the Guru?*

**Chadda:** *Baba, tell us something about the Guru. Who can be called a Guru?*

**Baba:** Only he who has merged himself completely in God can become a Guru. The Guru has achieved total unity with God; therefore, the Guru is also called Parabrahman (the supreme Self).

Many ornaments are made of gold, but the gold in all of them is the same. Similarly, all the various objects in this world have emerged from the same God. It is because different qualities are superimposed upon pure Consciousness that diversity is seen, just as the walls of a room create the illusion that the space inside the room is different from the space outside the room. In reality, space is all one. If you remove the walls, you will find that the inside space and the outside space are one and the same. Similarly, the Self is not different from God. The Guru is one who has given up all external attributes and has merged with God. The Guru is one who has the power to bestow grace on his disciples. He alone is considered fit to guide others. You can call him a Guru, a saint, or God—all are the same. The scriptures say that Self, Guru, and God are one; hence, worship them as such.

> Although he is as all-pervasive as space, he assumes the threefold division of God, Guru, and Self. I bow to such a Guru.[3]

The Guru is he who has the ability to show others what he himself has seen. Since nothing in this world is different from God, then why not accept the Guru as God? He is not like God—he is God Himself.

SUNDAY, FEBRUARY 20, 1966

*Barrister Raman Vyas, the brother of Pandit Hariprasad Vyas of Secunderabad, came today. He asked Baba some questions.*

## *The Nature of Happiness*

**Raman:** *What is the happiness of Self-realization like? Is it like the happiness we experience through the senses or is it different from that?*

**Baba:** Happiness is of two kinds: permanent and temporary, transient. The happiness you derive from sensual enjoyments is transient, whereas the happiness experienced within yourself is permanent. It should not be called happiness; it should be called supreme bliss.

We have two kinds of instruments: the outer instruments and the inner instrument. The outer instruments, or sense organs, are directed toward objects in the outer world. It is the inner instrument that gives you an experience of exalted inner bliss.

**Raman:** *Does one also obtain material pleasures after receiving the grace of God?*

**Baba:** Material pleasures are dependent on one's destiny. By receiving God's grace, you obtain God Himself. After attaining God, getting material pleasures or losing them are both the same. One person may become completely detached from the material world, while another seems to get deeply involved in it. For example, after realization, King Gopichand left his palace and went to live in a cemetery, whereas Shikhidhvaja returned to his kingdom.

One gets the results of one's karmas from previous lives, but a wise person will say that it was all given to him by God.

## SUNDAY, MARCH 6, 1966

*As is usual on Sunday, many people were gathered in the satsang hall. Ram Chadda recently attended the discourses of Arthur Osborne in Bombay, and he spoke to Baba about them.*

**Chadda:** *Baba, in all his discourses, Osborne repeats the same instruction, which is to contemplate the question "Who am I?" Many people in the audience told him that they found this very difficult, and asked him how it could be done. In reply, Obsorne told them to drive all worldly thoughts away from their minds, to make their minds vacant, and then it would be possible to contemplate "Who am I?" He was then asked how the thoughts could be driven away, but he was unable to answer this question.*

### *See the World as a Form of the Self*

**Baba:** If he were to tell me to practice this, I would ask him, "Have you yourself driven the thoughts from your mind and then contemplated 'Who am I?'" If he replied "Yes," I would then ask him a second question: "You have come here and you are talking to us. Are you performing these activities while thinking about the world or without thinking about it?" He would certainly reply, "While thinking about the world." That means that when one is immersed in the Self, thoughts about the world cannot remain, and when one is engaged in thoughts about the world, the experience of the Self cannot remain. Therefore, you would sometimes be in that state (immersed in the Self) and sometimes in this state (thinking about the world). What is the use of achieving such an unstable state? The state of true Self-realization always remains the same.

The truth is that we do not have to eliminate all thoughts; we have to make them assume the form of the Self. We have to see this world as a form of the Self. Nothing is different from the Self.

## Monday, March 7, 1966

*Vaidya Shri Antarkar has been here for seven days. Today his brother, who is a professor of philosophy at Ruparel College and a seeker, also came with him.*

### *The Need for Sadhana*

**Professor:** *Many thought-waves arise in my mind, but during meditation, I drive away all extraneous thoughts and concentrate on only one thought such as a sound, an idol of God, or the letters of a mantra and become one with it. But this does not satisfy me because my aim is to drive away all thoughts, while in this practice one thought-wave remains constant.*

**Baba:** Because there are waves in the mind, there is meditation. If there were no waves, how could there be any meditation? Meditation is practiced until the Truth is realized, until knowledge of the Truth is obtained. Sadhana is done according to one's own worth, because perhaps only one among millions is so worthy that, without doing any sadhana, he is able to obtain knowledge immediately upon receiving the Guru's teaching, "Thou art That." Therefore, as long as thought-waves arise in the mind, as long as the mind engages itself in thoughts, sadhana has to be practiced.

Until knowledge of the Truth is attained, the various triads will remain, namely, the meditator, meditation, and the object of meditation; the seer, seen, and seeing; the knower, known, and knowledge; the seeker, sadhana, and the goal. In fact, the person who meditates, the object on which he meditates, and meditation are all one and the same, but for one who cannot grasp this subtle truth, various types of sadhana are prescribed.

**Professor:** *Yes, but one does experience peace through meditation.*

**Baba:** Do meditate, but at the same time keep in mind that whether or not waves arise in the mind, they do not bring about any change in the Self, which is never affected by anything. The Self can never be bound by anyone. What difference does it make to your Self whether the mind becomes agitated or remains quiet? Does it make any difference in the state of your Self whether a gale wind is blowing, carrying everything with it, or whether the air is calm and all objects remain steady?

These thought-waves can be compared to the phenomenon of flowers and fruit appearing on trees in the proper season and dropping off when the season passes. Know and recognize the Self as separate from the thought-waves. Agitation or quietude are only mental states; the Self has no connection with them.

**Professor:** *Sankhya philosophy says that it is prakriti that is liberated, not the purusha.*

**Baba:** That which is dirty needs to be washed, not that which is already clean. The Self is always pure. How can it be contaminated or impure? As long as one does not understand this truth, one has to practice sadhana.

## Sunday, March 20, 1966

*Today G. N. Vaidya, Yogendrabhai, Bhaskar Desai, and Pratap Yande were present for satsang.*

### *Ashes Do Not Come From the Abode of God*

**Vaidya:** *Last night I went to see a sannyāsī at Gwalior Palace. He materializes sacred ash from his hand and his devotees consider it to be prasād from God.*

**Baba:** It is worth analyzing where this sacred ash comes from. *Chidākāsha* is absolutely pure and objectless. It is the dwelling place of the supreme Self, or God; it is where the light of the Self shines. Where the pure Self alone exists, there is no room for sacred ash. Ashes are an impurity, whereas *chidākāsha*, the abode of God, is without any taint or impurity, so how can ashes exist there? One thing is certain: the ashes do not come from the abode of God.

Moreover, ashes represent the earth element of the five great elements. They can be seen, smelled, tasted, and touched. These qualities of *prakriti* are found in the world created from the five elements. The sacred ash, therefore, belongs to this very world. Hence, there is a vast difference between such magic and the abode of God.

## Monday, May 2, 1966

*Mr. Korgaonkar came today. He asked Baba some questions.*

## Shāmbhavī Shakti (The Shakti of Shambhu)

**Korgaonkar:** *Which Shakti is transmitted in shaktipat?*

**Baba:** The science of shaktipat has come down from time immemorial. It is also known as *shāmbhavī vidyā.* Discussions of it can be found in such books as *Trika Siddhānta* and the *Āgama Shāstra.* According to Shaivism, the absolutely pure and spotless state is Shiva, in whom Shakti dwells. This Shakti pervades the whole universe, performing innumerable wonders. The description of this Shakti is awe-inspiring.

Shakti is inseparable from Shiva. She cannot be divided into portions—nor can She be multiplied. She is infinite and omnipresent. Her wonderful power enables Her to remain as water in water and as fire in fire. She is not concealed; She is manifest. She dwells in a human being in the form of *prāna.* She dwells in the *mūlādhāra chakra* in the form of a coiled serpent called Kundalini. When this Kundalini is awakened by shaktipat from the Guru, one experiences this Shakti. Until then, one cannot understand anything about Her.

**Korgaonkar:** *Why does Jnaneshwar Maharaj refer to this world as "my play"?*

**Baba:** Because that is his actual experience. When one experiences this entire world as one's own expanse and play, that is the true state of Self-realization.

## Saints Also Abide by the Laws of God

**Korgaonkar:** *Why was it necessary for Jnaneshwar to take live samādhi?*

**Baba:** Great beings always abide by God's laws. They practice what they preach. Once even Mr. Nehru waited in line to obtain a ration card in accordance with the laws made by his government. The laws of God are also applicable to his messengers; therefore, all the Siddhas act in conformance with these laws.

Jnaneshwar convinced the great yogi Changdev that he should give up his desire for a long life, so how could he himself harbor such a desire? Changdev was a great yogi and had earned a life span thousands of years long through *kāyakalpa.* Jnaneshwar advised him not to lengthen his life with stolen time and gave him knowledge of the Truth. So why would Jnaneshwar have tried to lengthen his own life? Life and death are equal for one who has realized the Truth. He has no desire to prolong his life. Such beings always act according to God's will. The changes they bring about are also in accordance with God's will. They never act contrary to the scriptures, and they understand religion in its real sense. One who has one-sided knowledge cannot be called a yogi or a Siddha.

Yogis who have attained a high state have knowledge of all three periods of time: past, present, and future. They have foreknowledge of their time of death. This is called the knowledge of time. Jnaneshwar Maharaj wrote some verses that indicate his knowledge of this subject. Such yogis withdraw into *samādhi* a day or two before their impending death and give up their *prānas* at the appointed time. Some Siddhas live till the end of the cycle, but what is the purpose of such a long life?

## *Three Types of Siddhas*

**Korgaonkar:** *Who can be called a Siddha?*

**Baba:** Siddhas are mainly of three types: one, *janma* Siddhas are those who are born as Siddhas; two, *kripā* Siddhas are those who obtain Siddhahood through grace; and sadhana Siddhas are those who become Siddhas as a result of their own sadhana.

Those who have practiced sadhana in many previous lifetimes and complete it in this life without the help of a Guru are called *janma* Siddhas. In their former life, such individuals were not able to completely give up their identification with jivahood (individuality) and hence, could not entirely realize their Shivahood. In this life, they take up sadhana on their own without a

Guru and become Siddhas. It is certain, however, that they must have had a Guru in their previous life. They resume sadhana in this life from whatever point they left it in their past life. They manifest *siddhis* at a very early age; for example, whatever they say comes true and they are able to foretell events.

Sai Baba of Shirdi and Nityananda Baba were Siddhas of this type. *Siddhis* reside in such great beings right from their birth, but they are not even aware of them. Their *siddhis* work for them in a natural way without any effort on their part. In spite of having great powers, they act according to the will of God. Such *janma* Siddhas complete their sadhana without any effort on their part. Shakti Herself ensures that they complete it. Those saints who attained perfection after receiving mantra initiation in a dream also belong to the class of *janma* Siddhas.

Those who attain Siddhahood as a result of an inner awakening by the grace of a Siddha Guru are known as *kripā* Siddhas. Later, they have the same powers as *janma* Siddhas, including the ability to bestow grace on others. One who becomes a Siddha by receiving a mantra from a Guru also belongs to this class of Siddhas.

Those who become Siddhas after practicing yoga and doing sadhana are known as sadhana Siddhas.

A *janma* Siddha has had a Guru in his past life, and his sadhana proceeds automatically in this life. A *kripā* Siddha receives the Guru's grace and attains liberation without any strenuous effort.

They are known as Siddha incarnations who come to this earth from Siddhaloka with a message from God, or who come to fulfill a special mission. They may remain here till the end of the cycle. They are unaffected by pleasure or pain and they have infinite powers, but they cannot be called incarnations of God.

*The Banavalikar family has been staying at the holiday camp in Ganeshpuri for the past three or four days. They are devotees of Shri Ramadevi. Every evening they come for satsang with Baba. One of them, Sulochanaben, has an especially keen interest in sadhana.*

## *Knowledge of the Self and the Mantra Given by the Guru*

**Sulochana:** *Baba, should one contemplate knowledge of the Self, or should one repeat the mantra given by the Guru?*

**Baba:** Knowledge of the Self is superior to all, but it is not so easy to obtain. You have to see That which cannot be seen, you have to catch That which has no form, you have to touch That which cannot be felt. Even the sages are wonder-struck by this Self. The *Bhagavad Gītā* says:

> Some see the Self as a great wonder, some speak of the Self as a great wonder, some hear about the Self as a great wonder, and yet even after hearing about Him, no one knows Him.[4]

In the *Katha Upanishad*, Yamaraja, the Lord of Death, says:

> Many never even hear about the Self; though hearing about it, many do not understand it. Wonderful is the one who imparts this knowledge of the Self, and wonderful is the one who attains the Self. The being who comprehends this transcendental divine Self is indeed supremely wise.[5]

If you were to see a being who has realized the knowledge of the Self, you would certainly be wonder-struck. Such is this knowledge of the Self.

That mantra by which the Guru was able to attain one with the supreme Self is given or taught by him to others repeating this mantra, a seeker spontaneously begins to experience the *So'ham* mantra within. Then the knowledge of the Self, "I am That," starts manifesting from within. After that, contemplation of the Self is no longer necessary.

## *Destiny Cannot Affect One's Worship of God*

**Sulochana:** *Is it true that one can worship God only if it is one's destiny?*

**Baba:** Destiny is related to the experiences of life in the world, not to the worship of God. One has to undergo painful and pleasurable experiences in relation to one's body and life in the world, according to his destiny. As far as the worship of God is concerned, one is absolutely free; it is entirely within one's own control. Saint Dayarnava says:

> Listen to this request of Dayarnava. You will undergo your destined life experiences, but make every effort to worship God. Understand that the worship of God is within your power.[6]

Let your destiny remain as it is; you can neither add anything to it nor subtract anything from it. Continue to worship God, paying no attention to destiny. One attains God while living out one's destined experiences. Even great saints cannot escape their destiny.

## SUNDAY, MAY 15, 1966

*Today Shri Shivajibhai, a Jain, came with a friend from Bombay. He asked Baba some questions about his sadhana.*

**Shivaji:** *I have done a lot of sadhana and yogic practices. As a result, I had various experiences and also attained siddhis. At one time when I sat for meditation, shakti would be transmitted from me to another. He would get up as if asleep and answer my questions. This all came to a halt six years ago. Now my sadhana does not bear fruit, nor do I have any experiences. I have sought the advice of many saints and sages regarding this lapse in my sadhana, but each one has a different explanation. Very few of our Jain sādhus have practiced yoga, very few have any knowledge of it. They are mostly ritualists. I did meet one Jain muni (holy man) who knows about kundalinī yoga. He told me that the kriyā in which the head touches the ground during meditation is harmful. According to him, I lost all my powers because of that kriyā. He taught me an āsana I practiced for three months, but without any benefit. My state has remained the same.*

**Baba:** Sometimes during meditation, the head touches the ground. This is one of the yogic *kriyās.* Whatever was happening to you was all right, nothing was wrong. In yogic practice, many such *kriyās* occur during the purification of the *nādīs.* There is no reason to have any fears or doubts about them. You must allow whatever is happening naturally to happen. Do not try to obstruct it.

## *The Divine Shakti Is Compassionate*

**Shivaji:** *Another Jain sādhu told me, "Chakreshvari, the deity of your lineage, is angry with you; hence, your sadhana has come to a halt."*

**Baba:** How could that have happened? Even our earthly mother who has given us birth tolerates all our faults and offenses, so how could Shakti, the divine Mother of the universe, get angry? The study and practice of yoga is not a reprehensible activity. It is the means by which you are trying to obtain the Mother Herself. Would this incur Her wrath? The Mother is extremely forgiving. Chakreshvari is Kundalini Shakti Herself. She is that Shakti who opens all the chakras. Do you consider the Shakti that you worship and experience during yoga practice to be different from Chakreshvari? Shakti is only one everywhere. For Christians, Parsis, Hindus, Muslims, Buddhists, and Jains, there is only one Shakti. People give this Shakti different names such as Sita, Radha, and Mary, but ultimately all are one. If your Shakti is different from that of other sects and religions, then is your Shakti true and theirs false? Do you think that the others will go to hell?

Moreover, if you seek someone's advice about your sadhana, and that person misguides you and your sadhana is disrupted, do you think that Goddess Chakreshvari will be angry with you? On the contrary, why wouldn't She be angry with the one who misled you? Your story is analogous to the following one: A man sold some land on which a cobra goddess lived, and the new owner removed her abode and disposed of it. Later on, the cow of the original owner died, and people started saying that the cobra goddess was angry with him. Is such a conclusion justified? The offense was committed by one man, so why would another man be punished for it? Wouldn't the cobra goddess be angry with the man who removed her abode?

God is never angry. The divine Shakti is extremely compassionate. Putana tried to poison Lord Krishna, but He still granted her liberation.

## *Past Lives Are Revealed in Meditation*

**Shivaji:** *Shri Rajachandra says that to know your past lives, you must regress yourself back into the past. If you are forty years old now, you must contemplate on what you were like at age thirty-nine, then at thirty-eight, and so on, continuing back to your past life. Is it possible to know about one's past life using this method?*

**Baba:** This is called *laya chintana* (contemplation in retrospect), but what is the need for practice when one's previous life is revealed automatically in meditation? All the impressions of former lives are stored in the *sushumnā.* After the awakening of the *kundalinī*, the door of the *sushumnā* is opened, and many seekers receive knowledge of their past lives spontaneously in meditation without any special effort.

**Shivaji:** *Is it necessary to know about one's past life? Of what use is such knowledge?*

**Baba:** Knowing about your past life is like knowing about past history; it is like knowing the succession of Indian kings from Babar to Aurangzib. There is no advantage in knowing your past. On the other hand, you will derive benefit from performing some meritorious actions in the present. By improving your present life, you will gain something; by trying to delve only into the past and the future, you will remain where you are. Think only of the present, and make good use of the time and opportunity available to you. Make some effort to attain God.

**Shivaji:** *There are two Jain sects. One sect, called Dehravasis, believes in idol worship; the other sect, called Sthanakvasis (to which I belong), does not believe in idols. What then should be the support for my meditation?*

**Baba:** Shakti Herself is the support. When you practice yoga, you have some experiences and *kriyās*. On what are they based? The support for all of them is Shakti. Why do you need any other support for your meditation?

## Wednesday, June 15, 1966

*Gita and Mark Obel arrived from South Africa five or six days ago. Today when everyone was assembled in the satsang hall, Gita asked a question about her sadhana.*

# *The Outlook of the Gopīs*

**Gita:** *Babaji, when I go into meditation, I see light. Sometimes I feel that I am that light and that the light is my Self.*

**Baba:** What you are now experiencing is only a glimpse of the Self. The Self is much greater than that. Are we able to see our entire body? We can see our arms and legs, but not our back. Similarly, you are seeing only a fraction of the Self.

I'll give you another example. If you put a bowl of water in the sun, you will see the sunlight reflected in it, won't you? In a small bowl, you will see a small light; in a big bowl, a big light. This reflected light is only a small fraction of the sun's widespread radiance. Similarly, the Self, or God, pervades everywhere. He appears to be limited in varying degrees due to the modifying factors of mind, intellect, ego, and subconscious mind in which He is reflected.

What is the object of your meditation? The one on whom you are meditating is within you. If the Self is sought outside of oneself, it is like the sun going out in search of heat or the moon in search of coolness. Sundardas says:

> Just as if the sun were searching for the sun to warm his body, or the moon were searching for the moon to cool her body, or a man safe inside his own house were frightened and wanted to seek shelter in his house, similarly, O Sundar, Brahman has forgotten His own nature and says, "Let Me try to find out what Brahman is like."[7]

The *gopīs* had become so completely united with Krishna that they entirely forgot themselves. They saw nothing in this world as different from Krishna. In this connection, I'll tell you a story about Krishna and Uddhava. Krishna imparted knowledge to Uddhava, enabling him to understand the inner lights, meditation, and so forth. Krishna knew, however, that Uddhava had not properly grasped his teachings. A teacher has unique ways of teaching a person who does not understand. Krishna gave

Uddhava a test. He told him to go to the *gopīs* and give them knowledge. Uddhava was very pleased and he went at once to Braj, where the *gopīs* were living. He announced his arrival by exclaiming, "*Gopāl kī jay!*" He saw the *gopīs* embracing all kinds of objects such as trees, cows, and water, saying, "O Krishna, O Krishna." Uddhava concluded that the poor *gopīs* were ignorant. He asked them, "What are you doing?" The *gopīs* replied, "What you are trying to attain through meditation, we see everywhere." Realizing the truth of their statement, Uddhava lost all his pride.

If we have the outlook of the *gopīs,* we need not practice any sadhana; lacking that outlook, any amount of meditation or any number of experiences are futile.

## Sunday, June 26, 1966

*Barrister Nain was among the devotees gathered in the satsang hall today. He commented that the ashram saplings and creepers grow very quickly, and even small trees yield large, delicious fruit.*

### *Nectarean Chaitanya*

**Baba:** The trees and creepers imbibe *chetana shakti* from the all-pervading *chaitanya* (Consciousness). Our clothes prevent this *chetana shakti* from entering our bodies. I keep most of my body uncovered so that the shakti can enter me easily. This is why my skin shines. This nectarean and radiant Consciousness is combined with air. Wherever the air enters, this Consciousness also penetrates. Where the vapor from boiling water diffuses in the atmosphere, you can see bright vibrations. Consciousness is something like that. If you watch the sun's rays entering a room through a skylight, you see movement in the sunbeam. Consciousness is something like that. These chairs, stones, clay, and so forth are inert forms of that Consciousness which pervades every place and every object. That Consciousness is the ultimate Truth, which is seen after practicing meditation for a long time.

**Nain:** *Baba, I recently read that as a man reduces his food intake and gradually loses weight, his mental power is enhanced.*

**Baba:** The mind should be sentenced to solitary confinement to increase its power. If the mind constantly runs after sense objects, it becomes unstable, but if it remains quiet and concentrated, it becomes more powerful. Let me tell you about an incident that happened this morning. While I was walking through the garden, it immediately struck me that a coconut had been stolen from the coconut tree. Everyone must have thought that Baba knows about everything, but that is not so. Such things arise automatically in a concentrated mind. There is, however, no special advantage in being able to know everything in this way. The coconut cannot be recovered just by knowing that it has been stolen.

## Monday, June 27, 1966

*Today L. R. Patel, who works with Amar Construction Company, came for Baba's darshan. He has come to the ashram before with Shri Ranchod Bapu. He brought two new visitors with him, Ramnath Mishra, a seeker, and Shantikumar Vaidya.*

# *Hatha Yoga and Siddha Yoga Sadhana*

**Mishra:** *What is the importance of the khecharī mudrā in yogic practice?*

**Baba:** There are two types of *khecharī mudrā*: the outer *khecharī* and the inner *khecharī*. Hatha yogis sometimes cut the frenum under the tongue in order to practice *khecharī mudrā*. This is the outer *khecharī* brought about by external means. In contrast, *khecharī mudrā* occurs spontaneously with the grace of the Guru. During sadhana, the tongue sometimes rolls back and presses against the upper palate, or even extends up and back into the nasal pharynx. This is the spontaneous, inner *khecharī*. It is the true *khecharī mudrā*, the one considered to be significant in yoga.

**Mishra:** *What is the place of ashtānga yoga (Patanjali's eight-limbed yoga) in Siddha Yoga sadhana?*

**Baba:** Siddha Yoga sadhana comes very easily to one who has already practiced *ashtānga yoga*. Generally, a person will not experience any difficulties in sadhana; but even if one does, they will be comparatively minor, because through the practice of *āsana, prānāyāma*, and so forth, the *nādīs* are already purified. One who has not purified the *nādīs* encounters a lot of difficulties in sadhana such as diarrhea, cough, and body aches. Purification of the *nādīs* occurs automatically as one does the Siddha Yoga meditation practices. As the *nādīs* are purified, even the clothes and sweat of the seeker no longer have a bad odor. One starts regulating one's food intake naturally, eating just the right amount of food required by the body, never too much or too little.

**Mishra:** *What is the correct time for meditation?*

**Baba:** Since hatha yoga is a yoga of self-effort and discipline, many rules and regulations must be observed, whereas in Siddha Yoga meditation it is not necessary to establish a set time for meditation. Siddha Yoga meditation happens naturally whenever you want it, regardless of time or place.

Since Siddha Yoga meditation is not antagonistic to the life of a householder, one need not give up one's home and family. Siddha Yoga meditation removes obstacles, it does not create them. It does not obstruct anyone's daily life. On the contrary, it is helpful. The seeker mentally renounces everything with ease.

**Mishra:** *Does the sleep state continue during wakefulness?*

**Baba:** Yes, it is called *jāgriti turīya*. With passage of time, this state becomes more and more steady. Eventually one remains in it all the time. Then even if he is abused, he will not get disturbed. Moreover, his state also affects everyone in his company. Even the trees, plants, and flowers are affected.

I fully believe in Patanjali's yoga; nevertheless, Siddha Yoga meditation is superior and easier to practice. A seeker does sadhana spontaneously and cannot give it up. Whenever anyone asks me for initiation, I tell him, "Come and stay here, you will receive it automatically." Many people receive initiation as soon as they arrive here. Initiation given intentionally by touch is inferior to that received automatically by staying in the ashram. I do not have to initiate anyone. The divine Shakti Herself does it. This initiation is beyond all differences of caste, sect, and religion. The seekers here include Jews, Christians, Hindus, Parsis, Jains, and others.

**Mishra:** *Do you give discourses?*

**Baba:** I speak according to the needs of the seeker and the subject under consideration.

**Mishra:** *Is it essential to have kumbhaka in yoga sadhana?*

**Baba:** It need not be practiced with effort in Siddha Yoga meditation; it takes place automatically.

**Mishra:** *Do prāna and apāna keep functioning during kumbhaka in Siddha Yoga meditation?*

**Baba:** *Kumbhaka* is of two types: one is external and requires effort, the other is internal and takes place automatically. The inner *prāna* is subtler than the outer *prāna.* When you have *kumbhaka* of this subtle *prāna,* the movement of *prāna* and *apāna* continues inside the *sushumnā.* This *kumbhaka* is permanent and gives the seeker satisfaction and happiness. When the internal *kumbhaka* occurs, just a small part of the *prāna* goes out.

This subject cannot be understood intellectually either through discussion or by reading books. It is understood only by direct experience.

*Today a bus driver came to the ashram with some relatives and friends.*

## *The Path of Devotion*

**Bus driver:** *For the past year or two I have completely lost interest in everything worldly. I don't feel like working or doing anything else. I can't hold down a job and feel like leaving my present job as a bus driver. My relatives noticed my condition and arranged a marriage for me two months ago, but I still have absolutely no interest in anything. I only feel like secluding myself and practicing bhakti. I have been doing japa of Bhagavati Ma for a long time.*

**Baba:** *Bhakti* is of two kinds. One kind is that which is suggested to you by your own mind, and the other is that which is prescribed by the Guru or the scriptures. If you follow the path shown by a Guru who is thoroughly versed in the scriptures and who is also adept in the life of the world, then you will find the true way of *bhakti.*

Marriage is determined by one's destiny, and a householder's life does not come in the way of *bhakti.* Shri Siddharudha Swami, who initiated me into Vedanta, was visited by many people like you who complained that their family life was creating difficulties in their sadhana. Swamiji used to show them the hundreds of stoves for cooking food in the ashram, telling them that he, a *sannyāsī,* had an even larger family than they.

Remain intoxicated with devotion to God, but at the same time love your wife and make her your partner in devotion. Merely chanting the name of Rama or Krishna with closed eyes is not real devotion.

Bhagavati Ma, whose name you have been using for *japa,* has full knowledge of your life in the world and will not let it affect your devotion. After doing your driving duty, do *bhakti,* as well as attending properly to your household. Bhagavati lives with

Shiva. Has any harm come to their life together? Remain devoted to Bhagavati with great love, and along with that, also do your other work.

## Sunday, August 21, 1966

*A student from the family of Shri Chandrashekhar Bharati, Shankaracharya of Sringeri Math, came to Baba today. Barrister Nain and other devotees were also there.*

# *True Samādhi*

**Student:** *I have heard and also read that if one remains in samādhi for twenty-one days, the body drops and one attains liberation. Is this true?*

**Baba:** A person's body may drop after a twenty-one-day *samādhi*, but the future of his soul depends on his karma and his destiny. If he has any remaining karma in store, he will have to take another birth. There are many cases, however, of yogis who remained in *samādhi* for more than twenty-one days without dropping their bodies. Two examples are Ramana Maharshi and Bhagawan Nityananda.

This kind of *samādhi* is not necessary to attain Brahman. One whose destined karmas are attenuated goes into *samādhi* spontaneously, as the example of Jadabharat illustrates.[8] But how many such persons can there be? You should talk about ordinary seekers.

*Samādhi* can be understood only by direct experience. It is *samādhi* when *dhi* (*buddhi*, or intellect) attains *sama* (equanimity). In *samādhi*, a *jñānī* experiences this entire world as full of God. He considers this very world to be the attributeless Brahman and acts accordingly in his daily life. He proclaims that what is considered nonexistent exists. While living his daily life, e is fully aware that he is superimposing this world on Brahman. Whatever he does, whatever he sees, is all Brahman and nothing else. There are no objects in his mind, so what should he meditate upon? There are no thoughts in his mind, so what mental waves should he eliminate? He sees the entire world as that Brahman who is One without a second. He is always in the same state wherever he may be, whether at home or in a forest. He is liberated even while living in the world. This is the highest kind of *samādhi.* In hatha yoga, however, one has to continually practice *kumbhaka* and enter into *samādhi* through effort, and even then its duration is limited.

## *The Mind*

**Student:** *What is the mind?*

**Baba:** The mind is a vibration of the Self; the Self is its support. As we go on doing sadhana and our intellect becomes extremely subtle, then we can know the mind. Just as I know myself, it is also possible to know the mind. The mind itself is comprehensible, and it also comprehends other objects, just as the sun illumines itself as well as illuminating the world.

So long as we do not understand the mind, we think that it is merely mind; but once we understand its true nature, we realize that, in reality, it is Chiti (Consciousness). It is Chiti who vibrates in the form of the mind. The *nirvikalpa* (thought-free) becomes *savikalpa* (with thoughts). The *savikalpa* state is to make worldly activities possible.

By what means do you know that you went into *samādhi* and experienced bliss? It is only by the vibration of the mind that these experiences are known. You are not the mind; the mind is yours. Just as such objects as your house, clothes, and ornaments belong to you, similarly, the mind also belongs to you and helps you in your daily life. Even saints and great beings who have attained *jīvanmukti* require the help of their minds to teach their disciples and write profound books on *jñāna.*

# *God Alone Is Everywhere*

**Nain:** *Which is the correct understanding: "I exist" or "I do not exist"?*

**Baba:** A seeker is confused about such matters only during the period of sadhana. After realization, he knows "I alone exist and none else."

This world is a manifestation of God. Just as the body with its various constituents such as blood, bones, flesh, and hair is formed from one semen, similarly, this world with its diverse objects has emerged from the one Consciousness. Though there are diverse names and forms, only one God pervades all. Everything is composed of Chiti; hence, there is unity in diversity. The world has emerged from Truth and will merge back into Truth. That (the world) which did not exist in the beginning and which will not exist at the end cannot be said to exist in between either. This is the truth. If anyone views it otherwise, his vision is faulty.

There are two types of understanding: one is gross, superficial, or outer; and the other is subtle, or inner. Subtle understanding is to know the true nature of things. Superficial, or gross, understanding perceives the same object in many different ways. Generally, people perceive an object after superimposing themselves (their own preconceptions, prejudices) onto that object. For example, a man was once relaxing under a tree. A student of the *Bhagavad Gītā* happened to pass by and said to himself, "This man appears to be a *sthitaprajña* (one centered in steady wisdom)." After some time, a *vaidyā* (Ayurvedic doctor) passed by, and he thought, "This man seems to be suffering from some disease. That's why he is lying unconscious under this tree." A little while later, a thief passed by and he surmised, "This man must have committed a theft last night. That's why he is sleeping." Still later, an exorcist passed by and he presumed that the man was afflicted by a ghost. When the man got up, someone asked him, "Why were you lying under that tree?" He answered, "I just wanted to rest for a while."

This story is similar to that of the five blind men who came across an elephant. Each of the five men gave a different description of the elephant, depending on which part of it he had felt. Truth is not like this. After realizing the Truth, one sees nothing but the kingdom of God everywhere. During the period of sadhana, one is trapped in such dualities as heaven and hell, *prakriti* and *purusha*, and so forth, but a *jñānī* sees everything as one.

**Nain:** *The scriptures say that there is neither bondage nor liberation for the Self.*

**Baba:** That is very true. Bondage and liberation are relative terms adopted only for the purpose of discussion and argument.

**Nain:** *Why are there discussions and arguments?*

**Baba:** You will understand this when you get into the state free from debate.

**Nain:** *Why do we experience pleasure and pain?*

**Baba:** Pleasure and pain are apparent in a particular state. Pleasurable and painful events occur even in the lives of great beings, but since they are beyond that state, they are not affected by them. Pleasure and pain seem very important to a seeker, but are insignificant to a *jñānī*.

**Student:** *Can a man become a doctor or an engineer in his next life if he cherishes such a desire at the time of death?*

**Baba:** That is what the scriptures say. This world has been described as an embodiment of desire, and one takes birth only because of desire. If you ask a child what he would like to be when he grows up, he would say a doctor, a barrister, and so forth. What he says is based on his awareness about his previous life. As he grows up, an urge arises within that he should become such-and-such.

*Baba has been in Bombay for the past four days. At about four in the afternoon, Rasik Kadakia, Rajendra Mahant, and other seekers came for his darshan and satsang.*

**Rasik:** *After realizing the Self, can one give an experience of the Self to others?*

**Baba:** Yes, one can give the experience to another who is worthy and deserving of it. One who has seen the Self can show it to others, but the one who wants to see must have the right vision. One person sees it and shows it to a second person, who in turn shows it to a third person; this verily is the Guru-disciple lineage.

**Rajendra:** *Swami Vivekananda did not write anything about his experiences.*

**Baba:** Other disciples of Ramakrishna Paramahamsa have written about their experiences.

**Rajendra:** *But does this indicate that Swamiji did not have any experiences?*

**Baba:** No, it doesn't. It is a saint's personal choice whether or not to relate his experiences to others.

**Rajendra:** *Even Shri Shankaracharya did not give an account of his spiritual experiences.*

**Baba:** Have you read the *āchārya's* own books? Read *Saundarya Laharī.* What is contained there could not have been written without personal experience.

Saints like Tukaram, Jnaneshwar, and Kabir all wrote about Svargaloka (heaven), *sahasrāra*, *nāda*, *bindu*, and *kalā.* Did they write without having experienced these things? A detailed description of the awakening of Kundalini is given in the sixth chapter of *Jñāneshvarī.* Could all that be false? Read Vivekananda's introduction to *Rāja Yoga* in which he has written about Kundalini.

One day a *sannyāsī* who was here said, "I do not believe in Kundalini." I replied, "Who cares what you believe? It is immaterial whether or not you believe in Kundalini. Just because you don't believe in Her doesn't mean that Kundalini does not exist."

**Rasik:** *A friend of mine says that only a celibate can become a Siddha. What would you say about that?*

**Baba:** Saints can be either *sannyāsīs* or householders. Householder saints can achieve everything according to the *varnāshrama*, the four stages of life. Maharishi Vyas, Kabir, and Tukaram were all householders. Ramana Maharshi renounced his home, and Bhagawan Nityananda was an *avadhūta.* He had neither a home nor a family, nor did he need them. For householder saints, worldly dealings are a part of their normal daily activities. They do not do these activities for gratification of the senses or for material enjoyment and pleasure.

> They act with the awareness that only the sense organs are being engaged in the sense objects to perform their work.[9]

Again, this is not your friend's subject, and he has no competence to make a judgment in this matter. This is the subject of the scriptures and *āchāryas.*

**Rasik:** *Can astrological predictions come true?*

**Baba:** If the inspiration of a pure mind combines with the science of astrology, they come true.

**Rasik:** *Can a true Guru destroy the karmas of his disciple?*

**Baba:** It is rare good fortune to get such a Guru. If you have incurred heavy debts and a millionaire becomes your friend, he can pay off all your debts. Similarly, if you seek refuge in a Guru, the burden of your karmas is relieved. He elevates you to such a state that outwardly you may be undergoing any amount of trouble or hardship, but inwardly you remain blissful and undisturbed.

# What Is to Be Renounced

**Rajendra:** *Is it essential to give up the material world to achieve God?*

**Baba:** If you want God-realization and liberation, give up the one thing that really needs to be given up: the idea of "I" and "mine," the idea that you possess that which really does not belong to you. A saint sings as follows:

> Ram is not attained by renouncing wealth or life.
> Only he attains Narayana who renounces
> the pride of his body.
> God can never be attained by renouncing
> all worldly affairs,
> By renouncing wife, children, family,
> or household matters,
> By eating only roots, tubers, and fruit,
> and renouncing other foods,
> By renouncing clothes and going about naked,
> by giving up women.
> Even by renouncing one's own life-force,
> Hari is not attained.
> Ram is not attained by renouncing wealth or life.
> Only he attains Narayana who renounces
> the pride of his body.[10]

To renounce that which really does not belong to you, but for which you have acquired the idea of "my"-ness, is like giving someone else's cow in charity and then looking upward expecting an airplane to take you to heaven.

This world created by God is not meant to be renounced. If it were, why would God have created it at all? What is the purpose of giving it up? It is like leaving one house just to take up residence in another, or like taking off one set of clothes just to put on another. How can that be called renunciation? It is like going to the barbershop for a haircut and afterward declaring, "I have sacrificed my hair." After a few days, your hair will grow back again. Similarly, that which you give up now will eventually return and present itself to you again. You need a house to stay in, you need clothes to protect the body, and you need food to sustain the body.

What did you bring with you when you were born? Nothing! You came into this world naked, with empty hands, without even teeth; yet now you lay claim to so many objects, saying, "This is mine and that is mine." In fact, nothing belongs to you. In the end, you will leave the world exactly as you entered it. Therefore, give up the idea of "my"-ness, not the world. A woman saint named Jayadevi says:

> The world consists of the idea of "I" and "mine"; apart from this idea, no world exists. Give up the idea of "I"-ness and "my"-ness, and you will have achieved liberation. After crossing this ocean of transmigratory existence, you will reach a place where there is no pain, sorrow, or misery. It is an ocean of bliss, ever full of happiness and contentment. O Jayadevi, give up attachment to the things of this world. Even this body does not belong to you. Why then do you say with pride, "This wealth is mine and this house is mine"?[11]

## SUNDAY, OCTOBER 16, 1966

*Many devotees attended satsang today, including Barrister Ramanlal Vyas.*

## *The Importance of Prāna*

**Ramanlal:** *Recently, after reading Hathayoga Pradīpikā, a question arose in my mind as to why so much importance is given to prāna and prānāyāma in hatha yoga.*

**Baba:** *Prāna* is the most important thing in this world. The *Katha Upanishad* says:

> All that lives in this world has arisen from the vibration of *prāna.*[12]

Because *prāna* is the first cause of creation, the Upanishads accord importance to the worship of it.

Life is sustained by the presence of *prāna* in the body. When *prāna* leaves, the body dies. Many different *prānas* function in the body. The five principal *prānas* are *prāna, apāna, samāna, vyāna,* and *udāna*; the five subsidiary *prānas* are *nāga, kūrma, kukāra, devadatta,* and *dhanañjaya. Prāna* moves through the seventy-two million *nādīs,* purifying the body. The mind becomes quiet through control of *prāna.*

## *Hatha Yoga Matured into Rāja Yoga*

**Ramanlal:** *Since hatha yoga is concerned with the body and the Self is separate from the body, then how can one attain knowledge of the Self through hatha yoga?*

**Baba:** You are right. Hatha yoga has no connection with the Self. The Self is nondual, unattached, and completely independent. The purpose of hatha yoga is to purify the body and the mind. The Self is always pure; it never becomes impure or tainted so there can be no question of purifying it.

As the name signifies, hatha yoga is practiced through discipline. It requires effort; it has certain prescribed rules, methods, and times for practice. Its main aim is to keep the body fit so that one may enjoy bodily pleasures and comfort. Hatha yoga makes the body healthy and strong. As a result, one appears younger and lives longer. It is said, "You need a healthy body to do sadhana."

**Ramanlal:** *Is hatha yoga the same as rāja yoga?*

**Baba:** No, they are different.

**Ramanlal:** *Then why does Hathayoga Pradīpikā refer to hatha yoga as rāja yoga?*

**Baba:** It makes no such statement. Read it again carefully. It says that hatha yoga takes you toward *rāja yoga.* This means that after hatha yoga has been practiced systematically, it eventually matures into *rāja yoga.* It says:

> Hatha yoga is the stairway for those who wish to ascend to the great height of *rāja yoga.*[13]

Just as after high school, there is college, similarly, mastery of hatha yoga leads to *rāja yoga.*

**Ramanlal:** *Can a householder practice yoga?*

**Baba:** Yes, you are already practicing it every day, but you have not given it any conscious thought. You sit in a particular, traditional way; that is *āsana.* You eat at a certain time, sleep at a certain time, and go to the office at a certain time—that is *yama* and *niyama.* You concentrate on your work, that is meditation.

## Wednesday, October 19, 1966

*Dr. Vipinbhai Modi and his family, who come every Sunday for Baba's darshan, were at the ashram today as well. The doctor's wife, Hansaben, has a great interest in spirituality and sometimes asks Baba questions.*

## The Goal of All Religions Is the Same

**Hansaben:** *People initiated into one religion or sect wear white clothes, while those initiated into another wear yellow or saffron clothes. What is the reason for these differences? What is the significance of the color of clothes?*

**Baba:** During his sadhana, a saint sees only a particular color in meditation and then wears clothes of that color. Later, his disciples follow his example and start wearing the same color.

There may be sects, many religions, but they all have the same final goal, which is to know the Truth, to know the Self. After this goal is achieved, all religions and sects are seen as one, undivided by superficial differences.

God is changeless, formless, and unattached. He has no name. One has to adopt some path in order to realize Him. It may be Hinduism, Islam, Jainism, or Christianity. The paths may be different, but their goal is the same. Once the goal is reached, the path has no further use. We serve food on a leaf plate, but after the food has been eaten, the leaf plate is of no more use and we throw it away. Another example: you came here by means of a car, but in order to enter the ashram, you had to leave the car outside.

Initially, when a seeker begins to meditate, he adopts some name or form of God for *japa* and meditation. It is by means of God with attributes that a seeker eventually attains the goal of realizing God without name or form.

## Tuesday, November 8, 1966

*This morning at nine o'clock, Professor Umedbhai Maniar came to the ashram with Mr. Umashankar Joshi, his daughter, Swati, and another friend. Umashankar is a well-known scholar and poet. Currently, he is head of the Linguistic Studies Department at Gujarat University, and on December first he will become vice chancellor of the university.*

*All the visitors went out to the garden where Baba was sitting, and Professor Maniar introduced everyone to him. Baba talked to them lovingly and started showing them the garden.*

**Baba:** The leaves, fruit, and other parts of these trees have so many uses. They often have medicinal value. The juice of guava is an antidote for liquor intoxication. A particular kind of abdominal pain can be cured by applying the leaves of swallowwort on the stomach.

**Umashankar:** *Yes, Baba, my father used to put them on his stomach.*

**Baba:** And if you walk around the swallowwort, you obtain wealth, but this is known only to the Marwaris (merchant community), not to others. (laughter)

**Umashankar:** *Yes, because they not only worship Narayana, they also worship Lakshmi Narayana (goddess of wealth).*

*Baba and the visitors discussed various topics in this way as they walked to the satsang hall.*

## *Kashmir Shaivism*

**Umashankar:** *I read the book Pratyabhijñāhridayam on Kashmir Shaivism, but I could not understand it.*

**Baba:** Such mystical books can be understood only by the grace of the Guru or God. It is stated in the very beginning of the book that:

> Only a few seekers who are full of devotion and who have a desire to achieve oneness with the supreme Self can, after shaktipat initiation, begin to grasp the teachings given herein.[14]

**Umashankar:** *Yes, the essence of the entire Shaivite doctrine has been given in just twenty sūtras.*

**Baba:** You have studied the book quite thoroughly, you even remember the number of *sūtras* it contains. These few *sūtras* express the entire essence of the philosophy that everything in the world is Consciousness. This Consciousness, or Chiti, is absolutely independent and creates this manifold world. She possesses the power to create many from one and one from many. This same Chiti dwells in man in the form of Kundalini.

**Umashankar:** *Yes, She dwells in human beings in a contracted form.*

**Baba:** She is also all-pervading.

**Umashankar:** *Everything is covered with impurities. Even the individual soul is said to be covered with impurities.*

**Baba:** Yes, as long as the divine Shakti is not awakened, one remains a *jīva* (individual soul); after Her awakening, one becomes Shiva.

> A human being without Shakti is a victim of transmigratory existence. When one's own Shakti unfolds, verily one becomes Shiva.[15]

**Umashankar:** *This scripture can be understood only with the help of the Guru.*

**Baba:** One needs a teacher to learn even the normal things of daily life, so why wouldn't one need a teacher for this? Various arts and sciences such as driving, cooking, carpentry, and so forth, are all learned either by observing someone else or through instruction. In the same way, spiritual knowledge has to be learned from a Guru. The Guru is said to be the grace-bestowing power of God.

**Umashankar:** *The Guru is also the same Chiti Shakti.*

**Baba:** Yes, the Guru is that power which bestows the grace of God on the disciple. God bestows His grace through the Guru. One of the *Shiva Sūtras* says, *gurur upāyah,*[16] "The Guru is the means."

**Umashankar:** *Gurur upāyah, that is, you must go to the Guru to receive this shakti.*

**Baba:** Yes, as soon as the disciple receives this shakti, his *sushumnā* begins to open and his own shakti is activated. Then the seeker experiences great inner bliss. Another *sūtra* says:

> By the opening of the middle one (*sushumnā nādī*), one obtains the bliss of the Self.[17]

In this connection, I will give you an illustration from Jnaneshwar Maharaj. In his book *Amritānubhava*, he writes about one of the *Shiva Sūtras: jñānam bandhah.*[18] This is quite surprising because he had no direct knowledge of the *Shiva Sūtras*; what he has written about them came from inner omniscience arising from shaktipat.

**Umashankar:** *Is the tradition of shaktipat still alive, or has it come to an end?*

**Baba:** It has not ended, nor will it ever come to an end. Jnaneshwar Maharaj has very clearly indicated his own lineage: Adinath, Matsyendranath, Gorakhnath, Gahininath, Nivrittinath, and then Jnaneshwar himself.

One must understand this science thoroughly. What can a *sādhu* achieve just by piercing his ears, applying sacred ash, wearing a loincloth, and repeating *shiva gorakh? Shiva gorakh* is not a mantra. The Guru's name is not the Guru mantra. The mantra given by the Guru is the Guru mantra. You must discover which mantra the Guru repeated to achieve perfection.

**Umashankar:** *Is it necessary to follow a technique in this branch of knowledge?*

**Baba:** You must know certain essential things such as who the Guru is, what Kundalini is, what shaktipat is, the meaning of *chitshakti*, and so forth.

**Umashankar:** *Is it good to awaken Kundalini through hatha yoga?*

**Baba:** Kundalini should never be disturbed or provoked. She must never be subjected to any force; otherwise, negative results will ensue. The simplest method of awakening Kundalini is by receiving the Guru's grace through shaktipat. There will be no obstacles on this path.

*Another satsang took place in the evening.*

**Umashankar:** *If all the work is performed by Chiti Shakti, then Shiva has no significance.*

**Baba:** Yes, that is so. It is said in *Saundarya Laharī*:

> Shiva is able to create the universe only when united with Shakti. Without Shakti, He cannot even vibrate.[19]

Shiva without Shakti is like a corpse.

According to Shaivite doctrine, Parashiva, Shiva, and Shakti are the three main principles. Parashiva is attributeless, motionless, and of the nature of supreme bliss. He is supreme existence and supreme knowledge. The first wave arising in Him as *idam* (this) is Shiva; the vibration of that wave is Shakti. She is also known as Parashakti or Paravak. She has three aspects: will, knowledge, and action. The ecstatic dance of Shiva and Shakti brings this world into existence. The myriad forms seen in the world are Shakti's own forms.

Once when Dr. Brahma Prakash, director of the Atomic Energy Plant in Trombay, was here, he explained that, according to the principles of physics, all matter is energy. I replied, "Then there is no difference at all between your doctrine and ours. What you call energy, we call Brahma or Chiti Shakti."

**Umashankar:** *The philosopher and the scientist have come very close to each other.*

**Baba:** Yes, you're right.

*At seven-thirty this morning, everyone again gathered in the hall. Yesterday evening, Shrimati Rajeshwariben, the wife of Dr. Brahma Prakash, brought a copy of Gītā Pañchashatī, a collection of poems by Rabindranath Tagore, to satsang. At Baba's request, she recited two of the poems.*

## *Inspired Poets and Ordinary Poets*

**Umashankar:** *Akha, a great Gujarati poet-saint and jñānī, used to say that a jñānī should not be called a poet because a jñānī has gone far beyond being a mere poet.*

**Baba:** There are two types of poets: inspired poets and ordinary poets. Those who write from divine inspiration or those who have received the grace of the Guru are inspired poets. Tukaram, Jnaneshwar, and Sundardas were inspired poets. Those who write with effort by applying the intellect are ordinary poets. Only the poems of inspired poets appeal to me. I read only those.

**Umashankar:** *One who has received the grace of God is an inspired poet. A Gujarati proverb says, "The poet reaches a place that the sun cannot reach, and the realized one reaches a place that the poet cannot reach."*

## *Shabda Brahman: The Sound-Form of the Absolute*

**Umashankar:** *It has been said that the sound aum can be heard even in the water flowing from the tap. The world has emerged from pashyantī (vibration of sound).*

**Baba:** In the Sanskrit alphabet, the vowel *a* is inherent in every letter from *ka* to *ksha*. This is the same *a* that is in the sacred syllable *aum*. Sound at the *parā* stage (the subtlest level of is devoid of attributes or manifestation; at the *pashyantī* s starts vibrating; at the *madhyama* stage, it assumes a subtl and at the *vaikharī* stage, it finds complete expression.

*Aum*, or *ham*, occurs in every word or sound. It can be heard in the gurgling of a stream, in the roaring of the sea, and in the gentle dance of raindrops. You utter *ham* even when you lift a bucket or some weight. The entire world has emerged from *aum*. Our *prāna* incessantly repeats the sound of *So'ham*.

The incoming breath makes the sound *ham*, and the outgoing breath makes the sound *sa*. We are constantly doing *japa* of this mantra, *Hamsa, Hamsa*.

**Umashankar:** *This is known as shabda brahman, the sound-form of the Absolute. Even the Bible says that the world came into being out of the Word, and there is also a theory regarding the process of dissolution.*

**Baba:** The world will dissolve in the same way in which it was born. Its sequence of evolution was from ether, to air, to fire, to water, and finally, to earth. At the time of dissolution, it will merge back in the reverse order.

## *Shaktipat Initiation*

**Umashankar:** *Is any special technique involved in shaktipat initiation?*

**Baba:** Initiation takes place spontaneously; nothing special has to be done. Even without the Guru's conscious knowledge, his shakti may enter an earnest seeker. Sometimes I get signals like those of a radar in my heart. Then I start looking around, and if I find someone swaying, I know that they have received shaktipat; that is, they have been initiated. If germs like those of tuberculosis can infect people so easily, why shouldn't the particles of this all-pervading shakti also be contagious? In the presence of one whose shakti is fully awake, one quickly experiences shakti's effects.

**Umashankar:** *Is the process the same for everyone?*

**Baba:** Yes, the same. All the saints have the same degree from the same university. Truth is only one.

## Saturday, November 26, 1966

*An American woman, Manjushri (formerly Irene Wolfington), has been staying in the ashram for two or three days. She has been in India for the past three years, visiting many ashrams and meeting numerous saints and sages, but she has not found what she is seeking. She is now living the life of a sannyāsīnī in the Bajarang Cave on Mount Abu. This morning she asked Baba some questions.*

### *Knowledge of the Guru Is Essential*

**Manjushri:** *I believe in devotion to the Guru and in surrendering completely to him.*

**Baba:** Very good, but along with devotion you must also have knowledge about the Guru; otherwise, you may lose your faith. It is very good to have faith in only one Guru. There is a story in the *Mahābhārata* about Eklavya, who imbibed all of his Guru's knowledge and expertise in archery solely through devotion to him.

**Manjushri:** *Yes, but I am not at all satisfied with that example. How can a Guru harm his disciple? Dronacharya asked for Eklavya's thumb*[20] *and thus deprived him of his art. Was that proper behavior for a Guru?*

**Baba:** The saints and sages in those days were the protectors of the world. Dronacharya was Guru to the king. He was as adept in worldly matters as he was in archery and spirituality. He acted after considering what Eklavya deserved. Eklavya was a boy from the Bhilla tribe. He had faith and devotion, but he lacked discrimination. Instead of using his skill in archery at a proper time and place, he used it on a dog. If higher knowledge and expertise fall into the hands of unworthy individuals, they are likely to be misused to the detriment of society. For example, atomic energy can be used for the world's benefit, and also for its destruction. For this reason, the Guru imparts his knowledge only to a worthy disciple.

**Manjushri:** *If we initially received shakti from one Guru and for some reason its unfoldment is obstructed, and then another Guru reawakens the shakti, will any harmful results ensue?*

**Baba:** All Gurus are one; throughout the entire world, the Guru principle is only one. The shakti dwelling in each and every individual is also one and the same, and all Gurus awaken the same shakti. Different Gurus do not awaken different shaktis. Before asking this question, however, you must first know who the Guru is. Do not limit the Guru to the frame of the gross body.

**Manjushri:** *If one has received guidance from more than one Guru, then it is very difficult to serve or worship all of them at the same time.*

**Baba:** Why do you give importance to the outer form of the Guru?

**Manjushri:** *Since it is God Himself who guides us in the form of the Guru, then why does God turn against us? It is God's duty to put us on the right path.*

**Baba:** God never turns against us. We feel so because of our own mental defects, not because of any fault on the part of God or the Guru. If we err in our own actions, we feel that the Guru turned against us. If you do not have thorough knowledge of the Guru, you will have many occasions to feel victimized.

**Manjushri:** *If the Guru's physical form is not important, does that mean a Guru is not necessary? Isn't it possible to progress without a Guru?*

**Baba:** Love God, contemplate Him, sing His glories. Eventually, you yourself will become the Guru. Remain where you are and keep doing whatever you are doing now. This is the best course for you.

*Gurudev Siddha Peeth, Ganeshpuri, India*

# Guide
## *to Sanskrit Pronunciation*

For the reader's convenience, the Sanskrit and Hindi terms most frequently used in Siddha Yoga literature and courses appear throughout the text in roman type with simple transliteration. *Śaktipāta*, for instance, is shaktipat; *sādhana* is sadhana, and so on. For less frequently used Sanskrit words, the long vowels are marked in the text. The standard international transliteration for each Sanskrit term is given in the Glossary of Texts and Terms and in the Notes.

For readers not familiar with Sanskrit, the following is a guide for pronunciation.

### Vowels

Sanskrit vowels are categorized as either long or short. In English transliteration, the long vowels are marked with a macron above the letter and are pronounced twice as long as the short vowels. The vowels *e* and *o* are always pronounced as long vowels.

| Short: | Long: | |
|---|---|---|
| *a* as in c*u*p | *ā* as in c*a*lm | *ai* as in *ai*sle |
| *i* as in g*i*ve | *e* as in s*a*ve | *au* as in c*ow* |
| *u* as in f*u*ll | *ī* as in s*ee*n | |
| *ṛ* as in w*ri*tten | *o* as in kn*o*w | |
| | *ū* as in sch*oo*l | |

### Consonants

The main differences between Sanskrit and English pronunciation of consonants are in the aspirated and retroflexive letters.

The aspirated letters have a definite *h* sound. The Sanskrit letter *kh* is pronounced as in in*kh*orn; the *th* as in boa*th*ouse; the *ph* as in loo*ph*ole.

The retroflexes are pronounced with the tip of the tongue touching the hard palate; *ṭ*, for instance, is pronounced as in an*t*; *ḍ* as in en*d*.

The sibilants are *ś*, *ṣ*, and *s*. The *ś* is pronounced as *sh* but with the tongue touching the soft palate; the *ṣ* as *sh* with the tongue touching the hard palate; the *s* as in hi*s*tory.

Other distinctive consonants are these:

| | |
|---|---|
| *c* as in *ch*urch | *ṃ* is a strong nasal |
| *ch* as in pit*ch-h*ook | *ḥ* is a strong aspiration |
| *ñ* as in ca*ny*on | |

For a detailed pronunciation guide, see *The Nectar of Chanting*, published by SYDA Foundation.

# NOTES

## Introduction

1. *Niti Śataka* 122
   *pari-caritavyāḥ santo yady-api kathayanti te na upadeśam /*
   *yās-teṣāṃ svair-akathāḥ tā eva bhavanti śāstrāṇi //*
2. *veda-udadḥi bina-guru lāgāi launa-samāna /*
   *bādara guru-mukḥa dvāra ḥai āmṛtāse ādḥikāna //*
3. *vedāntānām-anekatvāt-saṃśayānāṃ bahutvataḥ /*
   *vedyasyāpy-atisūkṣmatvān-na jānāti guruṃ vinā //*
4. *Bhagavadgītā* 4.34
   *tad viddhi prāṇipātena paripraśnena sevayā /*
   *upadekṣyanti te jñānaṃ jñāninas tattvadarśinaḥ //*
5. *ekam-apy-akṣaraṃ yas-tu guruḥ śiṣye nivedayet /*
   *pṛthivyāṃ nāsti tad-dravyaṃ yad-dattvā tvan-ṛṇībhavet //*
6. *Bhagavadgītā* 10.18
   *bhūyaḥ kathaya tṛptir-hi śṛṇvato nāsti me'mṛtam /*

## 1962

1. *Bhagavadgītā* 9.22
   *teṣāṃ nityābhiyuktānāṃ yoga-kṣemaṃ vahāmy-aham /*
2. *Bhagavadgītā* 4.18
   *karmaṇy-akarma yaḥ paśyed-akarmaṇi ca karma yaḥ /*
   *sa buddhimān-manuṣyeṣu sa yuktaḥ kṛtsna-karma-kṛt //*
3. *Bhagavadgītā* 5.18
   *vidyā-vinaya-sampanne brāhmaṇe gavi hastini /*
   *śuni caiva śvapāke ca paṇḍitāḥ sama-darśinaḥ //*

4. *Bhagavadgītā* 4.11
*ye yathā māṃ prapadyante tāṃ tathaiva bhajāmy-aham /*

## 1963

1. *Bhagavadgītā* 10.42
*viṣṭabhyāham-idaṃ kṛtsnam-ekāṃśena sthito jagat /*

2. *Bhagavadgītā* 9.21
*kṣīṇe puṇye martya-lokaṃ viśanti /*

3. *avaśyam-eva bhoktavyaṃ kṛtaṃ karma yubhāyubham /*
*nābhuktaṃ kṣīyate karma kalpa-koṭi-śatair-api //*

4. *Bhagavadgītā* 11.12
*divi sūrya-sahasrasya bhaved-yugapad-utthitā /*
*yadi bhāḥ sadṛśī sā syād-bhāsas-tasya mahātmanaḥ //*

5. *Bhagavadgītā* 18.17
*yasya nāhaṃ-kṛto bhāvo buddhir-yasya na lipyate /*

6. *isā akḥila viśvā meṃ bharā eka tū ḥī tū /*
*tujḥameṃ-mujḥameṃ 'tū meiṃ-tū 'tū 'tū ḥī tū //1//*
*nabḥā meṃ tū jalā-tḥala vāyu atāla meṃ bḥī tū /*
*megḥadhvani dāmini vṛṣṭi pralayā meṃ bḥī tū //2//*
*sāgara atḥāha saritā/pravāḥa meṃ bḥī tū /*
*śaśi/śitalatā dinakara-pradāḥa meṃ bḥī tū //3//*
*tū pāpa-puṇya-meṃ naraka-svārga meṃ bḥī tū /*
*paśu-pakṣī surāsura manujavarga meṃ bḥī tū //4//*
*hai miṭṭi-lauḥa pāṣāṇa-svarṇa meṃ bḥī tū /*
*caturāśrama meṃ tū caturvarṇā meṃ bḥī tū //5//*
*ḥai dḥanī-raṃka jñānī-ajñānī meṃ tū /*
*ḥai nirābḥimānī meṃ ati abḥimānī meṃ tū //6//*
*ḥai śātru-mitra meṃ bāḥara-gḥara meṃ tū /*
*ḥai ūpara nīce madḥya carācara meṃ tū //7//*
*'ho' meṃ 'nā' meṃ tū 'tū 'meṃ 'maiṃ 'meṃ tū /*
*ḥai tū-tū-tū-tū-tū-tū basa! tū ḥī tū //8//*

7. Kashmir Shaivism delineates four different *upāyas,* or means, for Self-realization. *Ānavopāya (ānava upāya)* is a means whereby the seeker uses the body, senses, breath, sound, etc. In *shāktopāya (shākta upāya)* the seeker primarily uses the power of the mind. In *shāmbhavopāya (shāmbhava upāya)* the power of the will is used. *Ānupāya* consists of instant recognition of the true nature of the Self through the Guru's grace.

8. *stuti kāṃḥīṃ na bolāṇeṃ / pūjā kāṃḥīṃ nā kārāṇeṃ /*
*samidḥīṃ kāṃḥīṃ nā ḥoṇeṃ / tujḥyā ṭhāyīṃ //*

9. *Vivekacūḍāmaṇi* 55
*yan-manasā na manute yenāhur-mano matam /*
*tad-eva brahma tvaṃ viddhi nedaṃ yad-idam-upāsate //*

10. The *kalā* of Chiti (literally, "the treasure of Chiti") refers to the inner lights that occur when the Blue Pearl bursts in meditation, granting the meditator the experience of Self-realization.

11. *jñāneśvarī pāṭhīṃ / jo ovī karila marhāṭhīṃ /*
*teṇe amṛtāce tāṭīṃ / jāṇa naroṭī ṭhevilī //*

## 1964

1. *Bhagavadgītā* 3.36
*atha kena prayukto'yaṃ pāpaṃ carati pūruṣaḥ /*
*anicchann-api vārṣṇeya balād-iva niyojitaḥ //*

2. *Bhagavadgītā* 3.37
*kāma eṣa krodha eṣa rajo-guṇa-samudbhavaḥ /*
*mahāśano mahāpāpmā viddhy-enam-iha vairiṇam //*

3. *yaṃ śaivāḥ sam-upāsate śiva iti brahmeti vedāntino*
*bauddhā buddha iti pramāṇa-paṭavaḥ karteti naiyāyikāḥ /*
*arhann-ity-atha jaina-śāsana-ratāḥ karmeti mīmāṃsakāḥ*
*so'yaṃ vo vi-dadhātu vāñchita-phalaṃ trailokya-nātho hariḥ /*

4. *pānyā-madhyeṃ māsā jhoṃpa gheto kaisā /*
*jāveṃ tyācyā vaṃśā tevhāṃ kaḷe //*

5. *Śiva Mahimnaḥ Stotram* 7
*rucīnāṃ vaicitryād-ṛju-kuṭila-nānā-pathajuṣāṃ /*
*nṛṇām-eko gamyas-tvam-asi payasām-arṇava iva //*

6. *tarī kīrtanāceni naṭanāceṃ / nāśile vyavasāya prāyaścittāṃce*
*je nāmaci nāhīṃ pāpāceṃ / aiseṃ keleṃ //*
*yamadamā avakaḷa āṇilī / tīrtheṃ ṭhāyāvarūni uṭhavilīṃ /*
*yama-lokīṃ khuṃṭilī / rāhāṭī āghavī //*
*yamu mhaṇe kāya yamāveṃ / damu mhaṇe kavaṇāteṃ damāveṃ /*
*tīrtheṃ mhaṇatī kāya khāveṃ / doṣa okhadāsi nāhīṃ //*
*aise mājheni nāmaghoṣeṃ / nāhīṃ karitī viśvācī duḥkheṃ /*
*avagheṃ jagaci mahāsukheṃ / dumadumita bharaleṃ //*

7. *brahmī-bhūta hote kāyā ca kīrtanīṃ /*
*bhāgya tarī ṛṇī devī aisā //*
*tīrtha-bhrāmakāsī āṇīna āḷasa /*
*kaḍu svarga-vāsa karina bhoga/*
*sāṃḍavīna tapo-nidhā abhimāna /*
*yajña āni dāna lājavīna /*
*bhakti-bhāgya-premā sādhīna puruṣārtha /*
*brahmīṃcā jo artha nijaṭhevā //*

8. *viṣaya to tyāṃcā jhālā nārāyaṇa*
*nāvaḍe dhana-jana mātā-pitā*

9. *rakta śveta kṛṣṇa pīta prabhā bhinna /*
*cinmaya añjana sudaleṃ ḍoḷāṃ //*

10. *jñānī iyetem̥ svasam̥viti / śaiva mhaṇatī śakti /*
*āmhī parama / bhakti āpulī mhaṇo //*

11. *Bhagavadgītā* 5.4
*sām̥khya-yogau pr̥thag-bālāḥ pravadanti na paṇḍitāḥ /*
*ekam-apy-āsthitaḥ samyag-ubhayor-vindate phalam //*

12. *ugā mī koṇā kāya mhaṇūm̥ //dhru //*
*sac-cit-sukha-maya ekaci asatām̥*
*kuṭhunī dvaita gaṇūm̥ ? . . . ugā mī /*
*brahma vilokunī sośīla kaisī*
*jagad-ābhāsa gaṇūm̥ ? . . . ugā mī /*
*amr̥ta-samudrīm̥ advaitācyā*
*kuṭhunī kūpa khaṇūm̥ ? . . . ugā mī /*

13. *Bhagavadgītā* 13.5
*r̥ṣibhir-bahudhā gītam̥ chandobhir-vividhaiḥ pr̥thak /*
*brahma-sūtra-padaiś-caiva hetumadbhir-viniścitaiḥ //*

14. *banā do buddhi-hīna bhagavān /*
*tarka-śakti sārī hī hara lo; haro jñāna-vijñāna /*
*bhara do hr̥daya bhakti-śraddhā se, karo prema kā dāna //*

15. *Yogasūtra* 1.37
*vīta-rāga-viṣayam̥ vā cittam /*

16. *jo mana nāri ki ora nihārata, tau mana hota hi tāhiku rūpā /*
*jo mana kāhasūm̥ krodha karai puni tau mana hai taba hī tada rūpā /*
*jo mana māya hi māya raṭai nita, tau mana būḍata māya ke kūpā*
*sundara jo mana brahma vicārata, tau mana hota hi brahma svarūpa //*

17. *Bhagavadgītā* 6.17
*yuktāhāra-vihārasya yukta-ceṣṭasya karmasu /*
*yukta svapnāvabodhasya yogo bhavati duḥkhahā //*

18. *Maitri Upaniṣad* 6.34.11
*mana eva manuṣyāṇām̥ kāraṇam̥ bandha-mokṣayoḥ /*

19. *Bhagavadgītā* 2.14
*mātrāsparśās-tu kaunteya śītoṣṇa sukha-duḥkhadāh /*
*āgamāpāyino'nityās-tām̥s-titikṣasva bhārata //*

20. *Kenopaniṣad* 2.3
*yasyāmatam̥ tasya matam̥ matam̥ yasya na veda saḥ /*

21. *Bhagavadgītā* 9.2
*rāja-vidyā rāja-guhyam̥ pavitram-idam-uttamam /*

22. *Taittirīyopaniṣad* 2.6.1
*tat-sr̥ṣṭvā tad-evānuprāviśat /*

23. *Bhagavadgītā* 18.46
*yataḥ pravr̥ttir-bhūtānām̥ yena sarvam-idam̥ tatam /*
*svakarmaṇā tam-abhyarcya siddhim̥ vindati mānavaḥ //*

24. *Kaṭhopaniṣad* 2.2.15
*na tatra sūryo bhāti na candra-tārakaṃ*
*nemā vidyuto bhānti kuto'yam-agniḥ /*
*tam-eva bhāntam-anubhāti sarvaṃ*
*tasya bhāsā sarvam-idaṃ vibhāti //*

25. *Yogasūtra* 3.2
*tatra pratyay-ekatānatā dhyānam*

26. *gupata hokara paragaṭa hove, jāve mathurā kāśī /*
*calatā hai pānī ke ūpara, mukha bole so hove //*
*phira bhī kaccā be kaccā, nahīṃ guru kā baccā //*

27. One who has mastered the *Bhrigu Samhitā* is a master of Vedic astrology.

28. Prahlad was the son of a demon and an ardent devotee of Lord Narayana. One day Prahlad and his father were arguing over the boy's religious beliefs, when Prahlad asserted with complete conviction that Narayana was everywhere, even in a nearby pillar. The father kicked the pillar, which then, before his very eyes, changed into a form of Lord Narayana.

Vishvamitra created another universe to accommodate King Trishanku, who wanted to stay in heaven in his earthly body. Vishvamitra, using his yogic powers, raised Trishanku to heaven, but the other inhabitants objected. Vishvamitra then created another heaven in which Trishanku could live.

The *gopīs* were the milkmaidens who were devoted to the young (*bāla*) Lord Krishna. Because of their ardent devotion and Krishna's love for them, those who could not leave their homes for the *rāslīlā* dance on full-moon nights found that Krishna came to their houses and danced with them there. *(Śrīmad Bhāgavatam)*

29. *deha ora dekhiye tau, deha pañca-bhūtana ko /*
*brahmā aru kīṭa laga, deha hī pradhāna hai //*
*prāna ora dekhiye tau, prāna saba hī ke eka /*
*kṣudhā puni tṛṣā dou, vyāpata samāna hai //*
*mana ora dekhiye tau, mana ko svabhāva eka /*
*saṅkalpa-vikalpa karai, sadā hī ajñāna hai /*
*ātama vicāra kiye, ātamā hī dīsai eka /*
*sundara kahata koū, dekhiye na āna hai //*

30. *Bhagavadgītā* 17.3
*sattvānurūpā sarvasya śraddhā bhavati bhārata /*
*śraddhā-mayo'yaṃ puruṣo yo yac-chraddhaḥ sa eva saḥ //*

31. *Bhagavadgītā* 2.60
*indriyāṇi pramāthīni haranti prasabhaṃ manaḥ //*

32. *govinda ke kiye jīva būḍata bhava-sāgara meṃ*
*sundara kahata guru kāḍhai dukhadvandva taiṃ //*
*aurahū kahāṃ lauṃ kacchū mukha teṃ kahūṃ banāya /*
*guru kī tau mahimā adhika hai govinda taiṃ //*

33. *deha devāce deūḷa, āmta bāhira nirmaḷa*

34. *saguṇī dhyātāṃ nirguṇī gelo, ātāṃ jhālo mī nārāyaṇa*

35. The *Satyanārāyana Pūjā* and *Shatachandi Yajña* are ritual ceremonies invoking the blessings of Satyanarayan and Chandi (the goddess Durga) respectively.

36. *Bhagavadgītā* 5.4
*sāṃkhya-yogau pṛthak-bālāḥ pravadanti na paṇḍitāḥ /*

37. *śyāya śyāma raṭata rādhe āpa hi śyāma bhaī /*
*pūchata phirata apanī sakhiyana se, pyārī kahāṃ gaī //*

38. *sac-cid-ānanda-rūpāya kṛṣṇāyākliṣṭa-kāriṇe /*
*namo vedānta-vedyāya gurave buddhi-sākṣiṇe //*

39. *dekhata brahma sunai puni brahmahi, bolata hai vahi brahma hi bānī /*
*bhūmihu nīrahu tejāhu vāyuhu, vyomahu brahma jahāṃ laga prānī*
*ādihu antahu madhyahu brahmahi, hai saba brahma yahai mati ṭhānī /*
*sundara jñeya ru jñānahu brahma hi, āpahu brahma hi jānata jñānī /*

40. *saba pānī gaṅgā bhayo, saba giri śāligrāma /*
*saba jaṅgala tulasī bhayo, hṛdaya basata jehi rāma //*

41. *Bhagavadgītā* 6.34
*cañcalaṃ hi manaḥ kṛṣṇa pramāthi balavad-dṛḍham /*
*tasyāhaṃ nigrahaṃ manye vāyor-iva suduṣkaram //*

42. *dekhai tau vicāra kari, sunai tau vicāra kari /*
*bolai tau vicāra kari, karai tau vicāra hai //*
*khāya tau vicāra kari, pībai tau vicāra kari /*
*sovai tau vicāra kari, jāge tau na ṭāra hai //*
*sundara tau vicāra kari, yāhī niradhāra hai //*

43. *Vairāgya Śataka* 35
*bhoge roga-bhayaṃ kule cyuti-bhayaṃ vitte nṛpālātbhayaṃ*
*maune dainya-bhayaṃ bale ripu-bhayaṃ rūpe jarāyā bhayaṃ /*
*śāstre vādabhyaṃ guṇe khalabhayaṃ kāye kṛtāntāb-bhayaṃ*
*sarva vastu bhayānvitaṃ bhuvi nṛṇāṃ vairāgyam-evābhayaṃ //*

44. *brahma-jñānācī killī, sāṃgate ekaca bolī*
*abhimāna nimālī, tūci brahma*

45. *Aparokṣānubhūti* 7
*viṣayebhyaḥ parāvṛttiḥ paramoparatir-hi-sā /*

46. *śāstra hai saba saccā /*
*hama samajhane meṃ kaccā //*

47. Vishvamitra: See 1964, Note 28.

48. A teaching story in Vedanta tells of a man who came across a rope on the road and became terrified and attempted to kill it because he mistook it for a snake.

## 1965

1. *aṃkhiyāṃ hari darasana kī pyāsī /*
*dekhyo cāhata kamalanaina ko nisi-dina rahat udāsī //*

2. *kyoṃ bana-bana ḍhūṃḍhata sāṃī sāṃī hai ghaṭa māṃhī ... kyoṃ ...*

3. *pānī meṃ mīna piyāsī, mohe suni-suni āvata hāṃsī*

4. *agara hai śauka milane kā to haradama lau lagātā jā /*
*jalākara khudanumāī ko bhasama tana para lagātā jā //*

5. *musallā chhoḍa, tasabī toḍa, kitābeṃ ḍala pānī meṃ /*
*pakaḍa dasta tū phariśtoṃ kā, gulāma unakā kahātā jā //*

6. *hameśā khā, hameśā pī, na gaphalata se raho ikadama /*
*naśe meṃ saira kara apanī, khudī ko tū jalātā jā //*

7. *na ho mullā, na ho bammana, duī kī chhoḍakara pūjā //*
*hukma hai śāha kalandara kā, analahak tū kahātā jā //*
*kahai mansūra mastānā, haka maine dil meṃ pahacānā //*
*vahī mastoṃ kā mayakhānā usī ke bīca ātā jā //*

8. This practice of exclusion is no longer prevalent.

9. *Bhaktisūtra* 72
*nāsti teṣu jāti-vidyā-rūpa-kula-dhana-kriyādi bhedāḥ /*

10. Kubja was a hunchbacked woman whose devotion pleased Lord Brahma so much that he gave her a place in Suryaloka, the world of the sun.

    Sudama was a childhood friend of Lord Krishna who became impoverished. Sent by his wife to beg a favor of Krishna, he was too embarrassed to do so and left after giving Krishna a humble gift: a handful of puffed rice, which Krishna eagerly accepted. Lord Krishna then caused food and riches to appear at Sudama's home.

    Vyadha had also been a childhood friend of Krishna. By adulthood he had sunk so low that he made his living by killing animals. One day while hunting deer, he mistakenly hit Lord Krishna himself. In fulfillment of a prophecy, the wound was fatal, and Krishna returned to Vaikuntha, his abode, as Lord of all.

    Gajendra was liberated by the touch of Lord Narayana even though he was an elephant, and consequently had no caste.

11. *Kulārṇavatantra*
*dīyate śiva-sāyujyaṃ kṣīyate pāśa-bandhanam /*
*ato dīkṣeti kathitā budhaiḥ sac-chāstra-vedibhiḥ //*

12. *yā devī sarva-bhūteṣu śakti-rūpeṇa saṃsthitā /*
*namas-tasyai namas-tasyai namas-tasyai namo namaḥ //*

13. *Bhagavadgītā* 14.4
*sarva-yoniṣu kaunteya mūrtayaḥ sambhavanti yāḥ /*
*tāsāṃ brahma mahad-yonir-ahaṃ vīja-pradaḥ pitā //*

14. *tāta milai, puni māta milai, suta-bhrāta milai, yuvatī sukhadāī /*
*rāja milai, gaja-bāji milai, saba sāja milai, manavāṃchita pāī /*
*loka milai, sura-loka milai, vidhi-loka milai, vaikūṭhahu jāī*
*sundara aura milai saba hī sukha, santa-samāgama durlabha bhāī //*

15. *Bhagavadgītā* 4.37
*yathaidhāṃsi samiddho'gnir-bhasma-sātkurute'rjuna /*
*jñānāgniḥ sarva karmāṇi bhasma-sātkurute tathā //*

16. *hṛdi-sthāne aṣṭa-dala-padmaṃ vartate tan-madhye rekhāvalayaṃ*
*kṛtvā jīvātma-rūpaṃ jyoti-rūpam-aṇu-mātra vartate /*

17. *yā sā tu mātṛkā devi para-tejaḥ samanvitā /*
*tayā vyāptam-idaṃ viśvaṃ sabrahma bhuvanāntakam /*
*sā nityā muktā sanātanī //*

18. *Bhagavadgītā* 2.51
*karmajaṃ buddhi-yuktā hi phalaṃ tyaktvā manīṣiṇaḥ /*
*janma-bandha-vinirmuktāḥ padaṃ gacchanty-anāmayam //*

19. *Bhagavadgītā* 4.16
*kiṃ karma kim-akarmeti kavayo'py-atra mohitāḥ /*

20. *Śivasūtra* 1.21
*śuddhavidyodayāccakreśatvasiddhiḥ /*

21. In the *Mahābhārata*, Sanjaya served as charioteer to the blind king Dhritarashtra, describing to him all that took place on the battlefield. Sanjaya listened to Lord Krishna's teachings to Arjuna and, by the end of the war, attained liberation. The king, however, only listened to hear who had won the battle and by the end of the war he was dejected and defeated.

22. *sarvatra prāṇināṃ dehe japo bhavati sarvadā /*
*haṃsaḥ so'ham-iti jñātvā sarva-bandhaiḥ pramucyate //*

23. In the *savikalpa* state, the mind recognizes a distinction between subject and object, knower and known, and so on.

24. *eko'haṃ bahu-syām*

25. *ādau bhagavān śabda-rāśiḥ*

26. *Bhagavadgītā* 10.25
*yajñānāṃ japa-yajño'smi*

27. *nāmā mhaṇe nāma caitanya nija dhāma*

28. *śuka sanakādika siddha muni jogī, nāma-prasāda brahma-sukha bhogī /*
*cahuṃ-yuga cahuṃ-śruti nāma-prabhāū kali viśeṣa nahiṃ āna upāū //*

29. *Yogasūtra* 1.28
*taj-japas-tad-artha-bhāvanam /*

30. *aiso rāma-nāma rasa-khāna,*
*murakha jāko marama na jāne,*
*pīvata catura sujāna /*
*rāma-rasa mīṭho aiso mīṭho nahīṃ aura koī //*

31. *rāma rasa mīṭha re, koī pīve sādhu sujāna /*
*sadā rasa pīveṃ, prema sauṃ, so avināśī pāna //*
*siddha sādhaka jogī jatī, satī sabai sukha devu /*
*pīvata aṃta na āvaī, aisā alakha abhevu //*
*ihi rasa rāte nāmedeva, pīpā aru raidāsa /*
*pīvata kabīrā nā thakyā, ajahūṃ prema piyāsa //*
*yahu rasa mīṭhā jina piyā, so rasa hī māhīṃ samāī /*
*mīṭhā mīṭhe milī rahyā, dādū anata na jāī //*

32. *Bhagavadgītā* 10.22
*indriyāṇāṃ manaś-cāsmi //*

33. *Bhagavadgītā* 4.7
*yadā yadā hi dharmasya glānir-bhavati bhārata /*
*abhyutthānam-adharmasya tadātmānaṃ sṛjāmy-aham //*

34. *saguṇī dhyātāṃ nirguṇī gelo, ātāṃ jhālo mī nārāyaṇa*

35. Markandeya's destiny was to live for only sixteen years. But he performed intense austerities with such ardent devotion, even as a child, that Lord Shiva saved him from death and granted him immortality.

36. *Bhagavadgītā* 10.6
*mad-bhāvā mānasā jātā yeṣāṃ loka imāḥ prajāḥ //*

37. *Bhaktisūtra* 6
*yaj-jñātvā matto bhavati stabdho bhavati ātmārāmo bhavati /*

38. Eight stages of yoga are described by Patanjali in his *Yoga Sūtras*, the authoritative text on yoga. The eight stages are self-restraint, daily practices, steady posture, breath control, sense withdrawal, concentration, meditation, and union with the Absolute. This practice is known as *ashtānga yoga*, literally, eight limbs of yoga.

39. *khudī ko na miṭāo taba taka khudā nahīṃ milatā /*
*miṭāo apanī hastī ko jo kuch maratabā cāhatā //*

40. *kṛṣṇa kṛṣṇa karata rādhā kṛṣṇa bana gaī /*
*pūchata sakhiyana se pyārī rādhā kahāṃ gaī //*

41. *Bhagavadgītā* 15.7
*mamaivāṃśo jīva-loko jīva-bhūtaḥ sanātanaḥ /*

42. *kaṃgāla ko mālomāla, daridra ko nihāla,*
*raṃka ko bhūpāla, śāha ko śāhanaśāha banātī hai /*
*papoṃ kī hananī, jñāna vairāgya kī jananī,*
*mūrkha ko paṇḍita, paṇḍita ko akhaṇḍita banātī hai /*

43. *kāyā hī paṇḍharī, ātmā hā viṭhṭhala, nāndato kevala pāṇḍuraṅga*

44. *bhramata bhramata kahūṃ, bhrama ko na āvai anta /*
*cira-kāla bītyo pai sva-rūpakuṃ na lahyo hai /*
*taise hī sundara yaha bhrama kari bhūlyo āpa /*
*bhrama ke gayeteṃ eka ātmā sadāī hai //*

45. *Bhagavadgītā* 14.5
*sattvaṃ rajas-tama iti guṇāḥ prakṛti-sambhavāḥ /*
*nibadhnanti mahābāho dehe dehinam-avyayam //*

46. *galitā śīra te kalevara re / udakeṃviṇa saritā bhayaṇkara re*
*ravi-śaśiviṇa ambara taseṃ / hariviṇa jiṇe asāra re /*

47. *Bhagavadgītā* 8.14
*ananya-cetāḥ satataṃ yo māṃ smarati nityaśaḥ /*
*tasyāhaṃ sulabhaḥ pārtha nitya-yuktasya yoginaḥ* //8.14//

48. *binu hari-bhajana na bhava tarie, yaha siddhānta apela /*

49. *rāma nāma raṭate raho, jaba lagi ghaṭa meṃ prāṇa*

50. *nāma saprema japata anayāsā / bhagata hohiṃ muda maṅgala bāsā/*

51. *yekāntī maunya dharūna baise*
*sāvadha pahātā kaiseṃ bhāse*
*so'haṃ so'haṃ aise śabda hotī*

52. In the Upanishads are four great statements, known as *mahāvākyas,* which assert the oneness of the individual self and God. These are: "I am the Absolute," *aham brahmāsmi (Yajur Veda)*; "The Self is the Absolute," *ayam ātmā brahma (Atharva Veda)*; "Consciousness is the Absolute," *prajñānam brahma (Rig Veda)*; "That thou art," *tat tvam asi (Sāma Veda).*

53. *pṛthaṅmantraḥ pṛthaṅmantrī na sidhyati kadācana /*

54. *mantrārathem mantra-caitanyaṃ yo na jānāti sādhakaḥ /*
*śatalakṣaṃ prajāpato'pi taysa mantro na sidhyati //*

55. *Vairāgya Śataka* 103
*dhanyānāṃ girikandare nivasatāṃ jyotiḥ paraṃ dhyāyatām /*

56. *gupata hokara paragaṭa hove, jāve mathurā kāśī /*
*calatā hai pānī ke ūpara, mukha bole so hove /*
*so hī kaccā be kaccā be, nahīṃ gurū kā baccā //*

57. *rakta śveta nīla kā nahīṃ jñāna /*
*tahāṃ mūrkha-paṇḍita eka samāna //*

58. *upara tau vyavahāra karai saba, bhītara svapna samāna ju bhāsai*

59. *bhramaṇa karata jyoṃ pavana teṃ, sūkho pīpaṛapāta /*
*śeṣa karma prārabdha teṃ, kriyā karata darasāta //*

60. *kabahuṃka caḍhi ratha bājigaja, bāga bāgīce dekhi /*
*nagnapāda puni ekale, phira āvata tihiṃ lekhi //*
*vividha veśa, śayyāśayana, uttama bhigana bhoga /*
*kabahuṃka sanaśata giriguhā, rajani śilā saṃyoga //*
*kari praṇāma pūjana karata, kahuṃ jana lākha-hajāra /*
*ubhaya loka teṃ bhraṣṭa lakhi, kahata karmī dhikkāra //*

61. *vāyu vahatī phara phara mujhameṃ mujhameṃ mujhameṃ /*
*nadī vahatī jhara jhara mujhameṃ mujhameṃ mujhameṃ //*

62. *jyūṃ bana eka aneka bhaye druma, nāma anantani, jāti hu nyārī*
*vāpi taḍāga ru kūpa, nadī saba, hai jala eka su dekha nihārī /*
*pāvaka eka, prakāśa bahuvidhi, dīpa cirāga masāla hu bārī /*
*sundara brahma vilāsa akhaṇḍita bheda-abheda ki buddhi su ṭārī //*

63. *Taittirīyopaniṣad* 2.2.1
*annād-bhūtāni jāyante jātāny-annena vardhante*

64. *Taittirīyopaniṣad* 2.1.1
*tasmād-vā etasmād-ātmana ākāśas sambhūtaḥ*

65. *dvaita kari dekhai jaba, dvaita hī dikhāī deta /*
*eka kari dekhai taba uhai eka amga hai /*
*sūrajakūṃ dekhai jaba sūraja prakāśi rahyo /*
*kiranakuṃ dekhai to kirana nānā ramga hai //*

66. *dekhata brahma sunai puni brahmahi, bolata hai vahī brahmahi bānī /*
*bhūmihū nīrahū tejahū vayuhū, vyomahū brahma jahāṃ laga prānī /*
*ādihu antahu madhyahu brahmāhi, hai saba brahma yahai pati ṭhānī /*
*sundara jñeya ru jñānahu brahmahi, āpahu brahmahi jānata jñānī //*

67. *Kathopaniṣad* 2.1.10
*mṛtyos sa mṛtyum-āpnoti ya iha nāneva paśyati /*

68. *Bhagavadgītā* 7.3
*manuṣyāṇāṃ sahasreṣu kaścid-yatati siddhaye /*

69. *Bhagavadgītā* 18.78
*yatra yogeśvaraḥ kṛṣṇo yatra pārtho dhanur-dharaḥ /*
*tatra śrīr-vijayo bhūtir-dhruvā nītir-matir-mama //*18.78*//*

70. *Yogadanda:* A stick that ascetics used to rest their chins on when meditating for long hours. Through the accumulation of shakti, accomplished yogis were said to perform miracles with these sticks.

71. *mānava! tujhe nahīṃ yāda kyā? tū brahma kā hī aṃśa hai /*
*kula-gotra terā brahma hai, sad-brahma terā vaṃśa hai //*

## 1966

1. *Bhagavadgītā* 18.66
*sarva-dharmān-parityajya mām-ekaṃ śaraṇaṃ vraja /*

2. *Bhagavadgītā* 18.66
*ahaṃ tvā sarva-pāpebhyo mokṣayiṣyāmi mā śucaḥ //*

3. *īśvaro gurur-ātmeti mūrti-bheda-vibhāgine /*
*vyomavad-vyāpta-dehāya tasmai śrī-gurave namaḥ /*

4. *Bhagavadgītā* 2.29
*āścaryavat-paśyati kaścid-enam-āścaryavad-vadati tathaiva cānyaḥ /*
*āścaryavac-cainam-anyaḥ śṛṇoti śrutvāpy-enaṃ veda na caiva kaścit //*

5. *Kaṭhopaniṣad* 1.2.7
*śravaṇāyāpi bahubhir-yo na labhyaḥ śṛṇvanto'pi bahavo yaṃ na vidyuḥ /*
*āścaryo vaktā kuśalo'sya labdhā āścaryo jñātā kuśalānuśiṣṭaḥ /*

6. *aikā dayārṇava-kṛta prārthanā bhoga prārabdha yoge jāṇā /*
*puruṣārthī sādhije bhagavad-bhajanā ye khūṇa manāmājī dharije //*

7. *jyūṃ ravi kūṃ ravi ḍhūṃḍhata hai kahuṃ, tapta milai tana śīta gamāūṃ /*
*jyūṃ śaśi kūṃ śaśi cāhata hai puni, śītala hai kari tapta bujhāūṃ /*
*jyūṃ sanipāta bhaye nara ṭerata hai ghara meṃ apane ghara jāūṃ /*
*tyūṃ yaha sundara bhūli svarūpahi, brahma kahai kaba brahmahi pāūṃ //*

8. Jadabharat was a brahmin in ancient times who was thought to be inert and dull (*jada*) by his family because he would spontaneously go into *samādhi* and remain in the same position for long periods of time, unresponsive to the outside world.

9. *indriyāṇi indriyārtheṣu vartanta iti dhārayana*

10. *nahiṃ mile dhana tyāge, nahiṃ mile rāmajī jāna taje /*
*nārāyaṇa to mile usī ko, jo deha abhimāna taje // ṭeka//*
*suta-dārā yā kuṭumba tyāge, yā apanā ghara bāra taje /*
*nahiṃ mile prabhu kadāpi, jagata kā saba vyavahāra taje /*
*kaṃda mūle phala khāya rahe, aura anna kā bhī āhāra taje /*
*vastra ko tyāga nagna rahe, aura ghara kī nāra taje /*
*to bhī hari nahiṃ mile yaha tyāge, cāhe apane prāṇa taje /*
*nārāyaṇa to mile usī ko, jo deha abhimāna taje /*

11. *maiṃ-merā saṃsāra hai, anya nahīṃ saṃsāra /*
*maiṃ-merā jātā rahe, beḍā hai bhava pāra //*
*beḍā hai bhava pāra, jahaṃ na duḥkha jarā hai /*
*sukha-sāgara bharapūra, eka sā nityabharā hai //*
*jayadevī taja moha, deha bhī nahīṃ terā /*
*kyūṃ karatī abhimāna, "gṛha merā, dhana merā" //*

12. *Kaṭhopaniṣad* 2.3.2
*yad-idaṃ kiñca jagat-sarvaṃ prāṇa ejati niḥsṛtam /*

13. *Hāṭhayoga Pradīpikā* 1.1
*bibhrājate pronnatarāja-yogam-ārodhum-iccher-adhi rohiṇīva /*

14. *śakti-pātonmiṣita-pārameśvara-samāveśābhilāṣiṇaḥ katicit bhakti-bhājaḥ teṣām-īśvara-pratyabhijñopadeśa-tatvaṃ manāk unmīlyate /*

15. *ayaṃ śakti-daridraḥ saṃsārī ucyate, sva-śakti-vikāse tu śiva eva /*

16. *Śivasūtra* 2.6

17. *Pratyabhijñāhṛdayam* 17
*madhya-vikāsāc-cid-ānanda-lābhaḥ /*

18. *Śivasūtra* 1.2

19. *Saundarya Laharī* 1.1
*śivaḥ śaktayā yukto yadi bhavati śaktiḥ prabhavitum /*
*na ced-evaṃ devo na khalu kuśalaḥ spanditum-api //*

20. Eklavya was a tribal boy who wanted to learn the princely art of archery from the great Guru of martial arts, Dronacharya. However, Dronacharya was retained by the king to teach only princes, so he could not accept Eklavya as his student. Unfazed by this rejection, Eklavya made a clay statue of Guru Dronacharya and worshiped it daily. In time, because of his devotion, Eklavya mastered the art of archery—including a shot that Dronacharya had not taught the princes. Dronacharya learned of Eklavya's mastery and knew it posed a problem, for the princes must be the best warriors in the country. It was the custom at that time that upon completion of his studies, the student would offer his teacher a gift, called *gurudakshinā,* which could be anything the Guru asked of him. So Dronacharya asked Eklavya for his right thumb. This would make archery impossible for Eklavya and maintain the princes' status. Eklavya willingly cut off his right thumb and gave it to Dronacharya. *(Mahābhārata)*

# GLOSSARY

## *of Poets, Philosophers, and Sages*

**ABHINAVAGUPTA**
(993-1015) A commentator and exponent of Kashmir Shaivism.

**AKBAR, KING**
(1542-1605) A great Moghul emperor who consolidated one of the most extensive Indian empires. His administrative skills, benevolent nature, and interest in culture and religion endeared him to his people.

**AKKAMAHADEVI**
An ecstatic twelfth-century poet-saint of South India. In her short life she composed many devotional poems in the Kannada language.

**ASHTAVAKRA**
(*lit.*, bent in eight places) A famous crippled sage of the Indian epics who taught King Janaka about the nature of Reality. His teachings are contained in the *Ashtāvakra Gītā*, which describes the path to liberation.

**AUROBINDO, SHRI**
(1872-1950) A yogi, poet, and scholar who wrote extensively on issues of social reform and on spirituality.

**BHARTRIHARI**
A legendary renunciant, poet, and sage; a king who gave up his throne to become a yogi.

**BIRBAL**
(1528-1586) A brilliant wit and poet; the friend and minister of King Akbar.

**CHAITANYA MAHAPRABHU**
(1485-1533) A God-intoxicated saint of Bengal who emphasized chanting as the means of attaining God. His consuming love for God inspired the lives of thousands.

**CHOKHAMELA**
A fourteenth-century poet-saint of Maharashtra, devoted to Lord Vitthal of Pandharpur. His *samādhi* shrine is located at the door to the Pandharpur Temple.

**DADU DAYAL**
(1544-1603) A learned poet-saint of northern India whose ecstatic experiences of God are recorded in his poetry, and whose *bhajans* are still sung today by the *sādhus* of the mission he established.

**EKNATH MAHARAJ**
(1528-1609) A householder poet-saint of Maharashtra; the author of several hundred *abhangas*. By writing on religious subjects in the vernacular, Eknath ushered in a spiritual revival among the people.

**GORAKHNATH**
(11th century) One of the nine masters of the Nath tradition who received initiation from Matsyendranath. Gorakhnath was the Guru of Gahininath, who initiated Nivrittinath, Guru and older brother of Jnaneshwar Maharaj.

**JANABAI**
A thirteenth-century saint who was the disciple and house servant of the Maharashtrian poet-saint Namdev. It is said that Lord Krishna was so moved by her devotion that He appeared to Janabai and helped her with her work.

**JANAKA, KING**
A royal sage who attained liberation through perfect fulfillment of his duties as king. He was a great supporter of the doctrines of the Upanishads. His Guru was the sage Yajnavalkya.

**JANARDAN SWAMI**
(1504-1575) A warrior-saint and the Guru of Eknath Maharaj. Janardan Swami was born in Chalisgaon and lived in Devagiri. His Guru was Narasimha Saraswati.

**JNANESHWAR MAHARAJ**
(1275-1296) Foremost among the poet-saints of Maharashtra. His older brother, Nivrittinath, was his Guru. At the age of twenty-one, Jnaneshwar took live *samādhi* (a yogi's voluntary departure from the body) in Alandi, where, to this day, his *samādhi* shrine continues to attract thousands of seekers. His best-known work is *Jñāneshvarī*, a commentary in Marathi verse on the *Bhagavad Gītā*.

**KABIR**
(1440-1518) A great poet-saint and mystic who lived his life as a simple weaver in Benares. His poems describe the experience of the Self, the greatness of the Guru, and the nature of true spirituality. They are still being studied and sung all over the world.

**KALIDAS**
A great classical sixth-century poet and playwright of India.

**MANSUR MASTANA**
(852-922) An ecstatic Sufi poet-saint who lived most of his life in Baghdad. He was hanged as a heretic for his pronouncement *ana'l-haqq*, "I am God," which orthodox Muslims of those days would not tolerate.

**MARKANDEYA**
A sage, the reputed author of the *Mārkandeya Purāna*. He was noted for his austeries and great age.

**MIRA; MIRABAI**
(1433-1468) A Rajasthani queen famous for her poems of devotion to Lord Krishna. She was so absorbed in love for Krishna that when she was given poison by vindictive relatives, Mirabai drank it as nectar and remained unharmed.

**NAMDEV**
(1270-1350) A poet-saint of Pandharpur in Maharashtra and friend of Jnaneshwar Maharaj. He realized the all-pervasive nature of God after meeting his Guru, Vishoba Khechar, and thereafter composed ecstatic *abhangas* to Lord Vitthal.

**NANAK, GURU**
(1469-1538) The founder and first Guru of the Sikh religion. He lectured widely, spreading liberal religious and social doctrines, including opposition to both the caste system and the division between Hindus and Muslims.

**NARADA**
A divine seer; a great devotee and servant of Lord Vishnu; author of the *Bhakti Sūtras*, the authoritative text on devotion to God.

**NITYANANDA, BHAGAWAN**
(d. 1961) A great Siddha master, Swami Muktananda's Guru, also known as Bade Baba ("elder" Baba). He was a born Siddha, living his entire life in the highest state of consciousness. In both

Gurudev Siddha Peeth in Ganeshpuri, India, and Shree Muktananda Ashram in South Fallsburg, New York, Swami Muktananda has dedicated a temple of meditation to honor Bhagawan Nityananda.

**NIVRITTINATH**
(1273-1297) Elder brother and Guru of Jnaneshwar Maharaj. He directed Jnaneshwar to write *Jñāneshvarī* and *Amritānubhava.*

**PATANJALI**
A fourth-century sage and the author of the famous *Yoga Sūtras,* the exposition of one of the six orthodox philosophies of India and the authoritative text of the path of *rāja yoga,* (the "kingly path;" the yoga of meditation).

**PIPA**
A righteous king of Gademandal, India. Upon hearing the glories of Vishnu, he renounced his kingdom and took to the forest, becoming a disciple of Ramananda. After serving his Guru for some time, he made a pilgrimage to the town of Dwaraka, where he had a vision of Lord Krishna. He remained in Dwaraka, chanting the Lord's name in ecstasy, for four months.

**RAIDAS**
An ecstatic saint of fifteenth-century Benares, India, who earned his living as a cobbler. Because this involved working with leather, a product obtained by killing sacred cows, cobbling was considered a low trade. Raidas's understanding and vision were such that he considered leather, as all things, to be only the Lord.

**RAMAKRISHNA PARAMAHAMSA**
(1836-1886) A great saint of Bengal; the Guru of Swami Vivekananda and the founder of the Ramakrishna Order of monks.

**RAMANA MAHARSHI**
(1870-1950) A saint who spent most of his life near Arunachala mountain in South India. After his spiritual awakening at age sixteen, he meditated intensely for many years and practiced Self-inquiry, the purpose of which is to focus the mind at its source. Once he had attained the ego-free state of realization, he composed a long hymn to Shiva, the lord of Arunachala.

**RAMANANDA**
A fifteenth-century North Indian saint who revitalized the path of *bhakti* (devotion).

**SAI BABA OF SHIRDI**
(1838-1918) One of the great Siddhas of modern times. Although he spent his entire life in a small country town, he became known all over India. His *samādhi* shrine at Shirdi, in central Maharashtra, is a powerful place of pilgrimage.

**SAMARTHA RAMDAS**
(1608-1681) A Maharashtrian saint who helped to unify and renew the Hindu religion in Maharashtra when it was threatened by extinction from Moghul invaders. He was the Guru of King Shivaji. His teachings, both social and spiritual, are contained in the *Dāsabodha.*

**SHAMS TABRIZI**
A tenth-century Sufi saint from Tabriz in Persia. He was the Guru of Jalalu'd-din Rumi, the great mystic poet of Persia.

**SHANKARACHARYA**
(788-820) One of the most celebrated of India's philosophers and sages, he traveled throughout India expounding the philosophy of Advaita (nondual) Vedanta. Among his many works is the *Vivekachūdāmani,* "The Crest Jewel of Discrimination."

**SHVETAKETU**
An Upanishadic sage, whose lessons from his father, Uddalaka, on the mystery of the universal soul appear in the *Chāndogya Upanishad.*

**SIDDHARUDHA SWAMI**
A great Siddha with whom Swami Muktananda studied Vedanta and took the vows of *sannyāsa.* In his ashram at Hubli in South India, the chanting of *Om Namah Shivāya* goes on continuously.

**SUNDARDAS**
(1596-1689) A renowned poet-saint born

in Rajasthan. The main collection of his *bhajans* in Hindi is the *Sundar Granthavāti.*

**TIRTHA, SWAMI RAMA**
(1873-1906) A distinguished professor of mathematics who, out of his longing for God, withdrew to the Himalayas and attained enlightenment. Rama Tirtha wrote many beautiful poems in the Urdu language, and in the last years of his life he lectured on Vedanta in Japan and the United States.

**TUKARAM MAHARAJ**
(1608-1650) A poet-saint who was a grocer in the village of Dehu in Maharashtra. He received initiation in a dream. Tukaram wrote thousands of *abhangas*, many of which describe his spiritual struggles and visionary experiences.

**TULSIDAS**
(1532-1623) The poet-saint of North India who wrote the *Tulsī Rāmāyana* in Hindi. This life story of Lord Rama is still one of the most popular scriptures in India.

**UDDALAKA**
A great Upanishadic sage who expounded the meaning of existence to his son Shvetaketu in the *Chāndogya Upanishad.*

**VALMIKI**
An ancient sage and the attributed author of the *Rāmāyana*, the epic account of the life of Lord Rama.

**VASISHTHA**
The legendary sage and Guru of Lord Rama, who epitomized the force of spiritual knowledge. He is the central figure of the *Yoga Vāsishtha*, which is one of the most detailed scriptures on the nature of the mind and the way to free it from illusion.

**VASUGUPTACHARYA**
The ninth-century sage to whom Lord Shiva revealed the *Shiva Sūtras*, which is the scriptural authority of Kashmir Shaivism.

**VISHVAMITRA**
A celebrated sage, said to be the author of a large portion of the *Rig Veda.*

**VIVEKANANDA, SWAMI**
(1863-1902) A disciple of Ramakrishna Paramahamsa and one of the most influential spiritual figures in modern India. During numerous trips, he introduced the teachings of Vedanta to the West.

**YAJNAVALKYA**
The Guru of King Janaka, whose teachings are recorded in the *Brihadāranyaka Upanishad.*

**YOGANANDA PARAMAHAMSA**
(1893-1952) A saint from Gorakhpur who wrote *Autobiography of a Yogi.*

# GLOSSARY
## *of Texts and Terms*

**ABHANGA** [*abhaṅga*]
A devotional song composed in the Marathi language expressing the longing of a devotee for God.

**ABHAYA MUDRA** [*abhaya mudrā*]
A symbolic gesture formed by raising one hand with the palm outward, meaning "do not fear." Many deities and saints are pictured with this gesture.

**ABSOLUTE, THE**
The highest Reality; supreme Consciousness; the pure, untainted, changeless Truth.

**ACHARYA** [*ācārya*]
A teacher.

**ADINATH PARASHIVA**
*See* SHIVA.

**ADVAITA VEDANTA**
*See* VEDANTA.

**AGAMA(S); AGAMA SHASTRA** [*āgama śāstra*]
Sacred Shaivite texts, revealed between the fourth and sixth centuries A.D., that explain religious philosophy and practices. *See also* KASHMIR SHAIVISM.

**AGNI ASTRA** [*agni astra*]
A fire missile charged with power by mantra.

**AHAM** [*aham*]
(*lit.*, I) The pure inner Self; the experiencing subject; I-consciousness.

**AJAPA** [*ajapa*]
The natural and effortless repetition of the mantra that goes on within every living creature in the form of the incoming and outgoing breath. *See also* HAMSA.

**AJNA CHAKRA** [*ājñā cakra*]
The spiritual center located between the eyebrows. *See also* CHAKRA(S).

**AMRITANUBHAVA** [*amṛtānubhava*]
(*lit.*, nectar of Self-awareness) A lyrical text, written in verse by the great sage Jnaneshwar Maharaj, on the nature of the supreme Lord, Shiva, and His power of creation, Shakti.

**ANAHATA NADA** [*anāhatanāda*]
(*lit.*, unstruck sound) The inner divine melody; the "unstruck" sound heard in meditation. *See also* NADA.

**ANTAHKARANA** [*antaḥkaraṇa*]
(*lit.*, inner psychic instrument) In yoga philosophy, the mind—which consists of the thinking mind (*manas*), the subconscious (*chitta*), the ego (*ahamkāra*), and the intellect (*buddhi*).

**APANA**
*See* PRANA.

**APAROKSHANUBHUTI**
[*aparokṣānubhūti*]
(*lit.*, the perception of what is not invisible) A work on Advaita Vedanta by Shankaracharya, explaining God-realization as the immediate and direct perception of one's own Self by means of inquiry.

**ARJUNA**
The third of the five Pandava brothers and one of the heroes of the *Mahābhārata*, considered to be the greatest warrior of all. He was the friend and devotee of Lord Krishna. It was to Arjuna that the Lord revealed the knowledge of the *Bhagavad Gītā*. *See also* MAHABHARATA.

**ASANA** [*āsana*]
1) A hatha yoga posture practiced to strengthen the body, purify the nervous system, and develop one-pointedness of mind. 2) A seat or mat on which one sits for meditation.

**ASHRAM** [*āśrama*]
(*lit.*, without fatigue) The abode of a Guru or saint; a monastic place of retreat where seekers engage in spiritual practices and study the sacred teachings of yoga.

**ASHRAMA(S)** [*āśrama*]
The four stages of traditional Hindu life. They are *brahmachārya*, the stage of a student engaged in scriptural study and the practice of celibacy; *grihastha*, the stage of a householder engaged in leading a family life; *vanaprastha*, the stage of retirement when one engages in scriptural study and other spiritual practices; and *sannyāsa*, the stage of complete renunciation in which one devotes one's life to the pursuit of Self-realization.

**ATMABODHA** [*ātmabodha*]
(*lit.*, Self-knowledge) A short treatise on Vedanta by Shankaracharya, teaching that our true Self is the Self of all beings; in this way, self-love leads to love for all creatures.

**ATMAN** [*ātman*]
Divine Consciousness residing in the individual; the supreme Self; the soul.

**AUM**
*See* OM.

**AUSTERITIES**
1) Rigorous spiritual practices. 2) Abandonment of the pursuit of worldly pleasure for the purpose of spiritual attainment. *See also* TAPASYA.

**AVADHUTA** [*avadhūta*]
An enlightened being who lives in a state beyond body-consciousness, and whose behavior is not bound by ordinary social conventions.

**AYURVEDA** [*āyurveda*]
(*lit.*, knowledge of life) The ancient Indian science of medicine which teaches that good health depends on maintaining the even balance of the three bodily humors: wind, bile, and phlegm.

**BABA; BABAJI** [*bābā, bābāji*]
A term of affection and respect for a saint, holy man, or father.

**BHAGAVAD GITA** [*bhagavadgītā*]
(*lit.*, song of God) One of the world's spiritual treasures; an essential scripture of Hinduism; a portion of the *Mahābhārata* in which Lord Krishna instructs His disciple Arjuna on the nature of God, the universe, and the supreme Self.

**BHAGAVATA PURANA**
*See* SHRIMAD BHAGAVATAM.

**BHAGAWAN** [*bhagavan*]
(*lit.*, the Lord) One endowed with the six attributes or powers of infinity: spiritual power, righteousness, glory, splendor, knowledge, and renunciation. A term of great honor. Swami Muktananda's Guru is known as Bhagawan Nityananda.

**BHAJAN** [*bhajan*]
A devotional song in praise of God.

**BHAKTA** [*bhakta*]
A devotee, a lover of God; a follower of *bhakti yoga*, the path of love and devotion.

**BHAKTI** [*bhakti*]
The path of devotion described by the sage Narada in his *Bhakti Sūtras*; a path to union with the Divine based on the continual offering of love and the constant remembrance of the Lord.

**BHAKTI SUTRAS** [*bhaktisūtra*]
The classic scripture on devotion composed by the sage Narada. *See also* BHAKTI.

**BHAVARTHA RAMAYANA**
[*bhāvārtha rāmāyaṇa*]
A sixteenth-century rendition of Valmiki's *Rāmāyana*, composed in the Marathi language by Eknath Maharaj.

**BINDU** [*bindu*]
*See* BLUE PEARL.

**BLUE PEARL**
A brilliant blue light, the size of a tiny seed; the subtle abode of the inner Self, and the vehicle by means of which the soul travels from one world to another either in meditation or at the time of death.

**BRAHMA** [*brahmā*]
The absolute Reality manifested as the active creator of the universe, who is personified as one of the three gods of the Hindu trinity. The other two are Vishnu, who represents the principle of sustenance, and Shiva, who represents the principle of destruction.

**BRAHMACHARI** [*brahmacārī*]
1) A celibate devoted to the practice of spiritual discipline. 2) The first of four traditional stages of life in ancient India—that of a student—which normally comprised the years between the ages of twelve and twenty-four.

**BRAHMAN** [*brahman*]
The Vedic term for the absolute Reality.

**BRAHMIN** [*brahmin*]
The caste of Hindu society whose members are by tradition priests and scholars.

**CAUSAL BODY**
*See* FOUR BODIES.

**CHAITANYA** [*caitanya*]
1) The fundamental, all-pervasive, divine Consciousness. 2) When used in reference to a mantra, *chaitanya* means that the mantra is enlivened with grace and thus has the capacity to draw one's mind spontaneously into meditative stillness.

**CHAKRA(S)** [*cakra*]
(*lit.*, wheel) A center of energy located in the subtle body where the *nādīs* converge, giving the appearance of a lotus. Six major chakras lie within the *sushumnā nādī*, or central channel. They are *mūlādhāra* at the base of the spine, *svādhishthāna* at the root of the reproductive organs, *manipūra* at the navel, *anāhata*, the "lotus of the heart," *vishuddha* at the throat, and *ājñā* between the eyebrows. When She is awakened, Kundalini flows upward from the *mūlādhāra* to the seventh chakra, the *sahasrāra*, at the crown of the head. *See also* KUNDALINI; NADI(S); SHAKTIPAT.

**CHANDIPATHA**
*See* DEVI BHAGAVATA.

**CHANDRALOKA** [*candraloka*]
The subtle world of the moon, experienced in meditation.

**CHETANA**
*See* CHAITANYA.

**CHIDAKASHA** [*cidākāśa*]
The subtle space of Consciousness in the *sahasrāra* and the heart.

**CHITI; CHITI SHAKTI** [*citi; citiśakti*]
The power of universal Consciousness; the creative aspect of God, portrayed as the universal Mother.

**CHITTA**
*See* ANTAHKARANA.

**CONSCIOUSNESS**
The intelligent, supremely independent, divine Energy that creates, pervades, and supports the entire universe.

**DAMA** [*dama*]
Self-restraint.

**DARSHAN** [*darśana*]
(*lit.*, to have sight of; viewing) A glimpse or vision of a saint; being in the presence of a holy being; seeing God or an image of God; experiencing God within one's heart.

**DASBODHA** [*dāsbodha*]
A seventeenth-century treatise by Samartha Ramdas in Marathi verse on leading a spiritual life and the pursuit of human excellence.

**DEVI BHAGAVATAM** [*devī bhāgavatam*]
A Purana devoted to the worship of the *devī*, or Shakti; a portion of the *Mārkandeya Purāna*, also called the *Chandīpātha.*

**DHARMA** [*dharma*]
(*lit.*, what holds together) Essential duty; the law of righteousness; living in accordance with the divine Will. The highest dharma is to recognize the Truth in one's own heart.

**DHYANA** [*dhyāna*]
Meditation; the seventh stage of yoga described by Patanjali in the *Yoga Sūtras.*

**DIKSHA** [*dīkṣā*]
Yogic initiation. *See also* SHAKTIPAT.

**DRAUPADI**
In the *Mahābhārata*, the wife of the Pandavas and a devotee of Lord Krishna.

**DRONACHARYA**
In the *Mahābhārata*, the weapons teacher of both the Pandavas and the Kauravas; he supported the Kauravas in battle.

**DUHSHASANA**
In the *Mahābhārata*, brother of the evil Duryodhana, who was head of the Kauravas.

**EGO**
In yoga, the limited sense of "I" that is identified with the body, mind, and senses; sometimes described as "the veil of suffering." *See also* ANTAHKARANA.

**EKLAVYA**
A tribal boy who wanted to learn archery from the great royal teacher Dronacharya. When Drona rejected him as a disciple because of his low caste, Eklavya mastered the skills of archery and equaled Arjuna, the greatest archer of all, by meditating on a clay image of the Guru with deep devotion.

**FIVE ELEMENTS**
Ether, air, fire, water, earth; according to ancient Indian philosophy, these comprise the elemental basis of the universe.

**FOUR BODIES**
The physical (gross), subtle, causal, and supracausal bodies, which are experienced respectively in the states of waking, dream, deep sleep, and *samādhi.*

**FOUR STAGES OF LIFE**
*See* ASHRAMAS.

**GANESHPURI**
A village at the foot of Mandagni mountain in Maharashtra, India. Bhagawan Nityananda settled in this region, where yogis have performed spiritual practices for thousands of years. The ashram founded by Swami Muktananda at his Guru's command is built on this sacred land. *See also* GURUDEV SIDDHA PEETH.

**GANGES (GANGA)**
The most sacred river of India, the Ganges is said to descend from heaven through Lord Shiva's hair. On earth, it flows down from the Himalayas, across all of North India to the Bay of Bengal. It is believed that all sins are purified by a dip in its holy waters; each year, many devout Hindus make the pilgrimage to its source in the ice caves of Gangotri.

**GITA**
*See* BHAGAVAD GITA.

**GOPI(S)** [*gopī*]
The milkmaids who were childhood companions and devotees of Krishna. They are revered as the embodiments of ideal devotion to God.

**GOVINDA** [*govinda*]
(*lit.*, master of the cows) 1) The lord of the senses and the mind. 2) A name for Krishna, who tended cows as a boy.

**GROSS BODY**
*See* FOUR BODIES.

**GUNA(S)** [*guṇa*]
The three essential qualities of nature that determine the inherent characteristics of all created things. They are *sattva* (purity, light, harmony, and intelligence); *rajas* (activity and passion); and *tamas* (dullness, inertia, and ignorance).

**GURU** [*guru*]
A spiritual Master who has attained oneness with God and who is therefore able both to initiate seekers and to guide them on the spiritual path to liberation; the grace-bestowing power of God. A Guru is also required to be learned in the scriptures and must belong to a lineage of masters. *See also* SHAKTIPAT; SIDDHA.

**GURUBHAKTI** [*gurubhakti*]
Devotion and love for the Guru. *See also* BHAKTI.

**GURUBHAVA** [*gurubhāva*]
(*lit., guru,* master; *bhāva,* becoming; being) A feeling of absorption in or identification with the Guru.

**GURUDEV SIDDHA PEETH**
(*lit.*, abode of the perfected beings) The mother ashram of Siddha Yoga meditation, located in Ganeshpuri, India; the site of the *samādhi* shrine of Swami Muktananda. *See also* ASHRAM; GANESHPURI.

**GURU PRINCIPLE**
The universal power of grace present as the inner Self of all beings.

**HAMSA; SO'HAM** [*haṃsa; so'ham*]
(*lit.*, "That am I"; "I am That") *Hamsa* and *So'ham* are identical mantras that describe the natural vibration of the Self that occurs spontaneously with each incoming and outgoing breath. By becoming aware of *Hamsa,* a seeker experiences identification with the supreme Self.

**HANUMAN** [*hanumān*]
A huge, white monkey, son of the Wind, and one of the heroes of the *Rāmāyana.* Hanuman's unparalleled strength was exceeded only by his perfect devotion to Lord Rama, for whom he performed many acts of magic and daring.

**HATHA YOGA** [*haṭhayoga*]
Yogic practices, both physical and mental, performed for the purpose of purifying and strengthening the physical and subtle bodies. *See also* YOGA.

**HATHAYOGA PRADIPIKA**
[*haṭhayogapradīpikā*]
An authoritative fifteenth-century treatise written by Svatmarama Yogi, which describes the practice of various hatha yoga techniques.

**HRIDAYA** [*hṛdaya*]
The space where the in-breath and out-breath merge; "the true heart"; the place where the breath is still in the state of merging.

**JAPA** [*japa*]
(*lit.*, prayer uttered in a low voice) Repetition of a mantra, either silently or aloud. *See also* MANTRA.

**JIVA** [*jīva*]
(*lit.*, living being) The individual soul, conditioned by the experiences and limitations of the body and mind.

**JIVANMUKTA** [*jīvanmukta*]
(*lit.*, liberated while living) One who is liberated while still living in a physical body.

**JIVANMUKTI** [*jīvanmukti*]
(*lit.*, liberation in life) Attainment of liberation while still alive.

**JIVATMA** [*jīvātman*]
The individual or personal soul. *See also* JIVA.

**JNANA** [*jñāna*]
True knowledge.

**JNANA YOGA** [*jñānayoga*]
The yoga of knowledge; a spiritual path based on continuous contemplation and self-inquiry.

**JNANESHVARI** [*jñāneśvarī*]
A majestic commentary in verse on the *Bhagavad Gītā,* written by Jnaneshwar Maharaj when he was sixteen. It was the first original scriptural work written in Marathi, the language of the people of Maharashtra.

**JNANI** [*jñāni*]
1) An enlightened being. 2) A follower of the path of knowledge. *See also* JNANA YOGA.

**KARMA** [*karma*]
(*lit.*, action) 1) Any action—physical, verbal, or mental. 2) Destiny, which is caused by past actions, mainly those of previous lives.

**KASHI**
The city of Varanasi, or Benares, sacred to Lord Shiva, located in North India on the banks of the river Ganges. According to Hindu tradition, whoever dies in this city attains liberation.

**KASHMIR SHAIVISM**
A branch of the Shaivite philosophical tradition, propounded by Kashmiri sages, that explains how the formless supreme Principle, Shiva, manifests as the universe. Together with Vedanta, Kashmir Shaivism provides the basic scriptural context for Siddha Yoga meditation.

**KATHA UPANISHAD** [*kaṭhopaniṣad*]
One of the principal Upanishads, containing the story of the sage Nachiketa, who, given a boon by Yama, the Lord of Death, asks for knowledge of the Absolute. *See also* UPANISHAD(S).

**KENA UPANISHAD** [*kenopaniṣad*]
One of the principal Upanishads, which establishes that Brahman is the supreme Reality by whom the mind, speech, and senses perform their functions. *See also* UPANISHAD(S).

**KHECHARI MUDRA** [*khecarī mudrā*]
An advanced yogic technique in which the tip of the tongue curls back into the throat and upward into the nasal pharynx.

**KRISHNA**
(*lit.*, the dark one) The eighth incarnation of Lord Vishnu. The spiritual teachings of Lord Krishna are contained in the *Bhagavad Gītā*, a portion of the epic *Mahābhārata*.

**KRIYA** [*kriyā*]
A physical, mental, or emotional movement initiated by the awakened *kuṇḍalinī*. *Kriyās* purify the body and nervous system, thus allowing a seeker to experience higher states of consciousness.

**KULARNAVA TANTRA** [*kulārṇavatantra*]
A Shaiva treatise about the Guru, the disciple, the mantra, and many traditional practices of worship.

**KUMBHAKA** [*kumbhaka*]
In hatha yoga, the holding of the breath after inhalation during the practice of *prāṇāyāma*. Esoterically, true *kumbhaka* occurs when the inward and outward flow of *prāṇa* becomes stabilized. When this happens, the mind also stabilizes, permitting the meditator to experience the Self, which lies beyond the mind.

**KUMKUM** [*kumkum*]
(*lit.*, red-red) A red powder used in worship; also worn as an auspicious mark between the eyebrows in remembrance of the Guru.

**KUNDALINI** [*kuṇḍalinī*]
(*lit.*, coiled one) The supreme power; the primordial shakti, or energy, that lies coiled at the base of the spine in the *mūlādhāra chakra* of every human being. Through the descent of grace (shaktipat), this extremely subtle force, also described as the supreme Goddess, is awakened and begins to purify the entire being. As Kundalini travels upward through the central channel (*sushumnā nāḍī*), She pierces the various subtle energy centers (chakras), until She finally reaches the *sahasrāra* at the crown of the head. There, the individual self merges into the supreme Self, and the cycle of birth and death comes to an end. *See also* CHAKRA(S); SHAKTIPAT.

**KURUKSHETRA**
A small plain north of Delhi; the battlefield on which the battle between the Kauravas and the Pandavas took place in the epic *Mahābhārata*.

**LIBERATION**
Freedom from the cycle of birth and death; the state of realization of oneness with the Absolute. *See also* JIVANMUKTI; MOKSHA.

MAHABHARATA [*mahābhārata*]
An epic poem that recounts the struggle between the Pandava and Kaurava brothers over the disputed kingdom of Bharata, the ancient name for India. Within this vast narrative is contained a wealth of Indian secular and religious lore. The *Bhagavad Gītā* occurs in the latter portion of the *Mahābhārata.*

MAHAMANDALESHVAR
*See* MANDALESHVAR

MAHANIRVANA TANTRA
[*mahānirvāṇatantra*]
(*lit.*, the tantra of great liberation) This text discusses liberation, the worship of the Absolute, righteous behavior, mantras, and rituals.

MAHARAJ [*mahārāja*]
(*lit.*, great king) A title of respect for a saint or holy person.

MAHARASHTRA
A state on the west coast of central India, where Gurudev Siddha Peeth, the mother ashram of Siddha Yoga meditation, is located. Many of the great poet-saints lived in Maharashtra, and the *samādhi* shrines of Bhagawan Nityananda and Swami Muktananda are there. *See also* GANESHPURI.

MAHASAMADHI [*mahāsamādhi*]
(*lit.*, the great union) 1) A realized yogi's conscious departure from the physical body at death. 2) The anniversary of a great being's departure from the physical body. *See also* SAMADHI; SAMADHI SHRINE.

MALA [*mālā*]
A string of beads used to facilitate a state of concentration while repeating a mantra. *See also* JAPA.

MANAS
*See* ANTAHKARANA.

MANDALESHVAR [*maṇḍaleśvara*]
A title conferred upon a well-known and respected monk who heads an ashram or monastery, and who is chief of the monks of a particular region.

MANTRA [*mantra*]
(*lit.*, sacred invocation; that which protects) The names of God; sacred words or divine sounds invested with the power to protect, purify, and transform the individual who repeats them.

MANTRA DEITY
The deity named by or identified with a mantra, to whom its repetition is offered as worship.

MANUS [*manu*]
The fathers of the human race, according to the ancient Indian scriptures.

MANUSMRITI [*manusmṛti*]
Ancient scripture giving a code of conduct.

MARKANDEYA PURANA
[*mārkaṇḍeya purāṇa*]
Scripture of the ninth or tenth century, which contains a succession of legends narrated by the sage Markandeya.

MATH [*maṭha*]
A monastery or ashram.

MATHURA
A town in the province of Agra, celebrated as the birthplace of Lord Krishna.

MAYA [*māyā*]
(*lit.*, to measure) The term used in Vedanta for the power that veils the true nature of the Self and projects the experiences of multiplicity and separation from God, creating the illusion that the real is unreal, the unreal is real, and the temporary is everlasting.

MOKSHA [*mokṣa*]
The state of liberation; enlightenment; freedom.

MUDRA [*mudrā*]
(*lit.*, seal) 1) A symbolic gesture or movement of the hand. Deities and saints are often pictured performing these gestures to bestow their blessings. 2) Hatha yoga techniques practiced to hold the *prāna* (life-force) within the body. *Mudrās* may occur spontaneously after one receives shaktipat.

MULADHARA [*mūlādhāra*]
The first chakra, the lowest of the seven major energy centers in the subtle body,

situated at the base of the spine, where consciousness is mainly concerned with survival. Here the *kundalinī* lies coiled three and a half times, dormant until awakened by grace. *See also* CHAKRA(S); KUNDALINI; SHAKTIPAT.

NADA [*nāda*]
(*lit.*, sound) Inner sounds heard during advanced stages of meditation; celestial harmonies; the spontaneous unstruck sound experienced in the *anāhata chakra.*

NADI(S) [*nāḍī*]
(*lit.*, duct, nerve) A channel in the subtle body through which the vital force flows. A network of 72 million *nādīs* spreads throughout the human body. The three main nadis are the central channel, or *sushumnā,* which is flanked by the *idā* and *pingalā nādīs.* The hubs or junctions of the *nādīs* are known as chakras. *See also* CHAKRA(S); KUNDALINI.

NAME, THE
A name of God. Silent repetition or audible chanting of the divine Name is considered to be the most effective means of redemption in the present age. *See also* JAPA; MANTRA.

NARAYANA [*nārāyaṇa*]
A name of Lord Vishnu meaning "the sole refuge of all creatures."

NATARAJ [*nāṭarāja*]
(*lit.*, king of the dance) A name of Shiva, referring to the dancing Shiva. The object of his dance is to free all souls from the fetters of illusion.

NATH [*nātha*]
A lineage of yogis. Originally there were nine Naths; Matsyendranath, the first, received initiation from Lord Shiva.

NETI NETI [*neti neti*]
(*lit.*, not this; not this) In Vedanta, the steady negation of all unreal aspects of oneself and the world.

NIRVIKALPA [*nirvikalpa*]
(*lit.*, without form) The yogic state beyond attribute, thought, or image.

NIYAMA [*niyama*]
Observances that are considered vital to one who is pursuing the yogic life, such as cleanliness, contentment, and mental and physical discipline.

OM [*oṃ*]
The primordial sound from which the universe emanates; the inner essence of all mantras.

PADUKA(S) [*pādukā*]
The Guru's sandals, objects of the highest veneration. Vibrations of the inner shakti flow out from the Guru's feet, which are a mystical source of grace and illumination and a figurative term for the Guru's teachings. The Guru's sandals are also said to hold this divine energy of enlightenment.

PANDHARPUR [*paṇḍharpūr*]
A place of pilgrimage and the center of worship for devotees of Lord Vitthal in Maharashtra state.

PANDURANGA [*pāṇḍuraṅga*]
A form of Lord Vishnu worshiped especially in Pandharpur.

PARAMAHAMSA [*paramahaṅsa*]
One who has completely mastered all of his senses; one who has attained Self-realization.

PARVATI [*pārvatī*]
(*lit.*, daughter of the mountain) The beloved of Lord Shiva and the daughter of the king of the Himalayas; a name of the universal Mother or Shakti.

PASHUPAT ASTRA [*pāśupata astra*]
Shiva's arrow, which is bright like the sun and burns all that it touches.

PRAHLAD [*prahlāda*]
The child of a demon, Prahlad enraged his father by becoming a devotee of Lord Narayana. Through faith, he transcended great persecution, proving to his father that the Lord protects His devotees.

PRAJNA [*prajñā*]
Wisdom, intelligence, knowledge, understanding.

**PRAKRITI** [*prakṛti*]
Primal undifferentiated matter; the source of the objective universe.

**PRALAYA** [*pralaya*]
The dissolution of the world at the end of a cosmic age.

**PRANA** [*prāṇa*]
The vital, life-sustaining force of both the individual and the entire universe. To carry out its work, *prāna* pervades the body in ten forms. The five most important are *prāna*, inhalation; *apāna*, exhalation; *samāna*, which distributes the nourishment from food to the body; *vyāna*, the power of movement within the *nādīs*; and *udāna*, which carries energy upward, giving strength and radiance to the body.

**PRANAM** [*praṇāma*]
To bow; to greet with respect.

**PRANAYAMA** [*prāṇāyāma*]
The yogic science through which the *prāna*, the vital force, is stabilized, a necessary condition in the Self-realization process. *Prānāyāma* may be practiced through specific breathing exercises, since there is a link between *prāna* and the breath.

**PRATYABHIJNAHRIDAYAM** [*pratyabhijñāhṛdayam*]
(*lit.*, the heart of the doctrine of recognition) An eleventh-century treatise by Kshemaraja that summarizes the *pratyabhijñā* philosophy of Kashmir Shaivism. It states, in essence, that individuals have forgotten their true nature by identifying with the body, and that realization is a process of recognizing or remembering one's true nature—the supreme bliss and love of the inner Self.

**PURANAS** [*purāṇa*]
(*lit.*, ancient legends) Eighteen sacred books by the sage Vyasa, containing stories, legends, and hymns about the creation of the universe, the incarnations of God, the teachings of various deities, and the spiritual legacies of ancient sages and kings.

**PURUSHA** [*puruṣa*]
The limited, individual soul.

**RADHA**
The childhood companion and beloved of Krishna, Radha is celebrated in Indian tradition as the embodiment of devotion to God.

**RAJAS; RAJASIC; RAJOGUNA**
*See* GUNA(S).

**RAKSHASA(S)** [*rākṣasa*]
A particular group of demons; said to be nocturnal wanderers.

**RAM; RAMA**
(*lit.*, pleasing; delight) The seventh incarnation of Lord Vishnu, Rama is seen as the embodiment of dharma (right action) and is the object of great devotion. He is the central character in the Indian epic *Rāmāyana*. *See also* RAMAYANA.

**RAMAYANA** [*rāmāyaṇa*]
One of the great epic poems of India; attributed to the sage Valmiki, the *Rāmāyana* recounts the life and exploits of Lord Rama.

**RAVANA**
The ten-headed demon who captured Lord Rama's wife, Sita, in the *Rāmāyana* epic, and who was finally defeated by Lord Rama.

**RIDDHI(S)**
*See* SIDDHI(S).

**RISHI** [*ṛṣi*]
A seer of Truth; usually refers to the sages to whom the Vedic scriptures were revealed.

**RUDRAKSHA** [*rudrākṣa*]
Seeds from a tree sacred to Shiva, strung as beads for *mālās*. Legend has it that the *rudrāksha* seed was created from the tears of Rudra, thus endowing it with great spiritual power.

**SACCHIDANANDA** [*saccidānanda*]
(*lit.*, absolute existence, consciousness, and bliss) In Vedantic philosophy, the three indivisible qualities of the Absolute.

**SADGURU** [*sadguru*]
A true Guru; divine master. *See also* GURU.

**SADHANA** [*sādhanā*]
1) A spiritual discipline or path. 2) Practices, both physical and mental, on the spiritual path.

**SADHU** [*sādhu*]
A wandering monk or ascetic; a holy being; a practitioner of sadhana.

**SAHASRARA** [*sahasrāra*]
The thousand-petaled spiritual energy center at the crown of the head, where one experiences the highest states of consciousness. *See also* CHAKRA(S); KUNDALINI.

**SAMADHI** [*samādhi*]
The state of meditative union with the Absolute.

**SAMADHI SHRINE**
Final resting place of a great yogi's body. Such shrines are places of worship, permeated with the saint's spiritual power.

**SAMSKARA(S)** [*saṃskāra*]
Impressions of past actions and thoughts that remain in the subtle body. They are brought to the surface of one's awareness and then eliminated by the action of the awakened *kundalinī* energy. *See also* KARMA.

**SANKALPA** [*saṅkalpa*]
Thought, intention, or will.

**SANKHYA** [*sāṅkhya*]
One of the six orthodox schools of Indian philosophy; a dualistic philosophy that views the world as comprised of two ultimate realities: spirit (*purusha*) and nature (*prakriti*).

**SANNYASA** [*sannyāsa*]
1) Monkhood. 2) The ceremony and vows of monkhood. 3) In India, traditionally, the final stage of life, which occurs after all worldly obligations have been fulfilled.

**SANNYASA ASHRAMA**
*See* ASHRAMAS.

**SANNYASI** [*sannyāsī*]
One who has become a monk by taking formal vows of renunciation.

**SATSANG** [*satsaṅga*]
(*lit.*, the company of the Truth) The company of saints and devotees; a gathering of devotees for the purpose of chanting, meditation, and listening to scriptural teachings or readings.

**SATTVA; SATTVIC**
*See* GUNA(S).

**SAVIKALPA** [*savikalpa*]
The state of absorption in an object of contemplation in which the knowledge of the object is retained. *See also* NIRVIKALPA.

**SELF**
The *ātman*, or divine Consciousness residing in the individual.

**SELF-REALIZATION**
The state of enlightenment in which the individual merges with pure Consciousness. *See also* SIDDHA.

**SEVA** [*sevā*]
(*lit.*, service) Selfless service; work offered to God, performed without attachment and with an attitude that one is not the doer.

**SHAIVISM**
*See* KASHMIR SHAIVISM.

**SHAIVITE**
1) One who worships the Supreme Reality as Shiva. 2) Of or relating to Shiva.

**SHAKTI** [*śakti*]
1) The divine Mother, the dynamic aspect of supreme Shiva and the creative force of the universe. 2) The all-pervasive, divine spiritual energy. *See also* CHITI; KUNDALINI.

**SHAKTIPAT** [*śaktipāta*]
(*lit.*, descent of grace) Yogic initiation in which the Siddha Guru transmits his spiritual energy into the aspirant, thereby awakening the aspirant's dormant *kundalinī*. *See also* GURU; KUNDALINI.

**SHAMBHAVI** [*śambhavī*]
Of or pertaining to Shiva, as the bringer of happiness.

**SHANKARA** [*śaṅkara*]
(*lit.*, giver of joy) A name of Shiva.

**SHASTRA(S)** [*śāstra*]
Hindu books of spiritual science and conduct.

**SHIVA** [*śiva*]
1) A name for the one supreme Reality. 2) One of the Hindu trinity of gods, representing God as the destroyer, often understood by yogis as the destroyer of barriers to one's identification with the supreme Self. In his personal form, Lord Shiva is portrayed as a yogi wearing a tiger skin and holding a trident.

**SHIVA MAHIMNAH STOTRAM** [*śiva mahimnaḥ stotram*]
(*lit.*, hymn on the glory of Shiva) A hymn on the greatness of Lord Shiva.

**SHIVASUTRA VIMARSHINI**
[*śivasūtra vimarśinī*]
Commentary by Kshemaraja on the *Shiva Sūtras.*

**SHREE GURUDEV ASHRAM**
Former name of Gurudev Siddha Peeth, the mother ashram of Siddha Yoga meditation in Ganeshpuri, India.

**SHRI** [*śrī*]
A term of respect.

**SHRIMAD BHAGAVATAM**
[*śrīmad bhāgavatam*]
One of the Puranas, consisting of ancient legends of the various incarnations of the Lord. It includes the life and exploits of Lord Krishna and stories of the sages and their disciples; it is also known as the *Bhāgavata Purāna.*

**SIDDHA** [*siddha*]
A perfected yogi; one who lives in the state of unity-consciousness; one whose experience of the supreme Self is uninterrupted and whose identification with the ego has been dissolved.

**SIDDHALOKA** [*siddhaloka*]
(*lit.*, world of the perfected beings) A world of blue light in which the great Siddha masters dwell in perpetual bliss.

**SIDDHA YOGA MEDITATION**
[*siddhayoga*]
(*lit.*, the yoga of perfection) A path to union of the individual and the Divine that begins with shaktipat, the inner awakening by the grace of a Siddha Guru. Siddha Yoga meditation is the name Swami Muktananda gave to this path, which he first brought to the West in 1970; Swami Chidvilasananda is its living master. *See also* GURU; KUNDALINI; SHAKTIPAT.

**SIDDHI(S)** [*siddhi*]
Supernatural powers attained through yogic practices.

**SITA**
(*lit.*, the daughter of the earth) An embodiment of Lakshmi and the wife of Lord Rama. Her story is told in the epic *Rāmāyana.*

**SO'HAM**
*See* HAMSA.

**SPANDA** [*spanda*]
The vibration of divine Consciousness that pervades all life; it is perceived by the yogi in higher states of meditation.

**SPANDA SHASTRA** [*spandaśāstra*]
A body of philosophical works in Kashmir Shaivism elaborating the principles of the *Shiva Sūtras.*

**STHITAPRAJNA** [*sthitaprajña*]
Possessing steady wisdom and firm judgment.

**SUBTLE BODY**
*See* FOUR BODIES.

**SUPRACAUSAL BODY**
*See* FOUR BODIES.

**SUSHUMNA** [*suṣumṇā*]
The central and most important of all the 72 million subtle nerve channels in the human body, the *suṣumṇā* extends from the *mūlādhāra* chakra at the base of the spine to the *sahasrāra*, or crown chakra, and contains all the other chakras, or subtle energy centers. *See also* CHAKRA(S).

**SUTRA** [*sūtra*]
Aphorism; any work consisting of aphorisms.

**SWAMI; SWAMIJI** [*svāmī*]
A respectful term of address for a *sannyāsī* or monk.

**TAITTIRIYA UPANISHAD** [*taittirīyopaniṣad*]
A scripture connected to the *Yajur Veda* whose mantras celebrate the bliss and the omnipresence of Brahman, the highest Reality.

**TAMAS; TAMASIC; TAMOGUNA**
*See* GUNA(S).

**TANTRA** [*tantra*]
Revealed scriptures of a tradition in which Shakti is worshiped as the divine Mother.

**TAPASVI** [*tapasvī*]
One who practices austerities; ascetic.

**TAPASYA** [*tapasyā*]
(*lit.*, heat) 1) Austerities. 2) The fire of yoga; the heat generated by spiritual practices.

**TULSI** [*tulasī*]
An Indian herb, a species of basil, that is used in the worship of Lord Vishnu. It has great medicinal virtues.

**TURIYA** [*turīya*]
The fourth, or transcendental, state that lies beyond the waking, dream, and deep-sleep states, and in which the true nature of reality is directly perceived; the state of *samādhi* or deep meditation. *See also* FOUR BODIES.

**TURIYATITA** [*turīyātīta*]
The state beyond *turīya*; the supremely blissful state of complete freedom from all duality and the awareness of the one Self in all; the ultimate attainment of human life.

**TWO-PETALED LOTUS**
*See* AJNA CHAKRA.

**UPANISHAD(S)** [*upaniṣad*]
(*lit.*, sitting close to; secret teachings) The inspired teachings, visions, and mystical experiences of the ancient sages of India; the concluding portion of the Vedas and the basis for Vedantic philosophy. With immense variety of form and style, all of these scriptures (exceeding one hundred texts) give the same essential teaching: that the individual soul and God are one. *See also* VEDAS; VEDANTA.

**VAIDYA** [*vaidya*]
A doctor in the Ayurvedic system of medicine. *See also* AYURVEDA.

**VANAPRASTHA ASHRAMA**
*See* ASHRAMAS.

**VARNA** [*varṇa*]
Caste.

**VARNASHRAMA**
*See* ASHRAMAS.

**VEDA(S)** [*veda*]
(*lit.*, knowledge) Among the most ancient, revered, and sacred of the world's scriptures, the four Vedas are regarded as divinely revealed, eternal wisdom. They are the *Rig Veda, Atharva Veda, Sāma Veda,* and *Yajur Veda.*

**VEDANTA** [*vedānta*]
(*lit.*, end of the Vedas) One of the six orthodox schools of Indian philosophy; usually identified as Advaita ("nondual") Vedanta, stressing its emphasis on the one supreme Principle that is the foundation of the universe. *See also* UPANISHAD(S); VEDA(S).

**VIDYA** [*vidyā*]
Knowledge.

**VISHNU** [*viṣṇu*]
One of the Hindu trinity of gods, representing God as the sustainer of the universe. Rama and Krishna are the best known of Vishnu's incarnations.

**VISHNU SAHASRANAMA** [*viṣṇusahasranāma*]
(*lit.*, the thousand names of Vishnu) A hymn honoring Lord Vishnu.

**VITHOBA**
*See* VITTHAL.

**VITTHAL** [*viṭṭhala*]
A form of Lord Krishna whose image is enshrined in Pandharpur, a famous place of pilgrimage in Maharashtra. Vitthal was eulogized by the poet-saints of Maharashtra and Karnataka. Also known as Vithoba.

**VIVARTAVADA** [*vivartavāda*]
Theory of phenomenal appearance.

**VIVEKACHUDAMANI**
[*vivekacūḍāmaṇi*]
(*lit.*, crest jewel of discrimination) A commentary by the eighth-century sage Shankaracharya on Advaita Vedanta, expounding the teaching that the Absolute alone is real. *See also* VEDANTA.

**VRITTI** [*vṛtti*]
Fluctuation or movement of the mind; thought.

**YAJNA** [*yajña*]
1) A sacrificial fire ritual in which Vedic mantras are recited while woods, fruits, grains, oils, yogurt, and *ghee* (clarified butter) are poured into the fire as an offering to the Lord. 2) Any work or spiritual practice that is offered as worship to God.

**YAMA** [*yama*]
Self-control.

**YAMALOKA** [*yamaloka*]
The realm of Yama, the lord of death.

**YANTRA** [*yantra*]
Mystical diagram.

**YOGA** [*yoga*]
(*lit.*, union) The spiritual practices and disciplines that lead a seeker to evenness of mind, to the severing of the union with pain and, through detachment, to skill in action. Ultimately, the path of yoga leads to the constant experience of the Self.

**YOGABHRASHTA** [*yogabhraṣṭa*]
One who practiced yoga but did not complete his sadhana in a former lifetime. He continues his spiritual practice at the level of attainment he achieved and attains perfection in a later birth.

**YOGAMAYA** [*yogamāyā*]
The Lord's power of illusion. *See also* MAYA.

**YOGA SUTRAS** [*yogasūtra*]
A collection of aphorisms, attributed to the fourth-century sage Patanjali. This is the basic scripture of *ashtānga yoga*, the "eight-limbed path" to Self-realization that takes a seeker through specific stages to the state of total absorption in God.

**YOGA VASISHTHA** [*yogavāsiṣṭha*]
A popular Sanskrit text on Advaita Vedanta, probably written in the twelfth century; ascribed to the sage Vasishtha. In it, Vasishtha answers Lord Rama's philosophical questions on life, death, and human suffering by teaching that the world is as you see it and that illusion ceases when the mind is stilled.

**YOGI** [*yogī*]
1) One who practices yoga. 2) One who has attained perfection through yogic practices. *See also* YOGA.

# Story Index

# INDEX

Jnaneshwar Maharaj, 147, 154, 175, 270, 278-79, 295-96, 313, 324; on action and inaction, 7; on chanting, 77; on devotion, 235; God's will and, 222; knowledge of, 40; lineage of, 52, 322; on sadhana, 51
*Jñānīs.* *See* Saints

Kabir, 85, 201, 228, 235, 313, 314
*Kalā,* 5-6, 52-53
Karma, 134, 186-87, 258, 291, 309, 314; rebirth and, 143; results of, 16-18; sadhana and, 69; of saints, 221; shaktipat and, 175
*Katha Upanishad,* 95, 105, 298, 316-17
Knowledge, 33-34, 40, 42, 144, 197-98, 228; destiny and, 82; of God, 253; Guru and, 146-47, 190-91, 321; heart and, 253-54; karma and, 187; means of gaining, 275-76; path of, 135; realization and, 153; saints and, 296; scriptures and, 3-4; of Self, 102-4, 106, 110, 114, 142; selfless service and, 38; shaktipat and, 184
Krishna, Lord, 53, 82, 119, 132, 134-35, 147, 162, 174, 178-79, 183, 189, 226, 231, 269, 301; teachings of, 303-4; true nature of, 172-73; on the world, 8
*Kriyās* (yogic movements), 183-84, 247, 273, 300, 302
*Kumbhaka* (breath retention), 107, 115, 307, 310
*Kundalinī* energy, 241, 247, 295, 313-14, 321-23; *ājñā chakra* and, 20; awakening, 25, 70, 96, 243-44; Blue Pearl and, 252; meditation and, 30-31; omniscience of, 71; shakti and, 120

Laldas, Mahatma, 200
Leadership, 61-62
Liberation. *See* Realization
Life span, 6, 154
Light, 83, 110, 252; in meditation, 45, 69, 111, 256; of Self, 105-6
Lineage, 63-64, 154
Love, 91, 110, 132, 147, 206

*Mahābhārata,* 82, 126
*Mahānirvāna Tantra,* 241
*Mahāsamādhi,* 80, 113
Mahashivaratri, 122, 125
*Maitri Upanishad,* 94
*Māndūkya Upanishad,* 252
Manpuri, 170
Mansur Mastana, 64, 170-71, 270
Mantra, 163-65, 240-41; enlivened, 4-5, 152-53; Guru and, 236, 298-99, 322; power of, 26, 224-25; sadhana and, 182; saints and, 297. *See also Japa*
Mantra repetition. *See Japa*
*Manusmriti,* 104
*Mārkandeya Purāna,* 178
Marriage, 149, 158, 180-81, 189, 266-67, 283, 308-9
Matsyendranath, 254
*Māyā* (illusion), 98-99, 179
Meditation, 111-12, 255-56, 272, 292-93; *ājñā chakra* and, 20; Bhagawan Nityananda and, 88; Blue Pearl and, 6, 53; experiences in, 118-19, 239, 285; four bodies and, 252; on God, 131-32; joy and, 205-6; *kriyās* in, 300; lights in, 45, 69, 83-84; mind and, 136, 148, 150, 151, 165, 192; nature of, 107-8; past lives and, 266, 301-2; *samādhi* and, 96, 211-12; Self and, 141, 303; shakti and, 302; shaktipat and, 30-31; visions in, 53-54, 287; yoga and, 179-80; Witness-consciousness and, 37, 55; worldly life and, 99

*Sahasrāra* (crown chakra), 20, 49, 67, 184, 247-48, 252
Sai Baba of Shirdi, 74-75, 86, 196, 297
Saints, 7-8, 32, 33-34, 52, 75, 90, 100-101, 133-34, 180, 208, 288, 299, 312, 314; actions of, 10, 40-42; belief in, 92; Bhagawan Nityananda and, 87; company of, 23, 54, 63, 109, 137, 140, 145, 186-87; experiences of, 47, 313; Gurus of, 147; *japa* and, 200-202; knowledge of, 286-87; the mind and, 230, 310; nature of, 76-80, 113-15, 256-59, 295-97; political figures and, 195; realization of, 85-88; rebirth of, 74-75, 220-21; renunciation and, 196-97; shaktipat and, 325-26; *siddhis* and, 248; teachings of, xvi, 89, 157, 170-71, 215, 242-43; vision of, 7-8, 119, 190, 227; work of, 61-62, 232, 245-46, 269-70
*Samādhi* (union with God), 27, 53-54, 72, 96, 180, 256, 296, 309-10
Samadhi shrines, 114-15, 196-97
Sanatkumara, 175
*Saundarya Laharī* (Shankaracharya), 313, 323
Science, 106, 323
Scriptures, 144-45, 188, 226, 263, 276; authenticity of, 157; authority of, 128-29; on the Guru, 289; God and, 3-4; knowledge of, 153; precepts of, 36-37, 122-24; sadhana and, 35-36; on shaktipat, 174-78; source of, 286-87; Truth and, 56-57; understanding of, 41, 231, 320-21
"See God in each other," 33, 103, 206, 249-50
Self, 8, 63, 212, 238-39, 260, 317; all-pervasiveness of, 136, 234-35, 303-4; Blue Pearl and, 252; contemplation of, 95; experience of, 108-10, 115, 285; forgetfulness of, 25; Guru and, 313; knowledge of, 142, 156, 197-98, 298-99; light and, 45, 83-84; meditation and, 108-10; mind and, 91, 244, 293, 310; *nāda* and, 97; nature of, 27, 104-6, 120, 184-85, 193, 271-72; sadhana and, 51; Vedanta on, 274; Witness-consciousness and, 37; world and, 117, 291-92; worship of, 131
Self-control, 161-62, 206-7
Self-effort, 99-100, 120, 134, 209, 231-32
Self-inquiry, path of, 79, 135
Self-realization. *See* Realization
Self-recognition, 117
Senses, 37, 105, 108; controlling, 93, 145, 161-62
Service, selfless, 20, 38, 101-4, 130, 180-81
Shaiva Tantra, 52
Shakti (energy), 19, 112, 115, 247; all-pervasiveness of, 24-25; contraction of, 194; development of, 119-20; Guru and, 327; meditation and, 302; nature of, 27-28, 177-78, 195-96, 289, 295, 300-301, 323
Shaktipat (initiation), 174-78, 182, 183-84, 248, 273, 301-2, 321-23, 325-26; ashram and, 307; degrees of, 52; Jnaneshwar Maharaj on, 278; knowledge and, 8-9, 40; meditation and, 30-31; mind and, 29; realization and, 47; sadhana and, 256; saints and, 297; science of, 295
Shams Tabrizi, 270

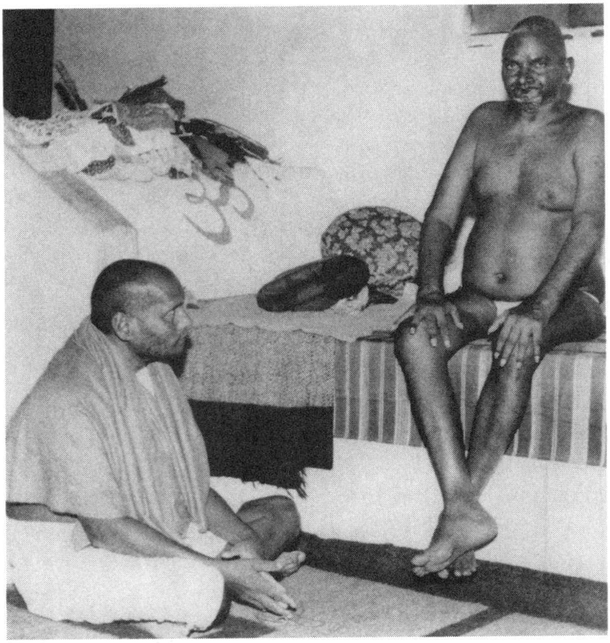

*Swami Muktananda with his Guru, Bhagawan Nityananda*

# SWAMI MUKTANANDA
## *and the Lineage of Siddha Yoga Meditation Masters*

Swami Muktananda was born in 1908 to a family of prosperous landowners near the South Indian city of Mangalore. Around the age of fifteen he met the renowned saint Bhagawan Nityananda, whom he would later recognize as his spiritual master. Within six months of this encounter, the boy set out from home in search of the direct experience of God, a journey that would ultimately last almost a quarter of a century and take him three times across the length and breadth of India. He met his first teacher, Siddharudha Swami, who was one of the renowned scholars and saints of that time, in an ashram in Hubli, two hundred miles to the north of his parents' home. It was there that he studied Vedanta, took the vows of *sannyāsa*, or monkhood, and received the name Swami Muktananda, "the bliss of liberation."

When Siddharudha died in 1929, Baba Muktananda began his pilgrimage to the holy sites of India. He met and learned from more than sixty saints, always looking for the one who would give him the experience of God. He searched for eighteen years, during which time he mastered the major scriptures of India, received training in an array of disciplines and skills—from hatha yoga to cooking and Ayurvedic medicine—and still he did not find what he sought.

At last one of the saints he met sent him to Bhagawan Nityananda, the Siddha Master (perfected spiritual teacher) he had seen so many years before. Bhagawan Nityananda was then living in the hamlet of Ganeshpuri, fifty miles northeast of Bombay. Recognizing Bhagawan Nityananda as the Guru he had been seeking, Baba later said that this meeting ended his wandering forever. From Bhagawan Nityananda he received shaktipat, the sacred initiation of the Siddhas by which one's inner spiritual energy is awakened. This energy, known in yoga as *kundalinī*, is a divine potential that exists within each human being; once awakened, it enables a seeker to reach the most sublime levels of inner experience.

With this initiation, Baba became a disciple, dedicating himself to the spiritual path set forth by his Guru. Thus began nine years of intense transformation, during which he fully explored the inner realms of consciousness through meditation and finally became steady in his experience of the fullness and ecstasy of the inner Self. In 1956, Bhagawan Nityananda declared that his disciple's inner journey was complete: Baba had attained Self-realization, the unchanging experience of union with God.

Even after he had achieved the goal of his discipleship, Baba remained a devoted disciple, continuing to live quietly near Ganeshpuri. Bhagawan Nityananda established him in a small ashram of his own, and for five years Guru and disciple lived less than a mile from each other. Then in 1961, just before his death, Bhagawan Nityananda passed on to Baba the grace-bestowing power of the Siddha Masters, investing him with the capacity to give spiritual awakening, or shaktipat, to others. On that day Bhagawan Nityananda told him, "The entire world will see you."

In the decades that followed, Baba traveled throughout India and, later, the rest of the world. During the course of three international tours, Baba imparted to others the same shaktipat initiation he himself had received, and he also introduced seekers to the practices and philosophy of the spiritual path he called Siddha Yoga meditation. People who had never before heard of meditation found that in Baba Muktananda's presence they were drawn

*Gurumayi Chidvilasananda*

into a stillness within that gave their lives new focus and meaning. He introduced programs to give shaktipat initiation to large groups and explained to people the ongoing process of transformation that was unfolding within them.

In 1982, shortly before his death, Baba designated his successor, Swami Chidvilasananda, who became known as Gurumayi. She had been his disciple since early childhood and had traveled with him since 1973, translating into English his writings, his lectures, and the many informal exchanges he had with his devotees. She was an advanced spiritual seeker with a great longing for God, and she became an exemplary disciple. Baba guided her in her sadhana and meticulously prepared her to succeed him as Guru. In early May of 1982, Gurumayi took formal vows of monkhood, and later that month Baba bequeathed to her the power and authority of the Siddha Yoga meditation lineage, the same spiritual legacy that his Guru had passed on to him. Since that time, Gurumayi has given shaktipat and taught the Siddha Yoga meditation practices to seekers in many countries, introducing them to Swami Muktananda's message:

*Meditate on your Self.*
*Honor your Self.*
*Worship your Self.*
*Understand your own Self.*
*God dwells within you as you.*

# Further Reading

## *Books Published by SYDA Foundation*

**From the Finite to the Infinite** — Swami Muktananda

This compilation of questions and answers is drawn from Baba Muktananda's travels in the West. In it, Baba addresses all the issues a seeker might encounter on the spiritual path, from the earliest days until the culmination of the journey.

**Play of Consciousness** — Swami Muktananda

In this intimate and powerful portrait, Swami Muktananda describes his own journey to Self-realization, revealing the process of transformation he experienced under the guidance of his Guru, Bhagawan Nityananda.

**Bhagawan Nityananda of Ganeshpuri** — Swami Muktananda

He rarely spoke, but a brief sentence from him spoke volumes, guiding the fortunate listener across the sea of illusion. This volume on the life of Bhagawan Nityananda is filled with the observations, thoughts, and offerings of praise—compiled from many sources, over many years—by his greatest disciple and his successor, the Siddha Master Swami Muktananda.

**Enthusiasm** — Swami Chidvilasananda

"Be filled with enthusiasm and sing God's glory" is the theme of this collection of talks given by Gurumayi Chidvilasananda. In these pages, she inspires us to let the radiance of enthusiasm shine through every action, every thought, every minute of our lives. This, Gurumayi says, is how we can sing God's glory.

**I Have Become Alive** — SWAMI MUKTANANDA

Here Baba Muktananda shows us how to integrate the inner quest with the demands of contemporary life. He illumines such topics as spiritual discipline, the ego, marriage, parenting, experiencing love, and attaining God while embracing the world.

**The Yoga of Discipline** — SWAMI CHIDVILASANANDA

"From the standpoint of the spiritual path," Swami Chidvilasananda says, "the term *discipline* is alive with the joyful expectancy of divine fulfillment." In this series of talks on practicing and cultivating discipline of the senses, Gurumayi shows us how this practice brings great joy.

**Nothing Exists That Is Not Shiva** — SWAMI MUKTANANDA

Above all else, Baba Muktananda loved inspiring spiritual seekers to make each moment of their lives a sacred celebration. He wanted people everywhere to recognize their identity with Shiva, the all-pervasive Lord. Here Baba comments on his favorite scriptures from Kashmir Shaivism, a revolutionary philosophy that venerates the divine Principle in every aspect of life.

**Ashram Dharma** — SWAMI MUKTANANDA

Meditation, one-pointedness of mind, inner stillness, and recognizing the divine in others are the essence of ashram dharma—the way to conduct oneself in the school of a spiritual Master. "An ashramite should not consider the ashram to be a particular place or area of land," writes Baba. "To him, the whole world is the ashram."

**Mukteshwari** — SWAMI MUKTANANDA

Baba Muktananda guides us through the stages of the spiritual path, inviting us to throw off our limitations and join him in the state of total freedom. These autobiographical verses are among Baba's earliest writings.

**Kindle My Heart** — SWAMI CHIDVILASANANDA

The first of Gurumayi Chidvilasananda's books, this is an introduction to the classic themes of the spiritual journey, arranged thematically. There are chapters on such subjects as meditation, mantra, control of the senses, the Guru, the disciple, and the state of a great being.

*You may learn more about the teachings and practices of Siddha Yoga meditation by contacting*

SYDA Foundation
371 Brickman Rd.
P.O. Box 600
South Fallsburg, NY 12779-0600, USA
Tel: (914) 434-2000

*or*

Gurudev Siddha Peeth
P.O. Ganeshpuri
PIN 401 206
District Thana
Maharashtra, India

*For further information about books in print by Swami Muktananda and Swami Chidvilasananda, and editions in translation, please contact*

Siddha Yoga Meditation Bookstore
371 Brickman Rd.
P.O. Box 600
South Fallsburg, NY 12779-0600, USA
Tel: (914) 434-2000 ext. 1700

*Call toll-free from the United States and Canada*
888-422-3334

*Fax toll-free from the United States and Canada*
888-422-3339